Praise for _Teachers of E_  **_f the Triratna_
Buddhist Order**

Though _Teachers of Enlighte......_ contains much useful information about
the figures on the Refuge Tree of the Western Buddhist Order [now called
the Triratna Buddhist Order], about the Buddhist scriptures, and about
the historical development of Buddhism, it is above all a call to spiritual
practice. – **Urgyen Sangharakshita**

I am delighted to see this new edition of _Teachers of Enlightenment_. As a
member of the Indian ordination team and a Public Preceptor I know how
crucial the visualization of the Refuge Tree and Prostration Practice are for
those who have asked for ordination within the Triratna sangha, as well as
for Order members. This practice is extremely helpful for deepening our
Going for Refuge and commitment to the Three Jewels. This book is a very
useful guide for the practice, and provides valuable information about the
figures on the Refuge Tree. Such a book is very much needed. I am very
happy to see that Dr Ambedkar and Anagarika Dharmapala have been
included in this new edition. This book will not only benefit those who wish
to practise within the Triratna sangha but any Buddhist who is interested to
know about the great spiritual beings on this Refuge Tree. – **Amoghasiddhi**,
Public Preceptor and member of the Indian ordination training team

For anyone exploring the Going for Refuge and Prostration Practice of
the Triratna Buddhist Order, _Teachers of Enlightenment_ has long been an
essential guide. Kulananda presents a wonderful description of each figure,
enabling our practice to come alive, a source of revelation and devotion.
This new edition now includes Vajratara's excellent introduction to Dr
Babasaheb Ambedkar and Anagarika Dharmapala, two more figures that
I can get to know through this precious practice. – **Kalyacittā**, women's
ordination team, Tiratanaloka Retreat Centre

Kulananda restores the central place of reverence on the Buddhist path
and shows how opening up to Other Power permits us to break free from
our self-preoccupation. This book is a timely reminder that Buddhism is
not reducible to a set of self-help techniques; it invites us to participate
in a cosmic myth, which is the compassionate liberation of all beings. –
Nagapriya, author of _The Promise of a Sacred World: Shinran's Teaching of
Other Power_

Since publication in 2000, Kulananda's *Teachers of Enlightenment* has been an invaluable source of information and inspiration for practitioners in Triratna, those ordained and those training for ordination, as well as anyone wishing to understand Triratna's spiritual roots and lineage. In the Preface to this new edition, Vajratara completes the presentation, outlining important clarifications and developments in Sangharakshita's thinking in the years following the first publication. One of the developments was the addition by Sangharakshita of two new figures, Dr Babasaheb Ambedkar and Anagarika Dharmapala, who are admirably introduced by Vajratara in two new sections of the book. There is no doubt that this publication would have given Sangharakshita immense pleasure, serving as it does to illuminate the spiritual lineage of Triratna, now a growing tradition taking its place in the contemporary Buddhist world. – **Mahamati**, Chair of Urgyen Sangharakshita Trust

The Triratna Refuge Tree is a unique, rich, and complex symbol. In order to understand its significance we have to become acquainted with it and ease ourselves into relationship with it. There is no better place to start than Kulananda's indispensable guide. He succinctly provides a clear overview of the Refuge Tree and then gives us an engaging snapshot of each of the figures and their teachings, which is a considerable achievement. He is a reliable companion helping us to navigate this compelling image, and he encourages us to take our first steps into the universe of potential spread before us. – **Punyamala**, Public Preceptor and founder member of the Sheffield Buddhist Centre

Kulananda offers a rich introduction to the Triratna Refuge Tree, its background and historical context. We meet the array of figures on the Tree, who together represent a stream of spiritual energy flowing from the historical Buddha down to us today. An invaluable guide to both the history and practice. – **Saddhaloka**, author of *Encounters with Enlightenment*

This book is a call to give yourself to the Going for Refuge and Prostration Practice and to allow it to act upon you. A call to enter a myth. A myth that develops as the significance of the Refuge Tree emerges. A myth that points beyond itself and helps you make sense of yourself and your place in the cosmos. – **Subhadramati**, author of *Not About Being Good: A Practical Guide to Buddhist Ethics*

TEACHERS OF ENLIGHTENMENT

The Refuge Tree of the
Triratna Buddhist Order

New Edition

TEACHERS OF ENLIGHTENMENT

The Refuge Tree of the
Triratna Buddhist Order

KULANANDA

New Edition with Vajratara

Windhorse Publications
38 Newmarket Road
Cambridge CB5 8DT
info@windhorsepublications.com
windhorsepublications.com

New edition 2023

Cover design by Akasajoti

Cover image: Shakyamuni (detail) © Aloka, used with permission
from Padmaloka Retreat Centre

Typesetting and layout by Tarajyoti
Printed by Bell & Bain
Illustrations by Aloka
Photographs © Urgyen Sangharakshita Trust

British Library Cataloguing in Publication Data:
A catalogue record for this book is available from the British Library.

ISBN: 978-1-911407-94-2

Contents

Preface to the New Edition, 2023   ix

About the Author   xiv

Preface to the 2000 Edition, by Sangharakshita   xv

Author's Acknowledgements for the First Edition   xx

Publisher's Acknowledgements   xxi

Part One

Introduction   1

Chapter One   The Refuge Tree of the Triratna Buddhist Order, and the Prostration Practice   5

Chapter Two   Visualization and Imagination   17

Chapter Three   Going for Refuge   29

Chapter Four   The Refuge Tree, Bodhicitta, and 'Other-power'   37

Part Two

Introduction   49

Chapter Five   The Buddhas of the Three Times   53

Chapter Six   The Five Jinas   71

Chapter Seven   The Arhants   89

Chapter Eight   The Bodhisattvas   113

Chapter Nine   Vajrasattva   135

Chapter Ten   The Dharma texts   141

Chapter Eleven   The Teachers of the Past   149
India   153
Tibet   171
China   191
Japan   207

Chapter Twelve   The Teachers of the Present   229

Conclusion   285
Notes and References   287
Selected Reading   293
Index   298

Contents

Preface to the New Edition, 2023

At the heart of the Going for Refuge and Prostration Practice is the enactment of Going for Refuge to the Three Jewels of Buddhism as represented by the Refuge Tree. We enter a myth in this practice, one that develops as the significance of the Refuge Tree emerges. In Tuscany in 1984 in the seminar 'The Bodhisattva Ideal: The Awakening of the Bodhi Heart', Sangharakshita talked of myth as having a definite impact on us, as something we necessarily experience, and as something we don't simply think about. As Sangharakshita mentions in his Preface to the 2000 edition, his own understanding of the myth and significance of Going for Refuge to the Three Jewels of Buddhism continued to change over the course of his life. With that, the image of the Refuge Tree – which represented his understanding of Going for Refuge – also changed and developed.

When the Western Buddhist Order was founded in 1967, Order Members did the Going for Refuge and Prostration Practice of the Nyingmapa School of Buddhism, which centres around the figure of Padmasambhava. This is the practice that Sangharakshita was introduced to in Kalimpong by his teacher Kachu Rimpoche. However, as the Triratna Buddhist Order developed into a distinctive Buddhist tradition, he felt it inappropriate to have a Going for Refuge and Prostration Practice that was taken completely from the Nyingmapa tradition. Therefore, in 1992, he changed the Refuge Tree on which the practice is based to reflect all the major traditions of Buddhism. On that Refuge Tree, the Buddha Shakyamuni was placed at the centre as 'the ultimate source of all Buddhist teachings'. When Kulananda published the first edition of *Teachers of Enlightenment* in 2000, it was this Refuge

Tree that formed the centre of his practice of the Going for Refuge and Prostration Practice.

Since that time, Sangharakshita changed the name of the Western Buddhist Order to the Triratna Buddhist Order to reflect that it was not just for the 'Western' world, but for the modern, globalized world. At the time of writing, about a third of the Triratna Buddhist Order lives in India, for example. In this edition of *Teachers of Enlightenment*, for ease of reference, therefore, we have changed previous references to the Western Buddhist Order to Triratna Buddhist Order.

The change of name of the Triratna Buddhist Order was significant, as it came out of a broader understanding of the Order and all the nationalities and cultures that make it up. For a long time it had been bothering me, and some of the Order in India, that a different image of the Refuge Tree had been recommended by Sangharakshita for our Order in India. That Refuge Tree included two of the key proponents of Buddhism in modern India: Dr Babasaheb Ambedkar and Anagarika Dharmapala. In effect, this left us with two Refuge Trees for the same Order: one for the Order in South Asia, and one for the rest of the world. In 2017, myself and some of the senior Order Members in India talked to Sangharakshita about this. It was 'mythologically divisive', as I put it. Sangharakshita agreed and asked the College of Public Preceptors to make changes as soon as possible, to include Dr Ambedkar and Dharmapala on all versions of 'The Refuge Tree of the Triratna Buddhist Order'.

It wasn't just because Dr Ambedkar and Dharmapala had significance for the Order and Movement in India that they were on the Refuge Tree. They had both been influential and formative influences on Sangharakshita's understanding of Buddhism and how it could be practised in the modern world. Along with the Buddha and Milarepa, he counted them as his greatest inspirations. As long ago as 1953, Sangharakshita wrote a biography of Dharmapala called *Flame in the Darkness*. In 1986, he wrote *Ambedkar and Buddhism*. At the time of changing the Refuge Tree to include them, he said that they belonged to the Order's lineage of inspiration and deserved a place on the Refuge Tree used by all Order Members. He also added that, for him, the Triratna Buddhist Order's Refuge Tree was now complete.

Preface to the New Edition, 2023, Vajratara

I have written the two new sections for this book to introduce the new figures. These can be found in the section: 'The Teachers of the Present'. The images of the Refuge Tree also had to be changed in the pictures depicting it. Cintamani was commissioned to do a new painting at the Order's new retreat centre, Adhisthana, and Aloka was asked to update his painting at Padmaloka retreat centre. This required more discussion with Sangharakshita as to where to put the new figures and how to depict them. In these talks, other changes to the iconography were developed in line with Sangharakshita's thinking.

The main change was to teachers of the past. Sangharakshita made it clear that he wanted them sitting on lotus thrones as a symbol of spiritual rebirth. He also wanted them to have the traditional auras of light around their bodies to signify the merit they had developed over their lifetimes. However, he did not want them to have the auras around their heads, which traditionally represent wisdom, as he did not want to make a statement about their attainments. This change was a result of his further thinking on what he called 'critical ecumenicalism'.

Sangharakshita saw the teachers of the past as 'great spiritual heroes', while the teachers of the present represent the Triratna Buddhist Community's 'immediate spiritual background'. He called the Refuge Tree 'The Tree of Refuge and Respect'. We can look to the figures on it for inspiration. We can admire them and respect them for their understanding of the Buddha's teachings and how they put those teachings into practice in their own culture. However, this doesn't mean that we have to accept everything they said or did uncritically or as a direct communication from an Enlightened mind. He encouraged his disciples to look at their teachings in the light of the broader Buddhist tradition.

Sangharakshita also recommended a few minor changes to the iconography: Nagarjuna was to sit under the Arjuna tree under which he was born, entwined by two snakes. Asanga was to have beside him the small dog which appeared to him after a long retreat. Santideva was to have his hands in the praying, or anjali, mudra. Perhaps the most surprising change was to ask that Padmasambhava appear in his 'pandit', or scholarly, form, as being closer to his historical reality than the more usual archetypal form with the three robes and magical staff.

So what of the future? After generations of changes from Sangharakshita, are we able to make more changes to the iconography since his death in 2018? There are some aspects of the Refuge Tree of the Triratna Buddhist Order that might sit uncomfortably with us. Some figures, historical or archetypal, that we are inspired by might be missed out. Some people struggle with the fact that there are many more male figures on the Refuge Tree than women. Some teachers may come to light from history and from different cultures that we may want to include. New teachers will come. There may be new archetypal Buddhas and Bodhisattvas that emerge as people deepen their meditation practice in different cultures.

Can we change the Refuge Tree again? Sangharakshita saw the Refuge Tree as being complete at the time of his death because it expressed his understanding of Going for Refuge to the Three Jewels. We could have other Refuge Trees, as individuals, or as groups of people, and we might suggest changes to the wider Order. But those Refuge Trees would cease to have the unifying influence of Sangharakshita at the heart of them. They would cease to be a Refuge Tree that unifies the Triratna Buddhist Order, which was founded by Sangharakshita. Ultimately, it was only he who could make changes to the Refuge Tree, just as it was only he who could change the name of the Order. However much different figures might be valued, they will not be part of our collective lineage in the same way.

As we remain with this Refuge Tree of the Triratna Buddhist Order, we must remember that its main purpose, as Sangharakshita points out in his Preface to the 2000 edition, is as a call to spiritual practice. As we practise together the Going for Refuge and Prostration Practice of the Buddha Shakyamuni, we will discover that it is a myth that points beyond itself to the heart of Reality: beyond words, beyond concepts, beyond images and descriptions, beyond even its own myth.

I would like to thank all those who have actualized one of Sangharakshita's last instructions: Saddhaloka and the College of Public Preceptors, who agreed it at the time after much reflection and discussion; Cintamani and Aloka, who went to such care to make iconographical changes to the paintings of the Refuge Tree; the team at Windhorse Publications, who went to enormous efforts to republish this book including all its changes; and to Kulananda, who accepted the changes to his original book simply and with encouragement.

Vajratara
Tiratanaloka Retreat Centre, January 2023

About the Author

Kulananda was born in South Africa in 1954 and emigrated to Britain in 1972. He joined the Order in 1977 and spent many years assisting in the development of what is now the Triratna Buddhist Community. Amongst other things, he worked at times as Sangharakshita's secretary; co-founded Windhorse:evolution and the Cambridge Buddhist Centre; has been president of various Triratna Centres and a member of the Preceptors' College.

More recently, he has worked teaching mindfulness and related approaches in the context of organizational leadership. Amongst his other books are *Western Buddhism*; *Principles of Buddhism*; *Mindfulness in Eight Weeks*; and *Mind Time*, all published by HarperThorsons, and *The Wheel of Life* published by Windhorse Publications.

Kulananda and his wife Dhirangama live in Cambridge, UK.

Preface to the 2000 Edition

'We needs must love the highest when we see it' is one of the best-known lines of a famous poet.[1] But what do we mean by the highest, how do we recognize it, and what makes us love it?

For me, the highest has always meant the True, the Beautiful, and the Good and whatever embodies them, whether separately or in combination and to whatsoever degree. Even in my pre-teen years I recognized that in certain poems, paintings, and pieces of music there was expressed a sensibility, a consciousness, even a state of being, that was immensely superior to my own, and the reason I was able to recognize it as superior was that this more developed sensibility, this higher consciousness or state of being, existed in me in germinal form. Nor was it a merely theoretical recognition. A positive emotional response was involved – a response of love.

Literature and the fine arts led me to religion and mysticism. In my teens I became acquainted with the teachings of the major world religions, as well as with the principal Western philosophies, and realized not only that I was not a Christian but that I was, in fact, a Buddhist, and always had been one. I therefore took the first opportunity of publicly affirming that I was a Buddhist by taking the Refuges and Precepts from a Buddhist monk on the occasion of a Wesak celebration. A few months later the Army transported me to India, where after demobilizing myself I spent two years as a freelance wandering ascetic before being ordained as a monk and going to live with my first teacher, the venerable Jagdish Kashyap, in Benares.

With Kashyapji I studied Pāli, Abhidhamma, and logic. One of the texts I studied with him was the *Dhammapada*, an anthology of the Buddha's sayings that at an early date came to be included in the Pāli Canon. In it occur the following verses:

> Many people, out of fear, flee for refuge to (sacred) hills, woods, groves, trees, and shrines.
>
> In reality this is not a safe refuge. In reality this is not the best refuge. Fleeing to such a refuge one is not released from all suffering.
>
> He who goes for refuge to the Enlightened One, to the Truth, and to the Spiritual Community, and who sees with Perfect Wisdom the Four Ariyan Truths – namely, suffering, the origin of suffering, the passing beyond suffering, and the Ariyan Eight-membered Way leading to the pacification of suffering, – (for him) this is a safe refuge, (for him) this is the best refuge. Having gone to such a refuge, one is released from all suffering.[2]

In 'taking' the Refuges and Precepts and thereby affirming that I was a Buddhist I was doing much more than simply joining a particular socio-economic group. The phrase 'taking the Refuges', though in common use, is in any case highly misleading, and does not even render correctly the original Indic expression. As the *Dhammapada* verses make clear, one goes for Refuge to the Buddha, the Dharma, and the Sangha, and it is this *going* for Refuge to the Three Jewels that makes one a Buddhist. In other words, a Buddhist is one who is committed to the actual realization of the supreme spiritual values of which the Three Jewels are the embodiment. For the Buddhist it is the Three Jewels that are 'the highest', and it is therefore the Three Jewels that he or she strives to see ever more clearly and love ever more ardently.

Going for Refuge is thus an act of the greatest importance. Though I realized this at the time I was studying with Kashyapji, I was then far from realizing the full extent of that importance. In particular I did not realize the absolute centrality of the act of Going for Refuge at *all stages* of the spiritual life, not just at the beginning; neither did I realize that the degree to which one was a Buddhist was determined not by one's ecclesiastical status – not by whether one was monk or layman, nun or laywoman – but simply and solely by the degree to which one went for Refuge to the Three Jewels. As I was later to declare, 'Commitment is primary, lifestyle secondary'. Realizing the absolute centrality of the act of Going for Refuge, and working out the practical and theoretical implications of the fact of that centrality, was a task that took me many years and is probably not complete even now. The various stages of the process are fully described in *The History of My Going for Refuge* and need not be recounted here. Suffice it to say that the turning point came in 1962, in Kalimpong in the eastern Himalayas, where I had been living for the last twelve years.

By what some would see as a coincidence, others as an example of Jungian synchronicity, on the morning after the very day on which I received the Padmasambhava initiation from Kachu Rimpoche I acquired, without knowing what it contained, a copy of a Tibetan text that described, *inter alia*, the Going for Refuge and Prostration Practice with Padmasambhava, the Greatly Precious Guru, as the central figure. The practice came as a revelation to me. It involved not just the mind, but also the body and one's speech. As such, it was a total practice. It exemplified, in highly concrete fashion, the fact that one went for Refuge not just mentally, but with one's whole being, and under Kachu Rimpoche's guidance I took it up enthusiastically.

The text I had acquired was a Nyingma text, and the reason for its having Padmasambhava as the central figure of the Going for Refuge and Prostration Practice was that the Greatly Precious Guru was the founder of the Nyingma School. The other schools of Tibetan Buddhism had their own founders as the central figure of the practice. There was thus a common iconic pattern, a pattern in which the school's founder was seated on an enormous lotus, with Bodhisattvas, Arhants, human Buddhas and teachers, and the volumes of the scriptures occupying, respectively, similar lotuses to his right and left, in front of him, and behind. All five lotuses were shown as springing from a common stem, in this way forming between them what was known as the Refuge Tree. Thangkas or painted scrolls usually contained several scores of such figures, including many that were of significance only for this or that school or lineage of Tibetan Buddhism.

For many years the members of the Western Buddhist Order did the Going for Refuge and Prostration Practice in accordance with

Nyingma tradition as I had done, i.e. with Padmasambhava as the central figure of the Refuge Tree. But the Western Buddhist Order was an 'ecumenical' Buddhist order, in that it did not identify itself exclusively with any one school of Eastern Buddhism but, on the contrary, respected them all, admired them all, and looked to them all for sources of inspiration and guidance. It was therefore increasingly felt that the way we performed the Going for Refuge and Prostration Practice should reflect the Order's ecumenical attitude. In 1992 I therefore devised and published a new Refuge Tree, a Refuge Tree in which the Buddha, as the ultimate source of all Buddhist teachings, occupied the central place, and in which were included key figures from the entire Buddhist tradition, whether Indian, Chinese, Tibetan, or Japanese, and whether historical or mythical. It is this new Refuge Tree – the Refuge Tree of the Western Buddhist Order – that Kulananda describes in this book.

According to a well-known art historian, if an iconography contains a number of sufficiently powerful symbols, it can positively alter a philosophical system. 'The points of dogma for which no satisfactory image can be created tend to be dropped and popular religious expression and episodes which have scarcely occupied the attention of the theologians tend to grow in importance if they produce a compelling image.'[3] Buddhism has produced a number of such compelling images, the most important of which have a close connection with its principal doctrines. Among the best known of these images are the Wheel of Life, the Mandala, and the Refuge Tree, the last of them being a composite image, incorporating as it does the symbols of the tree and the lotus, both of which are images in their own right. It is because it is a compelling image that the Refuge Tree is able to function as the object of the Going for Refuge and Prostration Practice and, in this way, to transform our lives and bring us nearer to our goal of Enlightenment for the sake of all living beings.

Though *Teachers of Enlightenment* contains much useful information about the figures on the Refuge Tree of the Western Buddhist Order, about the Buddhist scriptures, and about the historical development of Buddhism, it is above all a call to spiritual practice. In particular it is a call to give oneself to the

Going for Refuge and Prostration Practice, a practice to which Kulananda has committed himself for many years. As such it will be of interest and value not only to members of the Western Buddhist Order everywhere in the world, but also to all Buddhists inasmuch as they themselves go for Refuge to the Three Jewels, and to those students of comparative religion who may be interested to see what it is that gives life, energy, and inspiration to a new Buddhist movement.

Urgyen Sangharakshita
Madhyamaloka
Birmingham
23 May 2000

Author's Acknowledgements for the First Edition

Vessantara, Aloka, Vajrabodhi, Tejananda, Ratnaguna, Suvajra, and Sthiramati read all or part of the text and made helpful comments, as did Urgyen Sangharakshita. What errors remain after their careful reading are definitely all mine.

I have drawn on many books in writing this one, and a full bibliography is given at the back, but I must acknowledge my particular debt to three that I have drawn on most extensively: Vessantara's *Meeting the Buddhas*, Nyanaponika Thera and Hellmuth Hecker's *Great Disciples of the Buddha*, and Subhuti's *Sangharakshita: A New Voice in the Buddhist Tradition*.

Aloka drew the illustrations and Sara Hagel, as editor, gave particularly perspicuous advice. Shantavira and Padmavajri at Windhorse Publications helped beyond the calls of duty. Guy Potter checked the quotations. My fellow community members respected my wish to write and the support team fielded my calls, leaving me free to do so. I am grateful to all of them. I would also like to thank Mahaprabha for his generous assistance in gaining permissions.

Publisher's Acknowledgements

Windhorse Publications wishes to gratefully acknowledge a grant from the Future Dharma Fund and the Triratna European Chairs' Assembly Fund towards the production of this book.

The publishers acknowledge with gratitude permission to quote from the following:

H. Saddhatissa (trans.), *The Sutta-Nipāta*, Curzon Press, London 1985.

Edward Conze (trans.), *Ratnaguṇa-samcayagāthā*, in *The Perfection of Wisdom in Eight Thousand Lines and Its Verse Summary*, Four Seasons Foundation, San Francisco 1983, copyright © Edward Conze 1973.

The Middle Length Discourses of the Buddha, A New Translation of the Majjhima-Nikāya, Wisdom Publications, Boston 1995, pp.339, 396, 403, 1097. Reprinted with the permission of the publisher.

Buddhist Scriptures, translated by Edward Conze, Penguin Classics, London 1959, copyright © Edward Conze 1959, pp.21–3, 48–9, 238–42. Reproduced by permission of Penguin Books Ltd.

Maurice Walshe (trans.), *The Long Discourses of the Buddha*, Wisdom Publications, London 1995, pp.116, 265, 403–4. Reprinted with the permission of the publisher.

Lama Anagarika Govinda, *The Way of the White Clouds*, Rider, London 1966, pp.9, 17. Reprinted with the permission of the Govinda Trust.

The Tibetan Book of the Dead, translated by Francesca Fremantle and Chögyam Trungpa, © 1975. Reprinted by arrangement with Shambhala Publications, Inc., Boston, www.shambhala.com

Entry into the Realm of Reality, translated by Thomas Cleary, © 1987. Reprinted by arrangement with Shambhala Publications, Inc., Boston, www.shambhala.com

Great Disciples of the Buddha, Wisdom
Publications in collaboration with
the Buddhist Publication Society in
Kandy, Boston 1997, pp.7, 103, 37,
118, 134–6, 142, 148, 153, 154, 179.
Reprinted with the permission of
the publisher.

K.R. Norman (trans.), *Theragāthā,
Elders Verses I*, Pali Text Society,
Oxford 1990, p.196. Reproduced
with the permission of the
publisher.

Buddhist Texts Through the Ages, ©
Muriel Conze. Reproduced by
kind permission of Oneworld
Publications.

A Buddhist Bible, edited by Dwight
Goddard, copyright 1938, renewed
© 1966 by E.P. Dutton, pp.257, 438–
40. Used by permission of Dutton, a
division of Penguin Putnam Inc.

'The Ocean of Clouds of Praises of
the Guru Manjughosa', in *Life and
Teachings of Tsongkhapa*, published
by the Library of Tibetan Works
and Archives, Dharamsala 1990,
pp.99–100, 192.

The Sūtra of Past Vows of Kṣitigarbha.
This sūtra is freely distributed by
the True Buddha School Net on
www.tbsn.org/english/library/
sutras/ksitigarbha, in order to
benefit sentient beings everywhere.

Martin Willson, *In Praise of Tārā:
Songs of the Saviouress*, Wisdom
Publications, Boston 1986, pp.179,
99–100. Reprinted with the
permission of the publisher.

*The Book of Gradual Sayings, (Aṅguttara-
Nikāya)* vol.i, Pali Text Society,
Oxford 1995, pp.171–2.

Cyril Birch (ed.), *Anthology of Chinese
Literature*, Penguin, London 1967.
Printed with the permission of
Grove/Atlantic, Inc.

The Lotus Sūtra, translated by Burton
Watson © 1993 Soka Gakkai.
Reprinted with the permission
of the publisher. Published by
Columbia University Press, New
York 1993, p.101.

Stephen Batchelor (trans.), *A Guide to
the Bodhisattva's Way of Life*, Library
of Tibetan Works and Archives,
Dharamsala 1979, pp.32, 120.

Śāntideva, *The Bodhicaryāvatāra*,
translated by Kate Crosby and
Andrew Skilton (Oxford World
Classics, 1998), translation © Kate
Crosby and Andrew Skilton 1995,
by permission of Oxford University
Press.

Buddhaghosa, *The Path of Purification
(Visuddhimagga)*, trans. Bhikkhu
Ñāṇamoli, Buddhist Publication
Society, Kandy 1991, pp.288–90,
300.

'The Song of a Yogi's Joy', in Garma
C.C. Chang, *The Hundred Thousand
Songs of Milarepa*, Shambhala
Dragon Editions, Boston and
London 1999, pp.74–5. Published by
arrangement with Carol Publishing
Group, Inc., Secaucus, NJ © 1962
Oriental Studies Foundation. All
rights reserved. Reprinted by
permission of Citadel Press.

Geshe Wangyal, *The Door of Liberation*,
Wisdom Publications, Boston,
revised edition 1995, pp.135–7.
Reprinted with the permission of
the publisher.

Yeshe Tsogyal, *The Life and Liberation
of Padmasambhava*, Dharma
Publishing, Berkeley 1978, pp.141,
142, 377–83, 388.

Samuel Beal (trans.), *Si-yu-ki: Buddhist
Records of the Western World*, Motilal
Banarsidass, Delhi 1981.

*Wild Ivy: The Spiritual Autobiography
of Zen Master Hakuin*, translated
by Norman Waddell, © 1999.
Reprinted by arrangement with
Shambhala Publications, Inc.,
Boston, www.shambhala.com

The Zen Master Hakuin, translated
by Philip B. Yampolsky © 1985
Columbia University Press.
Reprinted with the permission of
the publisher.

Trevor Leggett, *A First Zen Reader*,
published by Charles E. Tuttle

and Company, Inc. of Boston, Massachusetts and Tokyo, Japan.

Kūkai: Major Works by Yoshito S. Hakeda © 1972, Columbia University Press, from pp.22, 27, 31–2, 47, 51–2. Reprinted with the permission of the publisher.

Reihō Masunaga (trans.), *A Primer of Sōtō Zen: a translation of Dōgen's Shōbōgenzō Zuimonki*, Routledge Kegan and Paul, London 1972. Printed with the permission of the publisher and the University of Hawaii Press.

Hisao Inagaki, Kosho Yukawa, and Thomas R. Okano (trans.), *The Kyō Gyō Shin Shō*, Ryukoku Translation Center, Kyoto 1983, pp.84, 107–8, 113–14.

Naomi Burton, Patrick Hart, and James Laughlin (eds), *The Asian Journal of Thomas Merton*, New Directions Publishing Corporation, New York 1973. Printed with the permission of the publisher and Laurence Pollinger Limited.

Sogyal Rimpoche, *The Tibetan Book of Living and Dying*, Rider, London 1992.

Matthieu Ricard, *Journey to Enlightenment: The Life and World of Khyentse Rimpoche, Spiritual Teacher from Tibet*, Aperture, New York 1996, pp.13, 33–4, 40, 82.

The Opening of the Dharma, Library of Tibetan Works and Archives, Dharamsala 1982, pp.9, 21, 25–7.

Every effort has been made to obtain permission to reprint the following, but if any omission has been made, please let us know in order that this may be acknowledged in the next edition.

Kenneth K. Inada, *Nāgārjuna: a Translation of his Mūlamadhyamakakārikā with an Introductory Essay*, Hokuseido, 1970.

Hsüan Tsang, *Ch'eng Wei-Shih Lun: Doctrine of Mere Consciousness*.

Dedicated to Urgyen Sangharakshita
with thanks, inexpressible,
for the gift of the Refuge Tree.

Part One

Introduction

All the time I have been writing this book I have been getting up just after 6 a.m. With one or two companions, I make my way down to the quiet basement shrine-room of Madhyamaloka community, where I live. It has been winter, and it is cold down there in the morning, before the heating comes on in the rest of the house. It is a beautiful room, quite bare and simple. The floor is clear varnished pine, the walls are painted a light ochre, and at the far end, in front of a blazing red silk backdrop, sits a fine bronze statue of the Buddha, made for us by a friend.

The cold mists our breath. We light candles and incense, salute the shrine, and take our seats for meditation. Clearing my mind of sleep and dreams, I try to establish some rudimentary concentration and good will. Then, relaxing into a sense of gratitude, I conjure up in my mind the Refuge Tree of the Triratna Buddhist Order.

I try to create a mental image, a 'visualization', of the Buddha Śākyamuni and all the figures, historical, legendary, mythical, and transcendental, who have contributed most significantly to the practice and understanding of Buddhism as we conceive of it in our Order.

Surrounded by a clear blue sky, five white lotus flowers appear, spreading out from a central stalk. On the middle lotus appear the Buddhas of the Three Times, on the lotus to their right sit five luminous Bodhisattvas, and, to their left, five of the Buddha's own Enlightened disciples; behind them are all the canonical Buddhist texts, and, on the lotus in front of them, is my teacher, Sangharakshita, the founder of the Triratna Buddhist Order, and *his* teachers. On either side of Sangharakshita and his teachers are two more figures on their own lotuses: heroes of modern Buddhism that have inspired and informed the work of Sangharakshita.

In the sky above the Buddha appear the teachers of the past, from whom Sangharakshita derives most of his teaching. Five of them are connected with Indian Buddhism, four with Tibet, three with China, and four with Japan. Above them appears the five Buddha mandala and, crowning it all, the ādi-buddha Vajrasattva. This is the Refuge Tree of the Triratna Buddhist Order. Gods and goddesses appear in the sky around the Tree, dancing, making offerings, and singing its praises, and the whole picture glows with luminous rainbow light.

Keeping the Tree clearly before us, my companions and I stand up, arrange ourselves in front of the shrine, and begin to prostrate before the Tree we have visualized, reciting aloud verses that express our dedication of body, speech, and mind. Twenty minutes later, we sit down again, keeping the visualized Tree before us, and, having been purified by its beneficent presence, we bring the practice to a close.

Well, that is the theory, at least.

I have never been much of a one for visualization. Clear blue skies tend to elude me – perhaps I have been living in England too long – and I don't usually 'see' the Refuge Tree very clearly in my mind's eye. I do, however, sense it in other ways.

To begin with, I have an immense gratitude to all the figures on the Tree. Through my contact with them, however fleeting and tangential, my life has been changed quite extraordinarily – it has meaning, purpose, and a spiritual orientation that I could never have achieved on my own. Had I not had the good fortune to meet my own teacher, and had he not introduced me, in many different ways, to the figures on the Refuge Tree, my life would have been incomparably poorer. Each of the figures on the Tree, in different ways, worked to spread the Buddha's teaching so that it might influence the lives of people, even those like me, who have little natural aptitude for it. I bow down to them in thanks for the unremitting effort and constant selflessness their tasks involved.

Every figure on the Tree, each in their own way, has changed the world for the better. Śākyamuni taught. His disciples taught and their disciples taught. The great teaching of the Dharma radiated outwards from north-eastern India eventually to encompass the whole of Asia. Half the world's people live in countries that have been deeply affected by it. About 150 years ago it began to affect Western cultures as well, and has continued to do so with increasing effect. The work of these figures has changed the mind of humanity for the better and I am grateful for that. The work they did now leaves its traces in our consciousness. The way we think and act in the world today is, in part at least, a result of their efforts. To that extent they live with us in the present, influencing the way we act, speak, think, and feel. They are a constant source of beneficence in the present. The historical figures have clearly left their traces on world culture. The archetypal figures, however, affect us in different ways. To me they express different facets of the highest potential of the mind, and wherever a wise or kind act is done, there – to some extent at least – we can see their work. They too, therefore, are constantly with us.

I have encountered all the different figures on the Tree in different ways at different times. I currently have the great good fortune to live with Sangharakshita, and I once met Dhardo Rimpoche in Kalimpong. I have studied texts written by several of the figures on the Tree and I have performed the visualization practice and mantra recitation of four of the archetypal figures for many years. All of that makes for a close sense of connection. As I've been writing this book that sense of connection has grown and deepened, and my admiration for each of the figures has increased as I have come to learn more about them.

'There's Yogi Chen,' I think to myself as he takes his place in my morning meditation, 'what a man he was! There's Dilgo Khyentse Rimpoche – he was so kind! There's the Arahant Dhammadinnā – imagine receiving a teaching from her!' I don't necessarily *see* these figures, but I have some kind of mental image of all of them – feelings, impressions, thoughts, memories; all of these go into making up my 'visualization' of the Tree.

I have been doing this practice all through this winter, but I have done it at other times as well. I last did it when I was writing my previous book, in a solitary retreat cottage in south-west England, just a few miles from the sea. It was an idyllic spot, a small, isolated cottage on a dairy farm run by a friendly, nature-loving couple.

There were two rooms, one up, one down, and I had with me all that I needed: sufficient food and clothing, my computer and printer, my meditation gear, and binoculars for the wildlife. I even had my trusty old office chair that is so kind to my back as I hunch over the keyboard. I was all set and the book was going well, but somehow I could not settle; it just didn't feel the right place for me. There were deer in the woods and badgers in the banks, foxes, squirrels, and rabbits. There were newts in the pond, brilliant dragonflies, and all kinds of wild flowers and birds. A fine spot, but I could not settle. I had a constant sense of being somewhat out of place. Nowhere I sat, nowhere I stood, felt altogether right. Why could I not settle?

And then, out of nowhere, I suddenly knew what I had to do. I took up the Going for Refuge and Prostration Practice and, like magic, it all became clear. That was my place. At the foot of the Refuge Tree. That is where I really belong.

That feeling has continued and strengthened as I've worked through this winter. The practice has the effect on me – to borrow a phrase from a friend – that a magnet has on iron filings. It points everything in the right direction and aligns all the kinks and quirks of my wayward mind. I hope this book will encourage those who are qualified to do so to take up this practice. It is open to all members of the Triratna Buddhist Order and to those who have requested ordination within it (though we ask that the latter take it up only under the guidance of a member of one of the ordination teams).

But I have not written this book only for those who might take up the practice. This book is also for those who have any interest in the Order and the Triratna Buddhist movement. It shows, I hope, where some of our chief doctrines come from, and how we fit into the scheme of Buddhism as a whole. The Refuge Tree is a symbol of the heart-essence of Triratna. It is what we are most deeply about.

I hope this book will serve as something of an introduction to the forty-six figures who between them make up the Refuge Tree. If I have managed to communicate even a little of the extraordinary spiritual stature of one or two of them, I will have gone a little way in repaying the enormous debt I owe to each of them.

Chapter One

The Refuge Tree of the Triratna Buddhist Order, and the Prostration Practice

Jamyang Khentse Chökyi Lodrö was one of the foremost Tibetan Buddhist teachers of his time. Sangharakshita met him in 1957 and received several significant initiations from him. One of Jamyang Khentse's chief disciples was Kachu Rimpoche, abbot of Pemayangse, the royal monastery of Sikkim. In 1960, at Jamyang Khentse's behest, Kachu Rimpoche initiated Sangharakshita into the practice of Guru Padmasambhava. At the same time, Rimpoche gave Sangharakshita a new name – 'Urgyen', the name of Padmasambhava's mythical homeland.

Sangharakshita had long felt a deep connection with Padmasambhava. He had first encountered him in 1950, in a temple in Darjeeling, in the form of a sculpture, three or four times life size. 'In seeing the figure of Padmasambhava,' he later wrote, 'I had become conscious of a spiritual presence that had in fact been with me all the time. Though I had never seen the figure of Padmasambhava before, it was familiar to me in a way that no other figure on earth was familiar: familiar and fascinating. It was familiar as my own self, yet at the same time infinitely mysterious, infinitely wonderful, and infinitely inspiring.'[4]

The day after the initiation, Sangharakshita came upon a Tibetan monk selling a few woodblock prints of text in the Kalimpong bazaar. Wanting to help the man, who was clearly in need, Sangharakshita gave him what little money he had and took the texts back to Kachu Rimpoche, who was then staying with him at his vihara. Rimpoche was delighted to find that they were Nyingma texts, mostly relating to Padmasambhava. He took this as an auspicious sign, and a mark of the success of the initiation. Among the texts was the *Tharpe Delam*, or 'Easy Path to

Emancipation', which, besides other things, gives an account of the 'four foundation yogas', or preliminary trainings. In particular, it described one of the Nyingma Refuge Trees and outlined a form of the Going for Refuge and Prostration Practice. Obtaining the necessary permission from Kachu Rimpoche, and translating the text with the help of Dhardo Rimpoche, Sangharakshita took up this prostration practice and continued with it for the remainder of his stay in Kalimpong.

The Refuge Tree, which is also known as the Refuge Assembly or Field of Merit, is a central symbol in Vajrayāna Buddhism. It is a visualization practice centred on the Three Refuges – the Buddha, the Dharma, and the Noble Sangha – represented by a vast array of figures, all of whom vary depending upon the system of thought and practice of the different schools of Tibetan Buddhism. For the Kagyupas, for instance, the central form is usually the Buddha Vajradhara, for the Gelugpas it is Je Tsongkhapa, and for the Nyingmapas it is Padmasambhava.

Traditionally, it is possible to visualize a Refuge Tree with any archetypal Enlightened form, or *yidam*, at its centre. You build up a visualization with whichever *yidam* you are most devoted to appearing at the centre, and then, according to traditional arrangements, you organize all the other Refuges around it. You can also condense the practice, visualizing only the central figure while sustaining a strong conviction that it embodies all the Refuges.

Although there are many different Refuge Trees, depending on the exact lineage within which one practises, they all more or less conform to a single pattern. The Refuges appear in the clear blue sky – the great scholars, the yogins, and the *yidams* that are central to the lineage in question, as well those *ḍākinīs* and *dharmapālas* with whom it has a particular connection. All these are ranged about the central figure, who is said to embody them all.

The practice of repeatedly prostrating before a visualized Refuge Tree is common to all the schools of Tibetan Buddhism. When this practice is performed as part of the set of Vajrayāna preliminary practices (such as those described in the *Tharpe Delam*), it is customary to perform 100,000 prostrations in all, usually over several years.

When he returned to the West and founded the Western Buddhist Order (now known as the Triratna Buddhist Order), Sangharakshita passed on the *Tharpe Delam* Going for Refuge and Prostration Practice, centred on Guru Padmasambhava, to those of his own disciples who wished to do it regularly, and for many years members of the Order followed the Nyingma approach to the four foundation yogas. Over time, however, Sangharakshita's thinking about the centrality of Going for Refuge to the Three Jewels and his understanding of the Dharma began to crystallize in a new way. Previously, he had more or less accepted the traditional Vajrayāna view of the path as ascending by degrees from the Hīnayāna, which was concerned primarily with self-liberation, to the Mahāyāna, which upholds the Bodhisattva ideal, to the Vajrayāna, the path of magical transformation. Sangharakshita later came to regard this view as the unfortunate result of what he called 'ultra-ism'.

Tibetan, Chinese, and Japanese masters, he now thought, had tried to make sense of the various teachings which had historically preceded them, and which had been given canonical status, by arranging them in complex sequences. This was the only way they could resolve certain contradictions. On the one hand, what had gone before was thought of as the direct teaching of the Buddha. On the other hand, it was often clear that reforms were needed and that the Dharma would be best expressed in ways that were in keeping with the needs of the time.

In this way, at each stage, new teachings arose that included – but claimed to go beyond – whatever had gone before. The Mahāyāna included but extended the teachings of what *it* called the Hīnayāna. The Vajrayāna claimed to include but go beyond the Mahāyāna. Eventually, in the case of the Nyingma tradition, nine different *yānas* (or ways) emerged.

But people today often cannot – and certainly need not – accept these traditional schematizations of the teachings. To begin with, they have no basis in history. We know that the Buddha did not *literally* teach many of the doctrines later attributed to him. This is not to deny the spiritual value of such doctrines, but they cannot be regarded as literally the word of the Buddha Śākyamuni. Moreover, at this point in history we stand as inheritors of the *whole* Buddhist tradition. As such, we are called upon to make sense of the various classificatory schemata that the different traditions present. But these conflict. The Tibetan traditions place the Theravāda in the Hīnayāna camp, but there are teachings in the Pāli Canon that the Theravādins follow which are clearly directed at individuals at a high level of attainment. Some Theravādins, for their part, regard Mahāyāna Buddhism as a later, Brahminical degeneration. And where do the Chinese and Japanese schools fit in? There seem to be close parallels, for example, between Zen and Dzogchen, the 'highest' teaching of the Nyingma Vajrayāna, but Zen is ranked as Mahāyāna, a stage beneath the Vajrayāna.

Besides the problems of trying to reconcile all the different systems of classification, there is also the issue of spiritual snobbery. Many modern Buddhists like to think they have the best, the highest, the most powerful teachings, and this often leads them to take up practices that are way beyond them, sometimes barely intelligible, and even literally fantastic. For most ordinary practitioners, for example, the idea that they themselves are literally Bodhisattvas, actually devoting their lives to saving all beings, can lead to a spiritual life that is divorced from reality. For many this might be nothing worse than a harmless dream, but at worst it can lead to inflation and arrogance.

In any case, the stack of teachings has simply become too high, and it is time to go back. Otherwise we will simply have stack upon stack of practices which claim to have superseded one another as the highest teaching. Instead, we should focus our attention on the earliest developments of the Dharma, which are closer to the Buddha's own time and to the Buddha himself. We are in the fortunate position of being able to do this on account of our peculiarly modern historical perspective and because of the tools of historical analysis we have inherited. Buddhists of former times lacked these means.

This return to basic principles does not mean ignoring or discarding later developments. Rather, it involves seeing them in the context of the earlier teachings. The entire later Buddhist tradition grew out of the Buddha's own teaching. It amplified and elaborated it, but did not supersede it or add new and higher stages. Behind the vast mass of the Buddhist tradition lies a continuous underlying transcendental unity.

So where did this all leave the *Tharpe Delam*, the Nyingma foundation yogas, and the Refuge Tree of the Guru Padmasambhava? As Sangharakshita's thought and teaching on this subject became increasingly clear, it also started to become clear to him, and to some of the senior Order members charged with leading the ordination training process of the Triratna Buddhist Order, that practices such as those outlined in the *Tharpe Delam* come to us freighted with an immense weight of assumptions which we no longer share. The foundation yogas, for example, are traditionally thought of as 'preliminary practices' – preliminary, that is, to entry into the Vajrayāna path, which one traditionally embarks upon only when one has first traversed the Hīnayāna and Mahāyāna paths. In other words, if one were to take this tradition at its word, one would need to be at least a fairly advanced Bodhisattva before taking one's first Tantric initiation. This rule has lately been more often broken than kept. Indeed, some Tibetan Buddhist teachers have developed the custom of giving out initiations *en masse*, sometimes with scant regard to proper preparation.

As it became increasingly clear that the Triratna Buddhist Order no longer shared some of the doctrinal assumptions that underpinned the Vajrayāna approach to practice, so it also became clear that a new approach was called for. In 1992, in consultation with a few senior members of the Order, Sangharakshita devised and published a new set of preliminary practices. Where relevant, these placed Śākyamuni, the historical Buddha, back at the centre of the Refuge Assembly, thus reaffirming his position at the very heart of the Order's teaching. The new Refuge Tree that Sangharakshita devised included figures from the entire Buddhist tradition – figures from different schools, traditions, and countries: India, Tibet, China, and Japan. The Order draws upon the whole Buddhist tradition for its teachings and inspiration. For the first time in Buddhist history a truly global, pan-Buddhist Refuge Tree had come into being.

Although based on traditional lines, this new Refuge Tree is simpler than most. It has far fewer figures upon it than the Tree from the *Tharpe Delam*, for example. Many people have difficulty visualizing even one Bodhisattva, let alone the hosts of beings one finds on many of the traditional Refuge Trees. Sangharakshita wanted to make the new Tree as easy as possible to visualize, without losing any of the major elements. At the same time, he has stressed that once one has become familiar with the primary figures one can always add further traditional elements to one's visualization. For instance, one can see beautiful offerings being made to the Refuge Tree.

One begins the practice by sitting down in meditation and establishing a working basis of concentration and emotional positivity. Then one visualizes a clear blue sky stretching out in all directions, vast and unimpeded. Out of the sky a rainbow-coloured cloud appears, and growing up from the cloud an enormous stem that soars upwards into the sky, bearing at its tip a huge white lotus flower in radiant full bloom. In the centre of the lotus flower appears the Buddha Śākyamuni, the Buddha of the present era, shining with golden light. To his right and left, slightly smaller than him, appear the Buddhas of the past and the future – Dīpaṅkara and Maitreya. Together, these three figures represent the principle of Enlightenment, in which is found the transcendental unity of Buddhism that transcends time and space.

Then four other lotuses appear, growing out from the central stem. One to the front and one behind the main flower, one to the left and one to the right. On the lotus flower in front of the Buddhas of the Three Times appear Sangharakshita and his eight main teachers, seated in three tiers. Sangharakshita finds his place here not as the centre of a 'cult of personality', but rather because he is the link between Order members and the wider Buddhist tradition. Each of the teachers is, in turn, a link with that tradition. Sangharakshita sits in the centre of the front tier. To his left is Bhikkhu Jagdish Kashyap, wearing the yellow robes of a Theravādin monk. To his right is Yogi Chen, wearing his grey Chinese scholar's robe, our link with the Chan tradition. On the next tier, above Yogi Chen, sits Chetul Sangye Dorje in his Tibetan costume. To his left is Kachu Rimpoche, dressed in Nyingma monastic robes. Dhardo Rimpoche, wearing the red monastic robes of a Tibetan gelong, appears next to him. On the third tier, above Dhardo Rimpoche, sits Dilgo Khyentse Rimpoche, next to him

Jamyang Khyentse Rimpoche, and then Dudjom Rimpoche – all wearing the robes of Tibetan yogi lay practitioners.

There is a significance in the arrangement of these figures that goes back to the story of the finding of the *Tharpe Delam* texts in the Kalimpong bazaar. Because of his spiritual eminence, and because of the significance of the initiations he received from him, Sangharakshita regards Jamyang Khyentse Rimpoche as his 'root guru'. Khyentse Rimpoche handed Sangharakshita over, as it were, to Kachu Rimpoche, who gave him the Padmasambhava initiation. This line of transmission is indicated on the Tree by the fact that Kachu Rimpoche sits above Sangharakshita's head, with Jamyang Khyentse Rimpoche above Kachu Rimpoche. Above both of them is the great guru Padmasambhava.

In 2018 Sangharakshita asked that two new figures be included on lotuses either side of Sangharakshita and his teachers, in line with the Refuge Tree used by the Triratna Buddhist Order in India. On the left is Dr Ambedkar, wearing white and with a garland of flowers, and on the right is Anagarika Dharmapala in yellow robes. Both were great inspirations to Sangharakshita and informed his work setting up a new Buddhist Order.

On the lotus flower to the left of the Buddha appear the five Bodhisattvas of the Refuge Tree. They demonstrate the Order's embracing of the Bodhisattva ideal in all its aspects and its drawing upon the highest resources of the Imagination. There is the Four-Armed Avalokiteśvara, brilliant white in colour; Mañjuśrī, golden-yellow with his sword and book; royal-blue Vajrapāṇi, with his golden Vajra; Kṣitigarbha with his monk's robes and mendicant's staff; and Green Tārā.

Opposite them, to the right of the Buddhas, are the five Arhants, some of the chief among the Buddha's own immediate disciples, who embody the basic teachings of Buddhism and are the source of their transmission to the present time. There are his two chief disciples – Śāriputra and Maudgalyāyana – Ānanda, the Buddha's friend and attendant, and Mahākāśyapa, who led the sangha after the Buddha's death. Dhammadinnā, the nun who excelled in Dharma teaching and whose insight into 'cyclic' and 'spiral' conditionality had an important effect on Sangharakshita's thinking, makes the gesture of Dharma teaching.

On the lotus behind the Buddhas is a vast stack of Dharma texts – the canonical teachings of the Buddha, the *Tripiṭaka*.

In the sky above the Buddha appear the teachers of the past. All of them sit on stylized lotus thrones, symbols for spiritual rebirth, and all have body auras that signify merit. These are the principal historical figures from whose teaching and commentaries we derive our inspiration and understanding of the Dharma. At the top are the teachers connected with Indian Buddhism. Ārya Nāgārjuna founder of the Madhyamaka tradition, is in front of the Arjuna tree he was born under, with two snakes entwined around the trunk; the brothers Asaṅga and Vasubandhu, who between them founded the Yogācāra, wear their pandit's hats, as does Śāntideva, the author of the *Bodhicaryāvatāra*, a text much studied in the Order and from which is derived the Triratna pūjā. Śāntideva sits on his lotus throne with his hands together in the 'praying' or añjali mudrā; Buddhaghosa, the great teacher of the Theravāda, holds up his *Visuddhimagga*.

Beneath these appear the teachers connected with Tibet – Milarepa, the 'poet-saint' of the Kagyupas, sits at ease, wearing his thin white cotton cloth; Atiśa, an Indian teacher who reformed much of Buddhism in Tibet, makes the gesture of teaching; Padmasambhava, who played a central part in establishing Buddhism in Tibet and who is especially revered in the Nyingma tradition, is in the robes of a pandit, or scholar; and Tsongkhapa, revered as the founder of the Gelug School, wears his yellow pandit cap.

Then come the teachers from China – Huineng, the sixth patriarch of the Chan school; Zhiyi, founder of the Tiantai, and Xuanzang, the great translator, scholar, and pilgrim.

Finally, there are the teachers from Japan – Hakuin, the great Rinzai Zen reformer, sits with his *kyōsaku*, or 'wake-up stick'; Kūkai, the founder of the Shingon Esoteric School, holds his vajra and rosary; Dōgen, founder of the Sōtō Zen School, sits on his teaching seat; and Shinran, founder of the True Pure Land School, clasps a rosary.

Above the Refuge Tree appear the Jinas, the archetypal Buddhas of the five directions, embodying the principal aspects of transcendental wisdom. White Vairocana, at the centre, makes the gesture of teaching; blue Akṣobhya, in the east, touches the earth; yellow Ratnasambhava, in the south, makes the gesture of boundless giving; red Amitābha, in the west, sits in meditation, and dark green Amoghasiddhi, in the north, wards off fear.

Finally, in the sky above the five Jinas the ādi-buddha, the pure white Vajrasattva, embodying the Dharma in its complete, wordless purity, sits holding his bell and vajra, radiating brilliant light. Gods and goddesses appear in the sky around this great Refuge Tree, singing and dancing, making all kinds of offerings, and luminous rainbow light fills the sky.

One sits for a time, holding the magnificent vision of the Tree in one's mind, developing a sense of its vast beneficent influence, and then one moves on to the next stage of the practice. Keeping the vision of the Tree before you, you imagine you are surrounded by all beings with your parents at each shoulder: traditionally your father and all men behind your right shoulder and your mother and all women behind your left. Then, with hands held in reverence at your heart, you recite this verse:

From now onwards
Until the attainment of Enlightenment,
With great reverence of body, speech, and mind,
I go for Refuge to the Buddha Śākyamuni.

Then you perform the first prostration. You bring your hands, still held in the gesture of reverence, to your head, then your throat, then your heart (representing body, speech, and mind) as you recite, '*Oṃ, āḥ, hūṃ*, to the best of all Refuges I go!'

Then you make a full-length prostration to the Refuge Tree in front of you. You go down on to your knees and stretch your whole body out on the floor, your arms in front of you. You then lift your folded hands up above your head in reverence. As you go down on to the floor, you recite to yourself:

To the Buddha for Refuge I go!
To the Dharma for Refuge I go!
To the Sangha for Refuge I go

Then you stand up and repeat the process:

Oṃ āḥ hūṃ – to the best of all Refuges I go!

and prostrate –

To the Buddha for Refuge I go!
To the Dharma for Refuge I go!
To the Sangha for Refuge I go!

over and over, as many times as you wish, always trying to keep a clear sense of the Refuge Tree before you.

Having done that for a time, you stand up and return to your seat, all the time maintaining the visualization. Now, clear white light streams down from the Refuges on to yourself and all beings, cleansing and purifying them. You sit for a time, basking in the radiance of purifying light, before the light is drawn back into the Refuges and you begin the final stage of the practice.

Vajrasattva, the five Buddhas, the teachers of the past, the Arhants, the Dharma texts, Bodhisattvas, and the teachers of the present – all, one group at a time, dissolve into white light which is absorbed into the Buddhas of the Three Times. Dīpaṅkara and Maitreya dissolve into light which is absorbed into the Buddha Śākyamuni. The Buddha himself dissolves into light which is absorbed into the clear blue sky, and then the sky itself gradually fades away.

You sit for a time, absorbing the impact of the practice, and then transfer the merits of having done it with verses such as these:

May the merit gained in my acting thus
Go to the alleviation of the suffering of all beings.
My personality throughout my existences,
My possessions,
And my merit in all three ways,
I give up without regard to myself,
For the benefit of all beings.

Just as the earth and other elements
Are serviceable in many ways
To the infinite number of beings
Inhabiting limitless space;

So may I become
That which maintains all beings
Situated throughout space,
So long as all have not attained
To peace.

With that you bring the practice to a close.

Not everyone is equally able to 'visualize', and some people, for health reasons, find making a full-length prostration very difficult. But such a prostration is not essential. One of my friends bows from his wheelchair; others make a half-prostration, like the Chinese *kow-tow*, or one can simply stand, or sit, and bow from the waist. The important thing is to make a physical gesture of reverence, receptivity, and submission; to express as vigorously as you can and with the whole of your being the act of Going for Refuge to the Three Jewels – the Buddha, the Dharma, and the resplendent Ārya Sangha embodied by the Tree.

The physical and verbal aspects of this practice are as significant as the mental ones. After reciting the threefold Refuge formula – 'to the Buddha for Refuge I go, to the Dharma for Refuge I go, to the Sangha for Refuge I go' – we usually recite a list of precepts, indicating our intention to live out that Going for Refuge in every aspect of our lives. This is important, for unless the act of Going for Refuge to the Three Jewels is extended into all areas of our lives it can easily remain a merely theoretical matter. By practising a set of ethical precepts we bring the nitty-gritty dimension of our daily life into line with our intention to go for Refuge.

The prostration practice has a similar effect. Joining our hands together and prostrating we engage the whole of our body, reciting the verses of Refuge we engage our speech, and by developing and maintaining the visualized image we engage our mind. In this way, the whole of our psychophysical organism is brought into relation with the mythic dimension of the Three Refuges. The spark of what is ultimate in us responds to the great blaze that is the Refuge Tree, and by acting out our relationship to the visualized Tree we take an active part in the cosmic drama of Going for Refuge, the drama of total transformation, from unenlightened being to Enlightened being, embodied by the Tree itself.

The effects of the practice are cumulative. The more time you spend in the presence of the Refuges, the more they are able to stir your depths. After a time you may come to feel that with each prostration you are, literally, throwing yourself more and more fully into the spiritual life. The more you do so the more natural it becomes, as all your stiffness of pride is gradually softened and worn away. It is a wonderful thing to be living in a universe in which beings as evolved as those on the Refuge Tree have emerged. It is our tremendous good fortune to be in contact with them, to be able to conjure them up in our minds and thereby, at least to some extent, enter their world. Step by step, prostration by prostration, the Refuges work their miracle of total transformation upon us. As we do this, our lives take on a deeper meaning. Being in contact to that extent with the Refuges and all they represent, living under their beneficial influence, we come to have more and more to offer to the suffering world we live in.

To begin with, we sit in meditation as a relatively fixed and solid self, building up the picture of the Refuge Tree. It is as if we are painting a picture in our minds, following a set of instructions – 'Avalokiteśvara has four arms, he is white, he holds a rosary and jewel....' In time, though, the figures on the Tree start to develop a life of their own. We feel less and less that we are building up a picture and more and more that we are actually contacting another dimension of reality. As we experience things in this way, our sense of our being fixed, unchanging entities starts to diminish, and the boundary between ourselves and the Refuge Tree, ourselves and others, becomes more translucent.

Over the years, the figures on the Tree may begin to take on as much life as the 'I' that supposedly creates them. The distance between us and them steadily decreases until, finally, we experience no distance at all. We become our own Refuge. In Going for Refuge more and more deeply, we ourselves become, in time, a Tree of Refuge.

Chapter Two

Visualization and Imagination

The act of visualizing a Buddha or Bodhisattva, as a spiritual exercise, is central to the Vajrayāna approach to Buddhism. But it is also present in the Mahāyāna, especially in those schools which focus on the Pure Land Sūtras, and the actual seeds of the practice go back very nearly as far as we can reach in Buddhist history. In the Pāli scriptures we read about Piṅgiya, the nephew and pupil of Bāvari (or Bāvarī), a Vedic master. At Bāvari's instruction, he once went with several fellow disciples to hear the Buddha teach. Piṅgiya was very elderly, and rather feeble, but his response to the Buddha was anything but weak. In the *Sutta-Nipāta*, one of the oldest Buddhist scriptures, we hear him telling his uncle what he found when he met the Buddha:

> 'I will sing you the praises of The Way to the Beyond,' said Piṅgiya (when he returned to where the brahmin Bāvari lives on the banks of the River Godhāvari). 'It was described to us by this man exactly as he saw it. But then, there isn't any reason why a man like him should lie – a mammoth of knowledge and completely pure, a man without desire.
>
> 'When a voice has none of the glibness of pride and none of the ingrained stains of ignorance, then its words are full of sweetness and beauty. It is such words that I praise now.
>
> 'They call him Buddha, Enlightened, Awake, dissolving darkness, with total vision, and knowing the world to its ends, he has gone beyond all the states of being and of becoming. He has no inner poison-drives: he is the total elimination of suffering. This man, brahmin Bāvari, is the man I follow.

'It is like a bird that leaves the bushes of the scrubland and flies to the fruit trees of the forest. I too have left the bleary half-light of opinions; like a swan I have reached a great lake.

'Up till now, before I heard Gotama's teaching, people had always told me this: "This is how it has always been, and this is how it will always be"; only the constant refrain of tradition, a breeding ground for speculation.

'This prince, this beam of light, Gotama, was the only one who dissolved the darkness. This man Gotama is a universe of wisdom and a world of understanding, a teacher whose Dhamma is the Way Things Are, instant, immediate and visible all around, eroding desire without harmful side-effects, with nothing else quite like it anywhere in the world.'

'But Piṅgiya,' said Bāvari, 'why then don't you spend all your time, your every moment, with this man Gotama, this universe of wisdom, this world of understanding, this teacher whose Dhamma is the Way Things Are, instant, immediate, and visible all around, eroding desire without harmful side-effects, and with nothing else quite like it anywhere in the world?'

'Brahmin, Sir,' said Piṅgiya, 'there is not a moment for me, however small, that is spent away from Gotama, from this universe of wisdom, this world of understanding, this teacher whose Dhamma is the Way Things Are, instant, immediate, and visible all around, eroding desire without harmful side-effects, with nothing else quite like it anywhere in the world.'

'You see, Sir', said Piṅgiya, 'with constant and careful vigilance it is possible for me to see him with my mind as clearly as with my eyes, in night as well as day. And since I spend my nights revering him, there is not, to my mind, a single moment spent away from him.

'I cannot now move away from the teaching of Gotama: the powers of confidence and joy, of intellect and awareness, hold me there. Whichever way this universe of wisdom goes it draws me with it.

'Physically, I cannot move like that – my body is decaying, I am old and weak – but the driving power of purposeful thought propels me with it without break.

'There was a time when, writhing in the mud of the swamps, I could only drift from one stone to the next. But then I saw the Sambuddha, fully awake and free from defilement.'

Then the Buddha spoke:

'Piṅgiya,' he said, 'other people have freed themselves by the power of confidence. Vakkali, Bhadrāvudha and Ālavi-Gotama have all done this. You too should let that strength release you; you too will go to the further shore, beyond the draw of death.'

'These words', said Piṅgiya, 'are the words of a man of wisdom. As I hear them I become more confident. This man is Sambuddha: he has opened the curtains and woken up. There is nothing barren there; his mind is clear and luminous.

'Everything accessible to knowledge is known to him, even the ultimate subtleties of godhood. There are no more questions for the doubtful who come to him: the teacher has answered them all.

'Yes, I shall go there. I shall go beyond change, I shall go beyond formations; I shall go beyond comparison. There are no more doubts. You may consider this as mind released.'[5]

Piṅgiya saw the Buddha in his mind, 'as clearly as with his eyes'. As far he was concerned, the Buddha was with him night and day. So strong was this sense, in fact, that the Buddha effectively communicated with Piṅgiya at a distance – assuring him that by the power of his confidence and trust he would soon gain Enlightenment, which, in fact, he did.

One can see how that might work. Piṅgiya had a strong sense of the Buddha's presence, night and day. The qualities of Enlightenment, therefore, accompanied him constantly. In time, there came to be no separation between Piṅgiya and the qualities of Enlightenment. They became his own qualities.

That is what one tries to do in visualization. Through symbolic imagery, one evokes, then dwells upon, particular aspects of the qualities of Enlightenment. *Ultimately* speaking, there is no separation between oneself and the qualities one evokes in meditation. To the extent that we experience them, they are *our* qualities. Practically, however, there is a huge gap between the qualities of Enlightenment that we evoke in meditation and the qualities of our day-to-day experience. The purpose of a visualization practice is to close that gap, to draw ever closer to the qualities of Enlightenment, and finally to realize, in lived experience, one's own innate Buddhahood. That is the work of lifetimes, but the closer one draws to the qualities of Enlightenment that are evoked in visualization practice, the more those qualities begin to manifest within one's own life.

This process of transformation is given symbolic meaning in the Vajrayāna by way of a twofold distinction. Buddhas and Bodhisattvas appear in the context of visualization practice in two forms. There is the *samayasattva*, or 'vow-body', and the *jñānasattva*, or 'knowledge-body'. The *samayasattva* is the form in which the Buddha or Bodhisattva appears to practitioners who have vowed to visualize them regularly. When one undertakes such a practice, one enters into a pact with that Buddha or Bodhisattva. One vows, for one's own part, to devotedly visualize them and recite their mantra on a regular basis. The Buddha or Bodhisattva, on the other hand, has their part in the pact. They assure one that if one practises faithfully, they will in time appear – fully and completely. The *jñānasattva*, or 'knowledge-body', is that appearance. When one first starts to practise one encounters the *samayasattva*. One makes an effort to visualize, and the form that one consequently 'sees' is the *samayasattva*. One does this faithfully, for many years, and then, when conditions are right, the *jñānasattva* 'descends into' the *samayasattva* and one encounters the form in its transcendental reality.

For Piṅgiya, the *samayasattva* was the form he saw through his complete faith in the Buddha. And since his faith *was* complete, *jñānasattva*, transcendental Buddhahood, soon manifested and 'spoke' to him – assuring him of complete Enlightenment. For many of us, however, the term 'visualization', is potentially problematic. The world we move in is by and large a visual world. As smell is for dogs and sound is for bats, so sight is for us. That is all very well as far as the day-to-day lives of the large majority of sighted people go. But when it comes to matters of the imagination, not everyone has an equal facility for working with visualized images.

Part of this is clearly a matter of temperament. Visual artists, for instance, incline more easily to the generation of visual images than the rest of us. It is important, therefore, not to be too literalistic when we consider the subject of visualization.

Try this exercise. Imagine your mother. One can be fairly sure that when most of us are asked to call our mothers to mind some kind of mental image is evoked. But how much of that mental image is strictly visual? In my own case, when I do this exercise, I always evoke a fairly clear sense of my mother. But that sense is not completely visual. It is not as if a kind of photographic representation appears in my mind, which I could, had I but the technology, print out and hand to my friends to show them what my mother looks like. When I call my mother to mind there is some degree of visual imagination involved, but it is more complex than that. I evoke a clear *image* of my mother, but the image is not strictly visual – there are other components as well. Feeling, memory, thought, sound, and touch come into it as well. I evoke, to use a German term, a gestalt – a perceptual pattern which has qualities as a whole that cannot be described merely as the sum of its parts.

So, when we set out to visualize the Refuge Tree, what we try to do is evoke its gestalt, and one of the first obstacles we may have to overcome is our tendency towards literalism.

Western Buddhists approach the image of the Refuge Tree today under a unique set of conditions. The image itself, as commonly depicted, follows the conventions of Indo-Tibetan medieval iconography. But we bring our own conditioning to bear upon the image when we look at it, and when it comes to visual images, that conditioning is strongly influenced by the conventions of European post-Renaissance pictorial representation, followed by a century or more of photography.

The conventions of post-Renaissance pictorial representation lead us to approach images as if they purported to be accurate depictions of the 'real' world. Pictures and photographs are an attempt to portray objects as closely as possible in two dimensions. If you can photograph something, we think it really exists, and it exists more or less as we see it in the photograph. The camera never lies. Of course, in the era of digital manipulation, this is no longer true, but nonetheless we continue to be in thrall to the conventions of pictorial representation in which the object and its depiction are thought to be very nearly identical. I know what the Sydney Opera House looks like, I've seen the pictures. When I go to Sydney and see it, it will be familiar. Allowing for the differences between the two-dimensional experience of photographs or paintings and the three-dimensional experience of the thing itself, there is an ineluctable correspondence between the object and the image.

Indo-Tibetan medieval iconography, however, like Western medieval sacred art and Eastern Orthodox iconography, is not like that. It is not an attempt to portray literalistically, in two dimensions, what actually exists in three. Rather, it is an attempt to evoke the sacred by way of the symbolic. But one can never – solely by way of colours, shapes, sounds, or concepts – get directly to the ultimate reality of the symbol. Such reality defies photographic, pictorial, or conceptual depiction. It exists on a plane of being where those activities have no hold. The iconographic images we depict are only very partial instantiations of a symbolic reality which goes far beyond them.

The Refuge Tree that is painted on canvas, or described in words, does not correspond to the *real* Refuge Tree in the way a photograph of the Sydney Opera House corresponds to a solid building beside Sydney Harbour. The real Sydney Opera House exists in the same dimension of being as its photograph. Broadly speaking, both partake very largely of human, historical time. The real Refuge Tree, however, exists at the intersection of a number of different dimensions of being. It appears at the intersection of human historical time with the legendary, the mythic, and the transcendental dimensions.

To begin to apprehend the real Refuge Tree, which stands behind the images we see and hear about, we have to approach it in a rather unfamiliar way. For a start, we need to get away from the idea that we are trying to generate in our minds a perfectly accurate pictorial representation of the Tree, as if that was the whole point of the exercise. Instead, we begin by evoking a gestalt of the Tree, and this gestalt will contain any number of elements. There will be visual elements, which follow from our knowledge of the traditional iconography of various figures on the Tree or from photographs we may have seen of the teachers of the present, but there will be other elements as well. Different people respond to different things at different times. One may have a strong feeling for the compassion of Tārā, so that felt response may for a time figure largely in one's apprehension of the Tree. Or one may recently have read a teaching of the Buddha and have a strong feeling for his kindness, so that may stand out. Or one may be moved by the gentle heroism of Kashyapji, and so on. Similarly, one may simply have a very strong response to the colour red, so Amitābha may predominate, or one may be deeply moved by the myth of Padmasambhava, or the clarity of Nāgārjuna. Whatever our personal responses, they are going to be manifold. We respond not only to one figure in one way, but to all the figures in different ways and to a different extent at different times. All these responses are facets of the overall gestalt of the Refuge Tree, which is larger than the sum of its parts.

That overall gestalt cannot be depicted directly, only pointed to. It is the gestalt of the ultimate meaning of Buddhahood and Going for Refuge, the gestalt, in fact, of the ultimate meaning of life. Our tendency to literalism, moreover, not only causes many of us to try to visualize the Refuge Tree as if we were trying to recreate in our minds a specific pictorial representation of the Tree. It also keeps many of us from engaging with the mythic, non-historical elements, and shuts us out from much of its symbolic significance.

In our own culture, the notion of the mythic has been greatly devalued. To an extent, we conceive it in opposition to the literal. In the modern West, literal truth has become the primary truth, and when we speak of something as mythic what we often mean is that it is actually untrue. During the medieval and classical eras, in both East and West, things were conceived differently. There wasn't such a stark division between literal and mythic truth. The world of the gods and the legends of history were apprehended as having the same degree of truth as the laws of mathematics and the discoveries of astronomy. The ancients lived in a world that was animated by vital spirits, their minds were peopled with the tales of myth and legend, and they had much easier access to what we might call the Realm of the Imagination.

The Realm of the Imagination corresponds, to some extent, to what C.G. Jung called 'archetypes of the collective unconscious'. Studying the dreams of his patients, Jung concluded that they often reproduced themes and motifs that play an important part in the various mythologies of mankind and in various religious teachings. He concluded that there were a number of basic psychic patterns, or archetypes, common to the human psyche which found expression in art, myth, dreams, and religious beliefs.

The Buddhist perspective, however, goes beyond that of Jung, and the archetypes that appear in Buddhist imagery have a different meaning. They exist ultimately on a transcendental level and are realized fully only at Enlightenment. But they also express themselves at lower levels, on different planes of archetypal form, in visions and in dreams. The visionary dimensions of archetypal form correspond to the various worlds of the gods that Buddhist imagery identifies, and these same archetypes emerge in our world of sense experience as the myths and symbols of human culture.

Myths and symbols, then, are the golden threads that lead us onwards and upwards to the refined world of the gods, and ultimately beyond that, to Enlightenment. But before most of us can embark on the journey through these different realms, we have first to overcome our conditioned tendency to literalism and materialism. And one of the ways we do this is by cultivating our imaginative faculty. Sangharakshita puts this very clearly in his essay *The Journey to Il Convento*:

> The imagination, or image-perceiving faculty, is not so much
> a faculty among faculties as the man – the spiritual man –
> himself. It is spoken of as a faculty because, in the case of
> the vast majority of people, it exists in such a rudimentary
> form that it appears to be simply a 'faculty' like, for instance,
> reason or emotion, or because it has not yet been developed
> or manifested at all. The imaginal faculty is, in reality, the
> man himself, because when one truly perceives an image one
> perceives it with the whole of oneself, or with one's whole
> being. When one truly perceives an image, therefore, one is
> transported to the world to which that image belongs and
> becomes, if only for the time being, an inhabitant of that

world. In other words, truly to perceive an image means to become an image, so that when one speaks of the imagination, or the imaginal faculty, what one is really speaking of is image perceiving image. That is to say, in perceiving an image what one really perceives is, in a sense, oneself.[6]

This, then, is what the Refuge Tree, as an image, represents. It is ourselves, Enlightened, and when we fully perceive it as such we will be at our journey's end. But that is some way off. In order to begin that journey most of us have to do some work developing our imagination.

We live today in a world of impoverished imagination, under the sway of literalism and materialism. Ever since the time of the Greeks, rationalism and its attendant preoccupation with literal truth have come increasingly to predominate within the Western mind. From the time of the emperor Constantine, moreover, the jealous god of the Israelites and his Christian devotees waged unremitting war against the paganism of the ancients. By the late Middle Ages it became clear that monotheism had triumphed and the psychic stage was swept clean for Jehovah's rule. Rationalism, however, which contrived for a time to coexist with monotheism, eventually gave birth to the eighteenth-century Enlightenment and, a mere one hundred years later, Nietzsche proclaimed the death of God. Reason killed him, and now struts alone on the psychic stage; a stark, alienated spectre – lonely, cold, and triumphant. The old myths and stories have been replaced by a welter of 'information'.

As a result of all this, reason and emotion have increasingly become separated in the modern mind, and, once separated, they become both weak and dangerous. The chattering, destructive, alienated intellect, separated from the emotions, has an endless capacity to explain everything away, but can find value in nothing. It has not the capacity, on its own, to discern what is truly valuable, so it wanders in the world, drawing and re-drawing the categories into which it compartmentalizes experience, all the time inhabiting a bleak, monotonous plane of sterile, deconstructive aridity. Emotion, on the other hand, separated from the intellect, moves in a world of whimsical self-preoccupation, endlessly infatuated with the minute details of its immediate experience.

Until these two are, to some extent, brought together, one cannot make any real spiritual progress. The intellect without the emotions cannot apprehend the truths that inhere in the world of spiritual imagination. Unable to let go of its own scepticism, and unable on its own to rise to higher levels of consciousness, it fails to distinguish imaginal truth from the mono-dimensional products of delusion and fantasy. The emotions without the intellect, lacking any critical faculty, are constantly swayed by passing fancies. Unable to distinguish what has genuine spiritual worth from what merely feels good, they too remain trapped on a single plane of value.

All human beings have the capacity to apprehend imaginal truth. But in most of us that capacity is not yet fully developed. There is, in each of us, some spark of apprehension that responds to the truth when we come upon it, however that may be, but all too often those responses are dimmed by the overriding calls of the mundane.

> The world is too much with us; late and soon,
> Getting and spending, we lay waste our powers.[7]

The spark of apprehension with which we respond to imaginal truth when we encounter it is known, in Buddhist terms, as *śraddhā*. Etymologically, this Sanskrit term means 'to place the heart upon', and the heart in Buddhism is not the seat solely of the emotions; the heart, the centre of the psyche, is also the seat of the intellect. That to which one responds with *śraddhā* is that upon which one places one's heart and mind.

In translation, *śraddhā* is often rendered as 'faith', but that can easily lead to confusion. Faith, in Western religious discourse, has many meanings, but it is not the same as *śraddhā*. In the monotheistic religions, faith is demanded by God. Loss of faith is sinful, and can even lead, in some cultures, to punishment. Faith is often presented as if it were opposed to reason. In that sense, it is blind: it is the capacity simply to accept what must be accepted, without the intervention of the intellect and without reference to experience. Concepts such as these are completely alien to the Buddhist approach. *Śraddhā* is a response of the whole mind – its reason and its emotions – to what is higher and more worthwhile. At its best, it is the response of what is highest in us to what is highest in the universe. It is the sympathetic resonance that occurs when the faculty for perceiving goodness, truth, and beauty, innate in all of us, encounters goodness, truth, and beauty in the world. It is our own innate potential for Buddhahood resonating with Buddhahood made fully manifest. When a potential Buddhist encounters the Dharma, *śraddhā* arises and one goes for Refuge to the Buddha, Dharma, and Sangha.

Śraddhā manifests as the act of Going for Refuge to the Three Jewels. When reason and emotion come together in perceiving one's highest ideals, action follows. In Going for Refuge to the Three Jewels one begins to enter the mythical world represented by the Refuge Tree. One embarks, in fact, on a pilgrimage in quest of the Grail of Enlightenment.

When one undertakes that journey in the context of the Triratna Buddhist Order, one does so both alone and in company. The act of Going for Refuge is both a public and a private matter. One can decide only for oneself to embark on that journey, and one's commitment to it is a highly personal affair. But having made that commitment one finds oneself in the company of a band of spiritual brothers and sisters who share one's ideals and become helpful companions. All the travellers on that mythic journey are guided by the same brilliant, shining beacon – the Refuge Tree of the Triratna Buddhist Order – however it appears to them.

Chapter Three

Going for Refuge

In the Pāli scriptures we read of many people coming to see the Buddha. He gives them a short teaching which so impresses them, so changes them, that they are impelled to reorient their entire lives as a result. 'It's as if something that had fallen over was put upright again. Things that were obscure are now quite clear,' they say. 'It's like light being brought into a dark room! I was completely lost and you've shown me the way. I go for Refuge to you, to your Dharma and your Sangha. May I be one of your disciples for as long as I live!'

The practice of Going for Refuge to the Buddha, Dharma, and Sangha is one of the most ancient in all of Buddhism, but the notion of ' going for refuge' can sit uncomfortably with some of our present-day ideas. The idea that we might need a refuge can seem a bit escapist, even weak. We don't like to think of ourselves as being unable to face up to life, of needing to take shelter from reality. But we deceive ourselves. The truth is that the very large majority of us *are* escapist. We hardly ever face up to the facts of life and we take refuge from them, in one way or another, all the time. The trouble is that we go for refuge to things that are not true refuges:

> Many people, out of fear, flee for refuge to (sacred) hills, woods, groves, trees, and shrines.
>
> In reality this is not a safe refuge. In reality this is not the best refuge. Fleeing to such a refuge one is not released from all suffering.
>
> He who goes for refuge to the Enlightened One, to the Truth, and to the Spiritual Community, – who sees with

perfect wisdom the Four Ariyan Truths, – namely, suffering, the origin of suffering, the passing beyond suffering, and the Ariyan Eight-membered Way leading to the pacification of suffering, –

(For him) this is a safe refuge, (for him) this is the best refuge. Having gone to such a refuge, one is released from all suffering.[8]

These days we may not, as in the time of the *Dhammapada*, 'flee for refuge to sacred hills, groves, trees, and shrines'. Instead, we dream of winning the lottery, finding the perfect partner, having the perfect holiday, being anywhere, in fact, rather than here and now – facing up to the truth of things. Unwilling to face up to the Buddha's first noble truth, that all conditioned things are intrinsically unsatisfactory, we conjure up visions and dreams as a refuge from our sense of inner incompleteness.

Our multiple strategies for avoiding facing up to the way things really are, however, inevitably come to nothing. Reality inexorably reasserts itself through all our vain efforts to deny it, and so we suffer. We may think that having the perfect partner will end our suffering for ever, but there *are* no perfect people out there; our friends and partners, being human and unenlightened, will inevitably let us down; and in any case, like everyone else, they will one day die.

There are no perfect partners, perfect friends, perfect jobs, perfect families, perfect holidays, or perfect meals. Despite everything the advertising industry tries to tell us, there are no perfect chocolate bars or ice-creams either. And yet, like hamsters on a wheel, we pass our time energetically scurrying about in quest of that perfect x-factor which will put a stop, finally and forever, to our innate sense of unsatisfactoriness, our own incompleteness.

Instead of taking refuge in dreams of wealth and power, or in the fleeting pleasures of chocolate bars, shopping, and television, we need to face the truth head on. Instead of taking refuge in delusion, we need to take refuge in the truth. In order to do this, however, we need to reverse a deep-seated process.

'I want this, I don't want that. I like this, I don't like that.' Responding in this way to the constantly changing circumstances of life, we build and rebuild ourselves as more or less stable ego-identities struggling to maintain their boundaries within the swirling tide of conditions. What we pull inside those boundaries: the food we like, the people we associate with, the things we watch and read; and what we push out: the people we don't want to be with, the clothes we won't wear, the places we avoid – all these define the shape and contours of our ego-identity. And this process runs on and on from minute to minute. We are constantly hard at work defining and redefining ourselves to ourselves and to the world, vainly struggling to get hold of that elusive x-factor that will give us some sense of peace and stability in the face of constant change. As long as we remain in denial of the facts of life, however, this process is doomed. 'All conditioned things are impermanent, insubstantial, and ultimately unsatisfactory.' So taught the Buddha, and until we face up to this and deal with life as it really is, we will suffer.

Previously, we took in distractions in one form or another and pushed out the painful truths of impermanence and unsatisfactoriness. Instead, we need to take in the truth and push out delusion. Going for Refuge to the Buddha, the Dharma, and the Sangha, we open ourselves to the highest truth, to the way in which that truth may be discovered, and to all those men and women throughout history who have made that truth their own and are able to impart it. Going for Refuge to the Buddha, Dharma, and Sangha is the exact opposite of escapism.

Living escapist lives, we use all kinds of strategies to avoid facing up to the deepest truth of things. We bury ourselves under our duvets or engage energetically with the world in order to amass wealth. We even escape into good works and humanitarian activity. But only by finally facing up to the true nature of things, with every aspect of our being, will we ever find any real peace and happiness, and only when we are deeply rooted in the truth will we be really effective in helping others.

The Buddha saw all this perfectly clearly, and everything he said and did was an expression of that fact. Communication with him must have been electrifying; it cut straight through people's cherished delusions, yet they responded wholeheartedly. It was as if light was brought into darkness. What they had always sought was suddenly right there before them, and right away they committed themselves to putting it into practice.

We ourselves may not have the good fortune to meet a Buddha face to face, but many people have such a response when they first hear the Dharma. For many of us it is an experience of 'coming home', of hearing what we had known deep in our hearts but which we had never before been able to articulate. So we go for Refuge to it.

The change that takes place at this point is spoken of in Pāli as the shift from *kāmachanda* to *dhammachanda*. *Kāmachanda* is the thirst for sense-experience. *Dhammachanda* is the thirst for the truth or the wholesome. Previously, we lived entirely under the sway of *kāmachanda*, the endless quest for distracting sense-experience, the thirst for those sense experiences that give us an apparently stable sense of ourselves. Now, we try increasingly to orient our lives towards the active pursuit of the truth.

In the case of some very rare individuals this reorientation happens fully and almost instantaneously. In the Buddha's lifetime that seems to have happened to many of the people he met; after hearing what he had to say many of them gained profound insights which changed them for ever. For most of us today it is a change which has slow beginnings and takes place by degrees. We gradually reorientate our lives so that they are increasingly informed by the values of the Three Jewels, and for the large majority of us the process of Going for Refuge to the Three Jewels involves a constant effort to reorientate our being away from the thirst for sense-experience towards the thirst for the Dharma. That effort is the very essence of the Buddhist spiritual life, and all Buddhist teachings and practices, in one way or another, have this as their object and focus.

Sangharakshita has made many important contributions to the understanding of the Dharma today, but perhaps the most important of these is his insight that the act of Going for Refuge to the Three Jewels is the principal Buddhist practice. Going for Refuge is primary. It is what makes one a Buddhist, and therefore something that all Buddhists have in common. The way in which that Going for Refuge is expressed, whether as a monk, householder, wanderer, or non-celibate full-timer, is secondary.

As well as this, Sangharakshita has seen that Going for Refuge deepens by degrees, and he has described different levels of Going for Refuge. For example, there are the cultural, provisional, effective, real, and absolute levels.[9] Cultural Going for Refuge is the level of those people who think of themselves as being Buddhists because they were born into a Buddhist family or Buddhist culture, although they have no commitment to spiritual practice. The provisional level of Going for Refuge is the level of all those who consciously begin to lead a Buddhist spiritual life, but are not yet fully committed to it. At the effective level one's commitment to the Three Jewels is the central axis of one's life to the extent that one's living conditions allow. Real Going for Refuge arises in dependence upon the arising of transcendental insight. After that has happened, one can no longer completely fall back under the sway of delusion. Absolute Going for Refuge is equivalent to Buddhahood.

Within all this there is one particular stage that different Buddhist schools and traditions have identified as the immediate goal of their spiritual endeavours, although it is described in different ways under different circumstances and within apparently very different systems of thought and practice. What Sangharakshita speaks of as the transition from Effective to Real Going for Refuge is spoken of in other traditions as, for example, Stream Entry, irreversibility (from full and perfect Enlightenment), the arising of Insight, the opening of the Dharma Eye, *satori*, the Turning About in the Deepest Seat of Consciousness, or the arising of the bodhicitta. All of these identify a single common experience: an irreversible change, in the basic emphasis of one's life, from an attraction to the mundane to an attraction to the transcendental. It is the shift from being primarily motivated by *kāmachanda* to being primarily motivated by *dhammachanda*, and forms the beginning of real spiritual creativity.

Sangharakshita's way of resolving all of these different ways of speaking of the goal of spiritual irreversibility into the language of Going for Refuge has the effect of demonstrating the essential unity of the Buddhist tradition. Once one sees that, much that was previously unclear falls neatly into place. What is more, since all the Buddhist traditions, in principle if not in practice, accept the central significance of the act of Going for Refuge, Sangharakshita's insight is, potentially, a major step forward in the establishment of understanding between the different traditions.

But one can push his insight still further. We can apply the template of provisional, effective, real, and absolute levels not only to the process of Going for Refuge, but also to all the many different aspects of spiritual life. We can speak of provisional, effective, real, and absolute insight, for example, and we can apply the same template to the practice of ethics, meditation, altruism, or devotion. In the context of the Refuge Tree, we can also apply it to the development of faith.

In the Triratna Buddhist movement, many people first take up the Going for Refuge and Prostration Practice in the context of a Going for Refuge retreat – that is, one of the retreats that form part of the ordination training process. The Going for Refuge and Prostration Practice is undertaken only by Order members or those who have asked for ordination, and the latter are asked to take it up only when they have been formally introduced to it in the context of a Going for Refuge retreat. In the context of the Triratna Buddhist Order, ordination signifies the transition from provisional to effective Going for Refuge. The ordination training process is designed to help people make that transition, so many of those who take up the prostration practice do so from the provisional level of Going for Refuge. Their faith in all the figures on the Refuge Tree is therefore provisional. Not yet ready to fully commit themselves to a life of spiritual endeavour within the context of the Order, their relationship to the Refuge Tree may be very important to them, but it is not yet the central fact of their lives. People practising at this level may have very strong feelings of confidence and trust in the figures on the Tree, but they will not yet have fully worked out all its implications for their future.

At the effective level of faith, once you have fully committed yourself and, in this case, joined the Order, the Refuge Tree takes its place firmly in the centre of your life. Whether you do the prostration practice regularly or not, it stands as an effective symbol of that in which you place your faith. You have taken your place in the field of spiritual influence that radiates out from the Refuges, and your life is now increasingly dedicated to opening

34

yourself up to that influence and passing it on. You are not yet spiritually irreversible – as conditions change, your faith in the Refuges waxes and wanes – but as long as you place yourself in beneficial circumstances your confidence in the Refuges and your heartfelt love of the Three Jewels will grow ever stronger.

At the real level of faith you have entered fully into the realm of the Refuge Tree. Your faith in the Refuges is unshakeable and the figures on the Tree become living presences in your life. At this level, being a member of the ārya Sangha, you yourself become an object of faith for others – you stand for the achievement to which they aspire, and you help them to move forward themselves.

At the absolute level there is no ultimate difference between yourself and the Tree. But that is a very long way away indeed.

The importance of faith in Buddhism should not be underestimated. Knowing the good, Socrates said, was sufficient. If one knew what was good one would do it. That is all very well for someone of Socrates' level of integrity. For the majority of us, however, the gap between knowing good and doing it is large. As Aristotle pointed out, Socrates' statement does not account for what Aristotle called 'the irrational parts of the soul'.

The Buddha was well aware of this fundamental human issue. Indeed, he took it into account in his formulation of the Noble Eightfold Path. The path begins with a moment of Perfect Vision. We have an intuitive flash of insight into the way things really are, and śraddhā – faith – arises. We see that what the Buddha said was true. We have a moment when we 'know' the truth. But that moment does not last. Because we are not yet emotionally ready to absorb the full implications of that 'knowing', and to live out all its implications in our daily lives, we soon lose it. The stage of Perfect Vision is followed by the stage of Perfect Emotion. We have to bring our emotional lives into line with the vision.

It is not enough simply to know; we also have to *feel* before we begin to act. The stage of Perfect Emotion, then, is where we begin to develop the feelings appropriate to our understanding of the Dharma. At this stage, we develop what Sangharakshita has called the emotional equivalents of our intellectual understandings, and we can do this using many different means. We can read devotional poetry and literature, listen to devotional music, and look at devotional pictures. We can engage in acts of pūjā and offering – whatever will engage our emotions and our imagination with that which we think of as the highest in our lives. We can also perform the Going for Refuge and Prostration practice.

Visualizing the Refuge Tree in front of us, in all its glowing glory, we create and adorn an image that stands as a luminous representation of all that we hold dear. Reciting verses of devotion and aspiration, we speak out and therefore concretize our heartfelt aspiration to arrange our lives in accordance with our highest values. Throwing ourselves down before the Tree again and again, we live out and deepen our feelings of faith and devotion, and we make our relationship to the Tree plain to ourselves and others. We have our place at the foot of the Tree. That is where we truly belong, below the Refuges, looking up.

In this and in other ways, acts of faith and devotion are a central part of our living out the provisional or effective levels of Going for Refuge that we experience in our lives. Engaging with such practices again and again, we make our Going for Refuge deeper and deeper. In time we might even make it Real.

Chapter Four

The Refuge Tree, Bodhicitta, and 'Other-power'

Sangharakshita writes in his memoirs how – when he was staying with his friend Dr Mehta in Poona and meditating more intensively – he found himself entering into dialogue with the Buddha in the course of deep meditation, asking pertinent questions and receiving direct replies. Later, we read that after receiving the Green Tārā initiation from Chetul Rimpoche he felt that his whole spiritual life was now guided from a higher dimension, and that he had at last found the inner guidance he had so long desired, beyond the level of his own ego.

How are we to make sense of all of this? What is this thing beyond the level of our ego? And how can it work in our lives? The Japanese Buddhist traditions are deeply concerned with such issues. They distinguish between 'self-power' and 'other-power'. Self-power is the effort we each make to grow and develop; other-power is the Buddha's response to that effort. To many of us this idea carries awkward overtones of theism. The Buddha, we know, is not a god. He is not the creator of the world, not its ruler or judge, and Buddhists are not required to believe in his omnipresent existence, yet there is this talk of 'other-power'. And what about all the other figures on the Refuge Tree? What are we doing when we throw ourselves down before them? Can they really do anything for us? What is the ultimate status of 'other-power'?

Ultimately, like everything else, it has no status at all. The mind of a Buddha, we are told, is free from all claims of 'me' and 'mine'. Buddhas do not, like us, automatically and unconsciously erect barriers between themselves and the flow of conditions about them. In the mind of a Buddha there is no boundary between self and other, no fixed ego-identity separating itself off from the flow of impressions, no unyielding barrier between the image and the imagination in which the image occurs. Ultimately, therefore, from the point of view of Enlightenment, there is no 'self' and no 'other', no subject, no object, and no existential status. There is just the flux of changing conditions in which nothing lasts long enough to claim the status of an independent existence, and the image of a Buddha that I conjure up in my mind in visualization has the same existential status as the computer on which I am typing this. Its status, ultimately speaking, is no-status. In the language of Yogācāra Buddhism, all things are 'mind-only', and this applies as much to the Buddha I visualize as to the computer here in my room.

You may not be able to see the Buddha I am imagining, but then you cannot see this computer either. As far as you are concerned, both are just images. But what if you were here with me, in my room, watching me type. Wouldn't you see my computer then? Would it not be more real than the Buddha I imagine? No, it wouldn't. All we ever apprehend are images. Memories, thoughts, sights, tactile impressions, sounds, smells, tastes – all are images, and we can never get behind them, to the 'real' world. Try as we might, all we ever encounter is another image, and we never get out of our minds and behind the image to the supposed 'thing itself'. There are no fixed, enduring essences underlying the images that we apprehend. All things are *Śūnyatā*, emptiness, manifesting as the myriad impressions that arise from changing conditions.

Now, that is all well and good in theory. All phenomena lack inherent existence; all good Buddhists know that – conceptually, at least. But in practice we still live and move in a world of apparently fixed and more or less stable entities – chairs and tables, laptops, and, above all, our own apparently unyielding ego-identities. We are not yet Buddhas. For us, the ideas of self and other seem to have real meaning, and it is because the notions of self and other have such a hold on us that the allied ideas of self-power and other-power also have meaning. Acknowledging that we actually see the world in dualistic terms, we can begin to use that dualism to overcome dualism.

At the start, our spiritual lives depend on self-power. For much of the time our attempts to go for Refuge to the Three Jewels involve making some degree of willed effort. We have to make the effort to meditate every morning, even though we may prefer to lie in bed. We have to curb our anger and our appetites. We do not lead spontaneously ethical lives, we have to make something of an effort to be unselfish. This is what spiritual life is like at the provisional and effective levels of Going for Refuge.

At this level we experience ourselves as having an ego – a more or less fixed sense of self. But as we progress along the path, our sense of the world is less and less firmly delineated by our ego. As we become kinder, more generous, more flexible, more sensitive, and more aware of the world about us in all its many dimensions, our ego begins to yield and to soften, and we begin to experience moments of genuine self-transcendence.

As we progressively open ourselves up to the process of self-transcendence, it can increasingly manifest as a kind of 'other-power' working through our lives. We begin to see that the notion of 'me' that we have constructed and spent so much time feeding and defending is not the final boundary of existence: reality is far greater than we are. This is what happens for some people when they are given a visualization practice and introduced to one or another of the archetypal Bodhisattvas. After contemplating the figure for many years they may begin to experience it as an active force in their lives, working through them and imbuing their thoughts and acts with greater significance and greater effectiveness.

This sense of a source of value external to the ego, drawing one onwards and upwards, is something upon which one may come increasingly to depend. As we make spiritual progress we depend more and more upon the Three Jewels, less and less upon petty, mundane things. This is the beginning of a deep shift in our identity. We stop deriving our security and sense of self-worth from our possessions, appearance, and social status and start to become more naturally concerned to help others and to see clearly how things really are. In other words, our Going for Refuge to the Three Jewels has become deeper and stronger.

But the Refuges are not something we have generated from within. They are not a part of the self, not a part of our ego-identity. Not being Buddhas ourselves, the very fact that we have heard of the Dharma depends upon its having been given us from outside. In one of the Perfection of Wisdom texts, the *Ratnaguṇa Saṃcayagāthā*, we read

> The rivers all in this Roseapple Island
> Which cause the flowers to grow, the fruits, the herbs and
>   trees,
> They all derive from the might of the king of the Nagas,
> From the Dragon residing in Lake Anopatapta, his magical
>   power.
>
> Just so, whatever Dharmas the Jinas' disciples establish,
> Whatever they teach, whatever adroitly explain –
> Concerning the work of the holy which leads to the fullness
>   of bliss,
> And also the fruit of this work – it is the Tathāgata's doing.
>
> For whatever the Jina has taught, the Guide to the Dharma,
> His pupils, if genuine, have well been trained in it
> From direct experience, derived from their training, they
>   teach it.
> Their teaching stems from the might of the Buddhas, and not
>   their own power.[10]

Just as the King of the Nāgas, residing at the bottom of Lake Anopatapta at the foot of Mount Kailash, sends forth his rivers into India to water all the plants there, so too there is a great river, a stream of spiritual beneficence, which has its origins in the Enlightened Mind, entirely beyond time and space, which streams forth into our world by way of the activity of the ārya Sangha. It is this that we come increasingly to depend upon, and, from the point of view of the ego, it is something other than ourselves. It is 'other-power'. When, at the level of Real Going for Refuge, we rely primarily upon the Three Jewels, and not upon mundane things, that amounts to a real dependence upon other-power. This idea of a stream of spiritual influence reaching towards us, even working through us, finds expression in the image of the Refuge Tree, which depicts in some detail how this process can actually work in our lives.

Above the Refuge Tree, beyond space and outside of time, is the image of Vajrasattva, who stands for the *dharmakāya*, Ultimate

Reality, Buddhahood, the final truth of things, which is the beginningless source and timeless origin of this vast river.

At the centre of the Tree is the Buddha Śākyamuni, who represents the irruption of that mighty river into the context of the current human, historical time-frame. On his left and right, the Buddhas Dīpaṅkara and Maitreya show that the river will always intersect with history.

To the right of Śākyamuni are the archetypal Bodhisattvas – idealizations of consummate skilfulness. They manifest at the interface between ultimate reality and the human imagination, urging us onward and upward, constant sources of spiritual nourishment. Wherever the imagination strives to apprehend Enlightenment, in whatever way, there, in whatever form, a Bodhisattva will appear.

To the left of Śākyamuni are his own Enlightened disciples – bearers of his teaching and exemplars of spiritual progress. He sent his Enlightened disciples out into the world to wander, 'for the sake of the many, for the welfare of the many'. Through their activity the Dharma spread far and wide.

Behind Śākyamuni are piled the great treasures of the Dharma texts that have preserved his teachings for the benefit of all. Above him sit the great teachers of our lineage who have made that Dharma their own and proclaimed it to the world. And above them, the five Buddha mandala represents Supreme Enlightenment made manifest in the imagination. Below Śākyamuni appear Sangharakshita, his eight teachers and Ambedkar and Dharmapala, who have introduced the Dharma to so many.

The fact that I am writing this book is a direct consequence of the great compassion of the Buddha Śākyamuni. When he gained Enlightenment, Buddhahood irrupted into the framework of human, historical time, and he taught out of his boundless compassion and concern for a suffering world. At that moment, for the first time in this historical era, Absolute Going for Refuge found expression in this world. At that moment, from the great ocean of Śākyamuni's Enlightened mind, vast streams of Going for Refuge were set flowing down the great course of human, historical time.

For the last two-and-a-half thousand years those great streams of Going for Refuge have passed from teacher to disciple, through many lands and civilizations, where they have watered magnificent cultures and brought flowers where previously there were deserts. And now, through the kindness of my own teacher, the great river of the Going for Refuge has come even to me. Śākyamuni taught, so my life has meaning. What can I do but open myself up to that stream and allow it to flow on?

When members of the Triratna Buddhist Order set up Buddhist centres, teach meditation and Dharma, work in Right Livelihood businesses, and welcome people into residential communities, it all derives from that. It is the same river of the Dharma, the same stream of Going for Refuge, at whatever level, reaching out to a suffering world.

The figures on the Refuge Tree, out of the fullness of their compassion, constantly reach out towards unenlightened beings. All of them dedicated their lives to helping the unenlightened move towards Enlightenment. That was all they cared for, and the spiritual efficacy of their work ripples ever onwards and outwards. This continues even today. It is present, to some degree at least, here and now, as you read this.

We reach up to the figures on the Refuge Tree. In doing so, we allow that same stream of spiritual influence to work upon us and through us. But Going for Refuge always has an altruistic dimension. Having derived so much benefit from the work of all the figures on the Tree, what can we do but reach out in turn to others? If we can bear this perspective in mind it puts all one's work for the Dharma into its true context. In helping to spread the Dharma, one is really helping to carry out the Buddha's work; one is helping to work out the great purpose of the beings on the Refuge Tree.

The primary task of most committed Buddhists is to make our provisional or effective Going for Refuge real. One of the great goals of the spiritual life is the achievement of spiritual irreversibility. Short of this point, all committed Buddhists are trying, in different ways, to grapple with the problem of the self. How do we overcome our fixed sense of ourselves? How do we move from being primarily self-regarding to being primarily other-regarding? How do we get beyond the constricting limitations of self-preoccupation? How do we overcome the ego?

It seems that however many times I return to the realization that my ego-identity is something truly insignificant – that it is the merest speck of delusion spinning out its little stories in the infinitely vast space of the cosmos – when I'm not looking, my ego again and again reasserts itself and swells to occupy the boundaries of space and time. Suddenly I turn round, and there I am again: the single most important entity in this vast universe; all of which must be arranged to serve my own interests. *My* needs, *my* comfort, *my* enjoyment, *my* achievements, *my* writing, even *my* Dharma teaching. All of these so easily and suddenly become paramount.

Whether our egocentricity manifests temperamentally as self-conceit or as self-contempt – or whether it is just an undue attachment to a fixed point of view – is neither here nor there. The point is that all of us who have not yet manifested the Real level of Going for Refuge are liable – at some time or other – to bouts of significantly delusive egocentricity.

This is the central problem of the spiritual life. Our ego is so slippery, so cunning, that it can easily turn all our good works and good intentions, all our spiritual practice, to its own ends. In no time at all our ego can appropriate what we do and turn our merit into ornaments.

So how do we overcome the ego? There is an old Zen saying: 'If you want to control a wild bull, give it a big field.' Some people take this as meaning 'Do what you want, don't be too disciplined.' It can be taken as a sort of easy rationalization for just giving in to our passing appetites, but its meaning is more profound than that. The 'big field' is much more than the field of our casual desires and impulses. It is really the field of bodhicitta.

Bodhicitta – the 'will to Enlightenment (for the sake of all beings)' – is the traditional focus of Mahāyāna Buddhist practice. Sangharakshita speaks of it as the altruistic dimension of Going for Refuge. Without an altruistic dimension, in fact, there is no Going for Refuge. Unless our Going for Refuge moves us – to some extent at least – away from self-preoccupation and towards a concern for others, it isn't really Going for Refuge at all. And because there is *necessarily* an altruistic dimension to Going for Refuge, to the extent that we go for Refuge we experience the arising of the bodhicitta.

By its very nature the bodhicitta is not something personal. To the extent that it arises within us, it diffuses the boundaries of our being and we experience it as much (if not more) outside us as within. Through the kindness of our teachers and the work of our spiritual ancestors, all Buddhists have some degree of access to the vast field of the bodhicitta that radiates outward from the Refuges. As Buddhists, that is our true context. We continue to have an ego-identity, but that ego-identity occurs within a context that extends well beyond it. We have an ego, but as men and women who are Going for Refuge to the Three Jewels that ego-identity is not the final boundary of our being.

In Going for Refuge to the Three Jewels, to whatever degree we do it, we place our ego-identity within the field of the bodhicitta, the field of spiritual influence which radiates out from the great Refuge Tree, and the more we go for Refuge, the more fully and deeply do we locate ourselves within it. In Going for Refuge more and more effectively we come in time to value the field within which our ego operates as much as – and in due course more than – the ego itself. That tipping of the balance, from predominantly valuing the ego to predominantly valuing the field of spiritual influence that surrounds the ego, is the Real Going for Refuge.

For my own part, when I reflect on it more deeply, I see that everything of lasting value in my life comes from the Refuge Tree, and any significant good I do derives from there too. If I can bear this in mind, I see that the true purpose of my life is not to serve my own ends, but to carry on the work of all the figures on the Refuge Tree. If only I can put myself at *their* disposal, and surrender myself to the stream of spiritual influence that radiates from the Buddha Śākyamuni, then I am living out of my own true place in the universe and my life has real meaning.

This perspective is shared by many members of the Triratna Buddhist Order. It motivates us in our work for the Triratna Buddhist Community. When we run our Buddhist centres, and start residential communities and Right Livelihood teams, what we are trying to do is open ourselves up to the great river of bodhicitta that flows out from the Refuge Tree. Every altruistic act we perform in the context of our Going for Refuge is a continuation of that great stream. Reaching out to a suffering world, we become, in our turn, tributaries of that great river. If we can only bear this perspective in mind, coming back to it again and again, then our ego-identities will find their proper place in the universal scheme of things and, over time, just fade away.

When I experience myself in this way – simply doing what is needed, not just doing what *I* want – I also experience the enormous relief of laying down the obsessive burden of ego-identity. I experience the sheer joy and relief of not having to bother – for a while at least – about *my* needs, how *I* sound, how *I* look, *my* preferences. It is an enormous relief to be free, even for a short time, from the burden of self-conceit or self-contempt and from my fixed point of view.

This is the practice of responding to the objective needs of the situation. It is not some dry, abstract, protestant wilfulness that is being evoked. We try to respond to the *objective* needs of any situation partly, at least, because in doing so we free ourselves from our carping, obsessive self-orientation. In freely responding to the objective needs of the situation we begin, oddly enough, to experience real freedom – freedom from the unceasing demands of egocentricity. This is the great work we all have to do this side of Real Going for Refuge, at the interface between effective and real bodhicitta.

The more we depend on the Refuges, the more skilful and effective our lives will be, until one day we find that we have come to depend upon them completely and we no longer depend upon anything else. Then we will find that we have laid down the burden of egocentricity and that we have, in effect, begun to embody the Refuges themselves.

The great river of the bodhicitta is not something we can possess. It is not something which we could ever claim as a personal attribute. It is far too big, it is far beyond us. It goes beyond the bounds of ego-identity altogether. If ever we think we've grasped it and encompassed it, we're mistaken, for this river is vast beyond our comprehension. Yet, somehow, through the endless beneficence of the Buddha and through the kindness of our teachers, we can locate ourselves within it, just Going for Refuge and handing it on, again and again and again, out of gratitude to our friends and teachers, for the sake of all living beings.

Part Two

Introduction

In Part 2 we will look, very briefly, at each of the figures on the Refuge Tree of the Triratna Buddhist Order. Each has their own story to tell. Some, such as the five Jinas and the Bodhisattvas, are clearly archetypal. Others, such as the teachers of the present, are clearly historical. In between come a number of figures who straddle the realms of myth and history – Padmasambhava and Milarepa, for example, left no writings (at least not in the ordinary, 'historical' sense), and what mythical biographies we have post-date them by many centuries.

So how should we view the following stories? In the modern world, we are used to discriminating between myth and history. History, we tend to think, presents us with the *real* truth. Myths, if not dismissed as *mere* myths, are often taken as diverting stories that cast some light on the way people used to think. In reality, myths have the capacity to contain far *more* truth than history. They can touch depths of experience that are beyond the scope of mere historical fact. History tells us that Padmasambhava may have come from the Swat Valley in what is now Pakistan. Myth tells us that he converted the demons of Tibet to the Dharma by discovering their secret names. The historical fact is interesting, but the myth communicates an immensely valuable psychological truth – that if we want to deal with the unconscious forces that trouble us, we must first uncover their names and natures. Only then can we harness the energies tied up in them and transform them into a force for good.

The distinction between myth and history is very much a modern phenomenon. I was fascinated to read Xuanzang's account of Nālandā Monastery, and I quote some of this in the relevant section. For Xuanzang, myth and history are completely indistinguishable – Avalokiteśvara walked about at Nālandā, as did the Buddha, and as did Xuanzang's immediate monastic forebears. All are given an equal 'historical' status.

In producing this account, I have not made very much of the distinction between myth and history. What we have here are stories – some almost entirely mythic, some largely historical, some a mixture of the two. Sometimes I have drawn on modern scholastic knowledge, sometimes not. My approach has been multifaceted, and – at this point in history – perhaps it cannot but be. When looking at the figures on the Refuge Tree we need to learn to shift perspective – to look at them now from a mythic, now from a scientific-historical, now from a devotional, now from a human perspective. Approaching the Tree from these different perspectives it becomes increasingly three- (or more) dimensional. If we are not careful, these different perspectives can cancel one another out ('History is more true than myth!', 'Myth is diminished by mere history!'), but, used with awareness, all these different perspectives can enrich our appreciation of the majestic figures on the Tree, imbuing them with more life and more meaning. In short, we need to approach the figures on the Tree in a spirit of open-mindedness. In that way we can allow them to speak to us as they will.

On this same note, although I have – for example in the accounts of the lives of the Arhants – based my accounts on canonical records, I have not always confined myself to quotations from the canon to tell the story. Sometimes I have created dialogues where none appear in the *suttas*. I have done this because I want to tell a story, to help bring the figures more alive, and because, in any event, I am aware that the *suttas* themselves are also stories – in the sense that none can be taken to be a historically accurate, factual account.

Some people, when they heard I was writing a book on this Refuge Tree, told me how much they were looking forward to its publication. This was, in part, because they really looked forward to finding out why Sangharakshita had chosen these particular figures. Out of all the vast panoply of Buddhist saints and teachers, why these? What do they mean to us in the Triratna Buddhist

Order? And for what teachings ought we to look to them? I'm afraid I shall perhaps disappoint some of my readers, for there is no single answer to this question, and I have not sought to address it.

The Refuge Tree is, above all else, a symbol. As such, its meaning can only be apprehended in the symbol itself. Any attempt to explain the symbol reduces it to a lower level. In trying to explain a symbol we often only explain it away. The Refuge Tree, of course, is not only a visual symbol. Each of its figures has a story, and these stories are also symbols. What we need to do is fully immerse ourselves in their teachings, histories, myths, and legends, and reflect on them. In doing so we will gradually discover what each of them means to us individually. In that way we allow them to stand as living symbols.

I have been able to provide only the briefest introduction to each figure. I have not attempted to give a connected account – there are too many of them, from so many different dimensions, and we know such varying amounts about each of them. Nor have I laid out the different sections in accordance with the pattern in which we normally build up our visualization of the Tree. For the purposes of exposition it made more sense to arrange this part of the book rather differently.

Each of the accounts that follows can be, perhaps ought to be, read independently. There is an enormous amount of information here – too much, perhaps, to be taken in in one sitting. I have tried to point out a number of approaches, and I hope that readers will, in their own time and in their own way, follow up some of these introductions for themselves, getting to know some of these towering figures in much greater depth. Any one of them would reward a lifetime of study and contemplation. I hope that for some of you a great journey of adventure and spiritual discovery will start right here.

Śākyamuni, making the gesture of 'touching the earth', is flanked by Dīpaṅkara on the left and Maitreya on the right, both making the gesture of teaching. The lotus blooming in Śākyamuni's begging-bowl symbolizes Compassion flowering in the bowl of Emptiness.

Chapter Five

The Buddhas of the Three Times

At the heart of the Refuge Tree sit the Buddhas of the Three Times: Dīpaṅkara, a Buddha of the distant past; Śākyamuni, the Buddha of our own era; and Maitreya, the Buddha-to-be. Blazing with light at the centre of the Tree, they represent the eternity of Buddhahood.

The Buddha Śākyamuni did not invent the Dharma, but rediscovered it. Buddhahood, the principle of Enlightenment, is beyond space and time. It is an eternal fact of life in all possible worlds. Buddhism thinks in terms of periods of time that are entirely beyond the grasp of the unenlightened mind. One of the traditional units of time in Buddhist thought is the *kalpa*. Suppose, the Buddha once said, there was a solid cube of rock, four leagues square, and at the end of every century a man was to stroke it once with a piece of the finest Benares muslin. The rock would be worn away before the kalpa came to an end.[11] Dīpaṅkara lived many, many kalpas ago.

As with time, space is incalculably vast. According to one simile, if a person were to take all the grains of sand in the River Ganges and were to deposit one grain of sand at the end of every period equalling in years the number of all those sand-grains, after exhausting all the grains of sand in that river they would be no closer to reaching the end of space than they were at the beginning.

From the Mahāyāna perspective, this vast extent of space contains innumerable world-systems, and each world-system has the potential for its own Buddha. Each Buddha represents the intersection between eternal Buddhahood, which exists beyond space and time, and the historical or mythic world of space and time which that Buddha inhabits.

The Buddhas of the Three Times, seated together at the centre of the Refuge Tree, symbolize the eternal presence of Buddhahood intersecting with our human world. They represent the constant possibility of change for the better and the prospect of unlimited self-transcendence at all times and in all places.

Śākyamuni

Unlike the other Buddhas at the centre of the Tree, Siddhārtha Gautama, the man who went on to become the Buddha of our era, was clearly a historical figure. Recent research places his birth around 485 BCE, in Lumbinī, near Kapilavastu, in the area below the foothills of the Himalayas which spans the current Nepalese border with India.

His father, Śuddhodana, was a member of the ruling oligarchy. Tradition later dubbed Siddhārtha a 'prince' and Śuddhodana a 'king', but whatever his correct designation, we know that Śuddhodana was rich and powerful and that the young Siddhārtha led a privileged life. Upon his birth a seer predicted that the young boy was destined for either political or spiritual empire. Śuddhodana, wishing his son to choose the former, tried to attach him to the advantages of wealth and power, providing him with every available luxury and keeping him sheltered from the harsher facts of the world. He arranged for Siddhārtha's marriage to a beautiful young woman, Yaśodharā, and she bore him a son, Rāhula.

But Siddhārtha experienced an acute sense of dissatisfaction. Whatever he had, whatever he did, there was always an aspect of himself that remained unfulfilled. Most of the people he met would have envied his privileged position. He had wealth, good looks and social status, a beautiful wife, and a healthy heir. But he also saw deeply into the fundamental emptiness of his life and his innate integrity would not allow him to pretend that everything was as it should be. What was the point of it all? Life seemed to be essentially meaningless, but he could not accept this and simply get on – as his companions did – with the usual daily round of the pursuit of power and pleasure.

Riding in his chariot one day, he became aware, for the first time, of an old man, and realized as never before the inevitable fact of old age. Similarly, he was confronted in turn by disease and by death. These experiences overwhelmed him. What was the point of living a life of ease and luxury when old age, disease, and death were waiting quietly in the wings – biding their time before coming to claim him, his family, and his friends? Finally, he saw a wandering mendicant, the sight of whom sowed in his mind the seed of the possibility that there was an alternative to the passive acceptance of old age, disease, and death. At the same time, he saw that to embark on such a quest would require radical, even painful, action.

His insight into the inevitability of old age, disease, and death left him with an acute and ineradicable sense of the painful hollowness of upper-class Śākyan life. Ancestral duty demanded that he join in and get on with the business of warriorship and government. Yet, at his core, he knew that a life which denied the fundamentals of reality was not for him. He had two stark options: he could deny reality, or he could deny family, luxury, and power. He chose the latter, and, at the age of 29, simply left home, leaving behind his wife, child, family, power, and social status. He cut off his hair and beard, swapped his warrior garb for the rag robes of a religious mendicant, and began his quest for truth and liberation.

It was an unsettled time. Rival kings were gradually absorbing and centralizing the earlier clan-oriented social structures. The old religion of the Vedas and its Brahminical priesthood was increasingly associated with these centralized governments and a new class of religious practitioner was emerging. These were the wandering ascetics who, dissatisfied with social conventions and the empty ritualism of established religion, gave up their homes and social positions to wander around, living on alms and seeking the truth. Siddhārtha became a 'wanderer', and his demeanour struck those who met with him with great force:

And as he, the Buddha, the one full of noble characteristics, walked about in search of food he came in time to Rājagaha, in Magadha.

The king, Bimbisāra, stood in his palace and, seeing the one possessing the noble characteristics, called out to his followers:

'Look carefully, friends, he is handsome, shapely and of beautiful complexion. His gait is pleasing with his eyes cast at only a little distance; with downcast eyes he is mindful and he does not seem to be from a low family. Send out the palace messengers to find out where he's going.'[12]

So the king's men went out in search of the Buddha-to-be and sent someone to report back to the king:

'Your majesty,' he said, 'the monk has settled down on the east side of Mount Pandava. He's sitting there in his mountain lair like a lion or a tiger or a bull!'[13]

The king went to meet Siddhārtha:

'You are only a young man, sir, a lad in the prime of your life. You are handsome and shapely. You appear to be a prince of noble birth.

'Adorning a splendid army, esteemed by a council of nobles, enjoy wealth which I can bestow upon you. However, can you please tell me what family you're from?'

'King,' came the answer, 'not far from Himavant, the snowland, is a country called Kosala. The people of Kosala are rich and they are strong.

'They come from the race of the sun and their family name is Sākya. That was the people I left when I walked away from the wish and the longing for pleasure.

'I have seen the miseries of pleasure. I have seen the security involved in renouncing them;

So now I will go,
I will go into the struggle,
This is to my mind delight;
This is where my mind finds bliss.'[14]

Siddhārtha sought out the most famous spiritual teachers of his time, but soon surpassed them in spiritual attainment and, realizing that even the lofty heights to which they had led him didn't provide the answers he sought, he left each of them in turn and eventually continued his quest alone.

It was commonly accepted at the time that one liberated the spirit by weakening the prison of the flesh, and for the next six years Siddhārtha engaged in extreme austerities:

> Because of eating so little my limbs became like the jointed segments of vine stems or bamboo stems.... my backside became like a camel's hoof.... the projections of my spine stood forth like corded beads.... my ribs jutted out as gaunt as the crazy rafters of an old roofless barn.... the gleam of my eyes sank far down in their sockets, looking like the gleam of water that has sunk far down in a deep well.... my scalp shrivelled and withered as a green bitter gourd shrivels and withers in the wind and sun.... my belly skin adhered to my backbone; thus if I touched my belly skin I encountered my backbone and if I touched my backbone I encountered my belly skin.... if I tried to ease my body by rubbing my limbs with my hands, the hair, rotted at its roots, fell from my body as I rubbed.[15]

Renowned for the extent of his asceticism, he soon attracted a following. But still he was not satisfied; six years after leaving home, he was no nearer to resolving the fundamental questions of existence. Realizing that his austerities had led him nowhere, Siddhārtha had the moral courage to abandon his previous course. Having almost starved himself, he began to eat in moderation and his former disciples, scandalized by this backsliding, left him in disgust.

He was now completely alone – family, clan, reputation, and followers all abandoned. All his attempts to break through the veil of ignorance had failed. Desolate, he didn't know which way to turn next. Only one thing was certain – he would not abandon his quest.

At this point a memory rose to the surface of his mind. When he was quite young, sitting in the shade of a rose-apple tree he had watched his father ploughing. Relaxed by the slow, steady rhythm of the ox team, sitting contentedly in the shade, he had spontaneously slipped into a concentrated meditative state – might that be the way to Enlightenment? In this state of acute existential solitude, his determination unshaken, Siddhārtha sat down under a tree with this declaration: 'Flesh may wither away, blood may dry up, but I shall not leave this seat until I gain Enlightenment!'

All night he sat there in meditation. Seeing Siddhārtha sitting determinedly in meditation, Māra, the Evil One, shook with fright:

> He had with him his three sons – Flurry, Gaiety, and Sullen Pride – and his three daughters – Discontent, Delight, and Thirst. These asked him why he was so disconcerted in his mind. And he replied to them with these words: 'Look over there at that sage, clad in the armour of determination, with truth and spiritual virtue as his weapons, the arrows of his intellect drawn, ready to shoot! He has sat down with the firm intention of conquering my realm. No wonder that my mind is plunged in deep despondency! If he should succeed in overcoming me, and could proclaim to the world the way to final beatitude, then my realm would be empty today,... but so far he has not yet won the eye of full knowledge. He is still within my sphere of influence. While there is time I therefore will attempt to break his solemn purpose, and throw myself against him like the rush of a swollen river breaking against the embankment!'
>
> But Māra could achieve nothing against the Bodhisattva, and he and his army were defeated, and fled in all directions – their elation gone, their toil rendered fruitless, their rocks, logs, and trees scattered everywhere. They behaved like a hostile army whose commander had been slain in battle. So Māra, defeated, ran away together with his followers. The great seer, free from the dust of passion, victorious over darkness' gloom, had vanquished him.[16]

Siddhārtha sat calmly beneath the tree, allowing his mind to become still. Gradually all the different currents of his psyche began to flow together. His concentration increased and his mind steadily became clearer and brighter. It was intensely pleasurable, but Siddhārtha wasn't distracted by the pleasure, and, letting it go, he entered states of increasingly profound equanimity. On and on he went, deepening and clarifying. Letting go of each preceding state he entered deeper and deeper into meditative

Teachers of Enlightenment

absorption. In the final watch of that full moon night in May, complete Enlightenment finally dawned. Siddhārtha Gautama became the Buddha:

> And the moon, like a maiden's gentle smile, lit up the
> heavens, while a rain of sweet-scented flowers, filled with
> moisture, fell down on the earth from above.[17]

Siddhārtha spent several weeks absorbing this profound experience. He pondered for some time whether or not he could make his discovery of Enlightenment known to others. It was so subtle. To penetrate it required calm and great concentration, but people were so caught up in their petty desires, getting and spending – so attached to family, friends, wealth, and reputation.

Then, the legend goes, a celestial being appeared and begged him to teach, for there were some beings in the world 'with but little dust on their eyes' who were perishing for want of the teachings. With the eye of his imagination, the Buddha surveyed all the beings in the world. He saw them as a vast bed of lotus flowers. Some were sunk deep in the mire, others had raised their heads to the level of the water, and yet others had risen quite above the water – though they had their roots in the mud they were reaching up towards the light. There *were* beings who would understand what he had to say. The Buddha decided to teach.

Leaving the place we now know as Bodh Gaya, he walked the hundred or so miles to Sarnath, near the ancient city of Vārāṇasī, where some of his former disciples were staying in a deer park. As he approached they looked at each other in disgust – here was the backslider Gautama, the former recluse. What did *he* want? They were certainly not going to receive *him* with respect. But as the Buddha approached they were so taken with his calm, radiant demeanour that they could not but defer to him.

These were stubborn men. Hardened by years of asceticism, fulltimers in the spiritual quest, they thought they had heard it all. But the Buddha seemed to be approaching life from an entirely new dimension. There was something inexplicably different about him. They got down to debate – tough, straight talking. The discussions went on for several days. The Buddha's conviction and confidence was absolute. He had found the skilful Middle Way to Enlightenment, a path leading between the extremes of hedonism and asceticism; nihilism and eternalism.

Finally, the ascetic Kauṇḍinya broke through. He saw what the Buddha was driving at and had the same kind of experience that the Buddha had under the tree at Bodh Gaya. His attachment to his own limited personality dropped away and he too was now free from the bondage of craving. The Buddha was delighted – ' Kauṇḍinya knows!' he exclaimed, ' Kauṇḍinya knows!' What the Buddha had discovered *could* be made known. If Kauṇḍinya could understand then others could too. Humanity *would* benefit from these teachings. Over the next few days the other ascetics also became Enlightened. Then a young man called Yasa came by. Engaging the Buddha in discussion, he too became convinced of the truth of the teachings and brought his family and friends along to hear them. In this way a new sangha came into being. Soon there were sixty Enlightened beings in the world and the Buddha sent them out to teach 'for the welfare and happiness of the many, out of compassion for the world'.

For the next forty-five years the Buddha wandered around northern India, either alone or accompanied by members of the community that was forming around him. As he wandered, he taught. Kings, courtesans, sweepers, and householders, all kinds of people came to hear his Dharma. In the course of his life, the Buddha's fame as a teacher spread throughout northern India, an area of fifty thousand square miles encompassing seven different nations. He was known as Śākyamuni – 'the Sage of the Śākya Clan' – and there was an immense interest in what he had to say. Enlightened at about 35, he lived until about 80, and all those forty-five years were given over to teaching. Except in the rainy season, when he and whatever followers were with him retired into retreat, he walked the hot and dusty roads, through villages and cities, living on alms, taking only what was freely offered to him, and addressing himself to whoever wanted to hear what he had to say, irrespective of sex, caste, vocation, or religion. Among his followers were two of the principal kings of the region, members of most of the leading republican families, and some of the wealthiest merchants. During his travels he came into close personal contact with wandering ascetics, peasants, artisans, shop-keepers, and robbers. People of all castes poured into his sangha, where they lost their separate designations of caste and class and became simply 'followers of the Buddha'.

Wherever he could, the Buddha tried to help people to see things as they really are, responding to every situation out of the depths of his wisdom and compassion. He was affectionate and devoted to his disciples, frequently enquiring after their well-being and progress. When staying in a monastery, he paid daily visits to the sick ward. Once, he himself attended a sick monk neglected by the others and made the comment that 'he who attends the sick attends me'. The Buddha did not accept the religious significance of the caste system, a long-established institution in India, and recognized the religious potential of men and women of all ranks:

> So what of all these titles, names and races? They are mere worldly conventions. They have come into being by common consent.
>
> This false belief has been deeply ingrained in the minds of the ignorant for a long time and (still) these ignorant ones say to us: 'One becomes a brahmin by birth.'
>
> (On the contrary,) no one is *born* a brahmin; no one is born a non-brahmin. A brahmin is a brahmin because of what he *does*; ....
>
> A brahmin is as a result of self-restraint, wholesome living and self-control. This is the essence of Brahmin.[18]

He appreciated both natural and physical beauty. On several occasions he was moved aesthetically, as he told Ānanda how delightful certain places were to him. He once told his monks that, if they had not seen the *devas* of the Tāvatiṃsa Heaven, they should look at the handsome Licchavis, beautifully and elegantly dressed in assorted colours.

The Buddha loved peace and quiet; even the followers of other teachers respected his wishes in this regard, silencing their discussions on his approach. He would not allow noisy monks to live near him and he often spent long periods in solitude, having one monk bring him his meals. King Pasenadi could not understand how the Buddha maintained such order in the sangha, when he, a king, with the power to inflict punishment, could not maintain it so well in his court. The Buddha told him that he kept order and discipline on the basis of the mutual love, affection, and respect that exists between teacher and pupil.

He had a quiet and ironic sense of humour. A conceited Brahmin, who was in the habit of denigrating others, questioned him as to the qualities of a true Brahmin. In a list of such high qualities as freedom from evil and purity of heart, the Buddha gently included 'not denigrating others'.

The Buddha's courage was shown on a number of occasions. He went out, single and unarmed, to confront the serial killer Aṅgulimāla; and when his cousin Devadatta launched various plots against his life, the Buddha refused his followers' offer of a bodyguard.

At the age of 80, his body worn out and racked with pain, the Buddha made one final teaching tour, giving all his friends and followers one last chance to ask any questions about the teaching. To the end he was completely aware and concerned only for the welfare of others. A wanderer called Subhadra came to see him on his death-bed and Ānanda, the Buddha's companion, turned him away, not wishing the Buddha to be disturbed at such a time, but the Buddha insisted on talking with him, and Subhadra, soon convinced of the truth of the Dharma, joined the sangha.

Then the Buddha asked if any of the assembled sangha had any doubts or questions about his teaching. With typical thoughtfulness, he allowed that those who were too embarrassed to ask for themselves might do so through a friend. The answer was a resounding silence. The Buddha had made the Dharma perfectly clear. Seeing this, he gave a final exhortation to his followers: 'All conditioned things are impermanent! With mindfulness, strive!' And with that he entered a state of deep meditation and passed away.

Dīpaṅkara

Over the course of aeons our own world-system has seen a large number of Buddhas. The Dharma dies out for a time and a Buddha arises who rediscovers it. They in turn teach the Dharma, which

Teachers of Enlightenment

lasts for a time and dies out. Then another Buddha arises and rediscovers it.

The Buddha Dīpaṅkara, whose name means 'Kindler of Lights', was, according to legend, the first in a line of twenty-four Buddhas who preceded Śākyamuni, the Buddha of the present age. He played a crucial part in Śākyamuni' s story, inasmuch as it was in his presence that the Bodhisattva who eventually went on to become Śākyamuni declared his intention to achieve full Enlightenment.

Legendary accounts of the Buddha Dīpaṅkara's life broadly follow the pattern we are familiar with from the life of Śākyamuni. His father was a king, he left home and practised austerities, gained Enlightenment under a bodhi tree and taught for many years. In some of the legends he is said, unlike the Buddha of our own era, to have been enormously tall – eighty cubits high according to some Pāli sources. He lived for 100,000 years and was always attended by an assembly of 84,000 arhants. When he died, he was entombed in a Stupa thirty-six *yojanas* high.

According to Pāli tradition, many aeons ago the Buddha-to-be was known as Sumedha. He was a very rich Brahmin from Amarāvatī , but he left the world and went forth to become an ascetic high in the Himalayas. While visiting a town he came upon a crowd of people decorating the road upon which the Buddha Dīpaṅkara was due to pass. Sumedha joined in the work, but before he was able to finish, the Buddha arrived. Seeing that the Buddha would have to walk over rough ground, Sumedha, in great devotion, lay down in a rut so that the Buddha might walk over him. At that moment his faith overflowed and he resolved that one day he too would become a Buddha. Dīpaṅkara, looking into the future with his supernormal powers, saw that Sumedha' s wish would come true and that one day, far in the future, when he had practised as a Bodhisattva for many aeons, he would eventually become the Buddha Śākyamuni, and he proclaimed this fact to the assembled multitude.

The Mahāvastu has a slightly different account. The young Brahmin Megha

decided to go to the royal city Dipavati, in order to see the city of a universal monarch, made of the seven precious things, and delightful to behold. When he entered the city, he saw that it was in festive array. He wondered to himself, 'What holiday do we have here to-day, or what dramatic performance, or what festival?'... And as he went on he looked for someone he could question.

Just then a young Brahmin girl came along, attractive, good-looking, reliable, gentle, and modest. She held a water jug and seven lotus flowers in her hands. Megha asked her, 'Is there a festival in the city to-day?' She replied with these verses:

You cannot, young man, be a native of this place.
A stranger from another city you must be.
You do not know that there is coming to this town
The Benefactor of the World, the Bringer of the Light!
Dīpaṅkara, the Leader of the world, the son
Of king Arcimat, He, a greatly famous Buddha,
Is drawing near. To honour him this city
Is decked in gay and festive garb.

Megha asked her: 'How much did you pay for those seven lotus flowers?' She replied: 'Five of them I bought for 500 coins; two were given to me by a friend.' Megha said to her: 'I will give you 500 coins. You then give me those five lotuses, and with them I shall worship Dīpaṅkara, the Lord. You can honour him with the remaining two.' She replied: 'You can have those five lotuses, but only on condition that for all future time you take me for your wife. Wherever you may be reborn, there I shall be your wife, and you my husband.' Megha replied 'My heart is set on supreme enlightenment. How can I think of marriage?'

The girl acquiesced, but Megha decided to marry her anyway – it was clearly a case of mutual love at first sight – but Megha was nonetheless not distracted from his desire to honour the Buddha. When he saw the Buddha Dīpaṅkara, Megha's body

was flooded with great joy and gladness, and a sublime decision arose in his mind. He ... threw himself down at the

feet of Dīpaṅkara, the Lord,... and aroused within himself
the following thought: 'Ah! May I too at some future period
become a Tathāgata, with all the attributes of a perfect
Buddha, as this Lord Dīpaṅkara is just now! May I too turn
the wheel of the highest Dharma, as this Lord Dīpaṅkara does
just now! Having crossed, may I lead others across; set free,
may I free others; comforted, may I comfort others – as does
this Lord Dīpaṅkara! May I become like him, for the weal and
happiness of the many, out of compassion for the world, for
the sake of a great multitude of living beings, for their weal
and happiness, be they gods or men!'[19]

And Dīpaṅkara, aware of Megha's deep devotion and his great
store of merit, predicted that in the future, 'after an immeasurable,
incalculable kalpa', he too would become a Buddha.

Because of the part he played in the former life of the Buddha
Śākyamuni, Dīpaṅkara is widely considered to be the most
important of all the Buddhas of the past. Together with Śākyamuni
and Maitreya he is one of the 'Buddhas of the Three Times' : past,
present, and future.

Maitreya

In the *Cakkavatti-Sīhanāda Sutta* of the *Dīgha-Nikāya*, the Buddha
tells some of his followers at Magadha about Metteyya, 'the
Friendly One', the Buddha-to-be:[20]

And in that time of the people with an eighty-thousand-
year life-span there will arise in the world a Blessed Lord,
an Arahant fully-enlightened Buddha named Metteyya,
endowed with wisdom and conduct, a Well-Farer, Knower
of the worlds, incomparable Trainer of men to be tamed,
Teacher of gods and humans, enlightened and blessed, just
as I am now. He will thoroughly know by his own super-
knowledge, and proclaim, this universe with its devas, māras,
and Brahmās, its ascetics and Brahmins, and this generation
with its princes and people, just as I do now. He will teach the
Dhamma, lovely in its beginning, lovely in its middle, lovely

in its ending, in the spirit and in the letter, and proclaim, just as I do now, the holy life in its fullness and purity. He will be attended by a company of thousands of monks, just as I am attended by a company of hundreds....[21]

Maitreya is currently residing in the Tusita Devaloka, the 'Heaven of the Contented Ones', which is the abode of all Bodhisattvas who are awaiting the right moment for their final rebirth when they will finally severe the bonds of craving and attain to Buddhahood.

Maitreya is the only celestial being accepted as such by both the Theravāda and Mahāyāna traditions. It is not uncommon for Theravādins to pray to be reborn when he appears and then to become monks so as to be able to proceed to Enlightenment under his tutelage, while in the Mahāyāna Maitreya's coming was sometimes seen to precede a kind of Buddhist millennium, when nothing but skilfulness will prevail. For example, in the *Maitreyavyākarava*, 'the Prophecy Concerning Maitreya', Śāriputra asks the Buddha Śākyamuni to tell the assembly about the Buddha-to-be. The Buddha replies:

At that time, the ocean will lose much of its water, and there will be much less of it than now. In consequence a world-ruler will have no difficulties in passing across it. India, this island of Jambu, will be quite flat everywhere, it will measure ten thousand leagues, and all men will have the privilege of living on it. It will have innumerable inhabitants, who will commit no crimes or evil deeds, but will take pleasure in doing good. The soil will then be free from thorns, even, and covered with a fresh green growth of grass; when one jumps on it, it gives way, and becomes soft like the leaves of the cotton tree. It has a delicious scent, and tasty rice grows on it, without any work. Rich silken, and other, fabrics of various colours shoot forth from the trees. The trees will bear leaves, flowers, and fruits simultaneously; they are as high as the voice can reach and they last for eight myriads of years. Human beings are then without any blemishes, moral offences are unknown among them, and they are full of zest and joy. Their bodies are very large and their skin has a fine hue....

The city of Ketumati will at that time be the capital. In it will reside the world-ruler, Shankha by name, who will rule over the earth up to the confines of the ocean; and he will make the Dharma prevail. He will be a great hero, raised to his station by the force of hundreds of meritorious deeds.

Because the world has now been made receptive to his teaching, Maitreya will leave the Tusita Heaven and take his last rebirth:

As soon as he is born he will walk seven steps forward, and where he puts down his feet a jewel or a lotus will spring up. He will raise his eyes to the ten directions, and will speak these words: 'This is my last birth. There will be no rebirth after this one. Never will I come back here, but, all pure, I shall win Nirvana!'....

As Maitreya grows up, the Dharma will increasingly take possession of him, and he will reflect that all that lives is bound to suffer. He will have a heavenly voice which reaches far; his skin will have a golden hue, a great splendour will radiate from his body,... and he will win his enlightenment the very same day that he has gone forth into the homeless life.

And then, a supreme sage, he will with a perfect voice preach the true dharma.... Under Maitreya's guidance, hundreds of thousands of living beings shall enter upon a religious life.

Then Sakra, the king of the gods, turned to the Buddha Śākyamuni and praised him. 'As a result of Maitreya's teaching, he proclaimed, 'gods, men, and other beings will lose their doubts and their cravings will be cut off'.

'Free from all misery they will manage to cross the ocean of becoming; and, as a result of Maitreya's teaching, they will lead a holy life. No longer will they regard anything as their own, they will have no possessions, no gold or silver, no home, no relatives! But they will lead a holy life of chastity under Maitreya's guidance. They will have torn the net of the passions, they will manage to enter into the trances, and theirs will be an abundance of joy and happiness; for they will lead a holy life under Maitreya's guidance.

'For 60,000 years Maitreya, the best of men, will preach the true Dharma, which is compassionate towards all living beings. And when he has disciplined in his true Dharma hundreds and hundreds of millions of living beings, then that leader will at last enter Nirvana. And after the great sage has entered Nirvana, his true Dharma still endures for another ten thousand years.

'Raise therefore your thoughts in faith to Shakyamuni, the Conqueror! For then you shall see Maitreya, the perfect Buddha, the best of men! Whose soul could be so dark that it would not be lit up with a serene faith when he hears these wonderful things, so potent of future good! Those therefore who long for spiritual greatness, let them show respect to the true Dharma, let them be mindful of the religion of the Buddhas!'[22]

In *The Way of the White Clouds*, Lama Govinda writes very movingly about a statue of Maitreya he encountered at Yi-Gah Chö-Ling, the gompa near Darjeeling where Dhardo Rimpoche was later to serve as abbot:

Whenever I happened to wake up during the night I beheld the benign features of Buddha Maitreya's golden face, which seemed to float high above the shadowy forms that filled the temple in the dim light of the Eternal Lamp. And in the golden, softly radiating face the large deep blue eyes seemed to be filled with supernatural life, and I felt their glance resting upon me with infinite tenderness.[23]

That statue had been placed there by Lama Govinda's teacher, the great Tomo Geshe Rimpoche, who was renowned for conjuring up visions of Buddhas and Bodhisattvas for people to see. Tomo Geshe had a strong connection with the Buddha Maitreya, and urged his followers to turn their feelings for Maitreya to a spiritually practical account:

He erected statues of Maitreya in many other places and made the followers of the Buddha-Dharma conscious of the fact that it was not sufficient to bask in the glories of the past, but that one must take active part in the shaping of the future, and thus make it possible for the coming Buddha to appear in this world by preparing our minds for his reception.[24]

Iconographically, Maitreya is usually golden in colour and often appears in the posture of royal ease. In his left hand he holds a lotus with a stupa rising out of it. He may also be shown holding a golden *dharmacakra* or 'wheel of the Dharma', or a sacred vase filled with the nectar of the Dharma which he will one day pour over the world. He may also be shown in the *bhadrāsana* pose, which is virtually unique in Buddhist iconography. He sits on a throne, his feet flat on the ground before him. This indicates that he is readying himself to step down into our world. In this pose he holds one hand to his cheek, with three fingers – representing the Three Jewels – extended. And he gazes with infinite compassion upon the world that he will one day light up with the radiance of his Dharma teaching.

Maitreya stands for the infinite compassion of the Bodhisattva. He could remain there, at ease, in the Tusita Devaloka, but one day he will descend to our plane of existence to spread the Dharma for the sake of a suffering world. He stands, therefore, as a sign of continuous optimism. Buddhas will appear and reappear wherever there are unenlightened beings to be saved.

Yellow Ratnasambhava makes the gesture of giving, red Amitābha sits in meditation, white Vairocana makes the teaching gesture, blue Akṣobhya touches the earth, and green Amoghasiddhi makes the gesture bestowing fearlessness.

Chapter Six

The Five Jinas

The Five Buddha mandala

Śākyamuni, the historical Buddha, made an important distinction when speaking about the nature of a Buddha. There was the *rūpakāya* – or 'form-body' – and the *dharmakāya* – the 'body of truth'. The *rūpakāya* alludes to the historical embodiment of the Buddha that exists under the conditions of space and time, the *dharmakāya* to the principle of Buddhahood that persists beyond space and time. In Śākyamuni's time, this idea received little elaboration. After all, both these ideas found full expression in his own person – he was an Enlightened individual, living within human, historical time, and he stood for, and expounded, the principle of Enlightenment. But in the years after his death the distinction between these two 'bodies' became increasingly meaningful. There might not be a human Buddha, such as Śākyamuni, present in the world today, but the principle of Enlightenment is always with us.

There is, however, a gap between the way in which we conceive of a human Buddha and the principle of Buddhahood. The former is much more immediate and, especially if one has the rare good fortune to meet such a being, to some extent apprehensible. The principle of Buddhahood, however, can be a rather distant, dry, perhaps even over-conceptual idea.

In the course of time Buddhist aspirants strove to bridge the gap between these two ideas. Seeking to apprehend the immense, mysterious nature of Buddhahood, they reached out towards it not only with their intellect, but also with their emotions and imaginations, and gradually another set of forms appeared. These are the ideal or archetypal Buddhas and Bodhisattvas, beings made entirely of pure light who manifest at the very highest reaches of the imagination and who represent the interplay between the human imagination and the principle of Enlightenment itself. Eventually, these developments crystallized into the *trikāya* doctrine, the doctrine of the 'three bodies of the Buddha'. These three bodies are the *nirmānakāya*, or 'created body', the Buddha who appears under the conditions of historical time; the *sambhogakāya*, or 'body of mutual enjoyment', the ideal Buddhas; and the *dharmakāya*, the 'body of truth', the universal principle of Buddhahood.

Later Mahāyāna and Vajrayāna Buddhism tended to focus their attention on the *sambhogakāya*. Śākyamuni, the human historical Buddha, the *nirmānakāya*, had long departed this world. Enlightenment in its purest form, the *dharmakāya*, was an ungraspable, abstract, and almost vague concept. But the *samhbhogakāya*, the Buddhas and Bodhisattvas of the Imagination, had a numinous spiritual presence that devotees could relate to and work with. Thus, in the Mahāyāna sūtras, the Buddha, although he often goes under the name of Śākyamuni, is clearly a trans-historical, archetypal figure, and in those sūtras too we begin to meet other Buddhas, many of them from eras and world-systems entirely different from our own.

These developments eventually came to be formalized iconographically. To begin with, Buddhahood began to be conceived of in terms of its two principal attributes, wisdom and compassion, and the archetypal Buddha appeared flanked by two other Buddha figures – Amitābha, who represents infinite love, and Akṣobhya, who stands for wisdom. Other figures gradually emerged, and in time the five Buddha mandala appeared – five Buddha figures who between them embody the five essential characteristics of Enlightenment.

Once begun, this process of development is potentially endless, for Enlightenment has an infinite range of qualities, and Enlightened beings strive to relate to the unenlightened using an infinite variety of means. But, for the Tantra at least, the five Buddha mandala is the central organizing matrix for its subsequent development. Each Buddha in the mandala came to be conceived of as the head of a particular Buddha family, comprising a whole range of other figures – Bodhisattvas, protectors, *ḍākas*, and *ḍākinīs*. Each of the Buddhas in the mandala, and therefore each of their families, had his own unique qualities, colours, directions, emblems, times of day, animals, gestures, seed syllables, mantras, skandhas, elements, pure lands, realms, magical functions, and so on. The five Buddha mandala, therefore, is the key to the vast treasury of spiritual imagination which is Vajrayāna Buddhism. By beginning to apprehend the mysterious qualities of each of the five Buddhas we begin to enter the world of the Vajrayāna Buddhist imagination.

Following the path of the sun, we shall now enter the mandala in the east, proceed to the south, the west, and the north, and finish in the centre.

Akṣobhya

Akṣobhya sits on a vast blue lotus throne supported by four massive elephants. His body is made of deep-blue light, he has dark, blue-black hair gathered into a topknot and he wears the flowing, richly ornamented robes of an archetypal Buddha. Seated in full-lotus posture, his whole body radiates light and imperturbable calm. His left hand rests in his lap, a golden vajra upright on his palm. His right hand, palm downwards, is lowered and his fingers just touch the white moon-mat on which he sits. This 'earth-touching gesture' communicates his unshakeable confidence. It stands for that ineffable, transcendental rootedness that is the paradoxical core of his nature – for he is rooted in *śūnyatā*, 'emptiness'. So deeply rooted is he, in fact, that nothing can ever shake his composure. In his heart the syllable *hūṃ* glows with a pale blue light, and his mantra resounds like the slow beat of a huge drum – *Oṃ vajra akṣobhya hūṃ*. Akṣobhya's mythical history is recounted in the *Akṣobhya-vyūha Sūtra*.

Aeons ago, in the land of Abhirati, 'intense delight', there lived a Buddha called Viśālākṣa. One day a monk came to him, wanting to vow to gain Enlightenment for the sake of all beings. The Buddha warned him that his task would be immense, as he would have to give up all feelings of anger. Undaunted, the monk took a series of great vows: never to give way to anger or to bear malice, never to engage in unethical conduct, and many others. Over succeeding ages he was unshakeable (*akṣobhya*) in holding to these vows, and as a result became a Buddha and created a pure land known as Abhirati.

Abhirati is situated at an unthinkable distance to the east of our own world. There, palm trees and jasmine, wafted by gentle breezes, give off heavenly sounds, surpassing all known music. Food and drink are abundant and all the inhabitants live joyfully, delighting only in the Dharma. Whoever is reborn there attains the state of non-regression. For them, Buddhahood is assured.

Akṣobhya is the head of the Vajra family. The vajra, the 'diamond thunderbolt', is an emblem of sovereignty – in the ancient Indian tradition it is borne by Indra, king of the gods, but in the Buddhist tradition it became far more than that. Indra's thunderbolt, like that of Zeus, is irresistible. It has all the immutable qualities of the diamond. In Buddhism this is the quality of the Truth, or transcendental reality. The mundane world is mutable, subject to change. The transcendental is immutable and unchanging. The vajra represents the unyielding nature of reality and the wisdom that perceives it. The Vajra family contains many illustrious members. Foremost among these are Vajrasattva and the 'family protector', Vajrapāṇi.

Akṣobhya's *mudrā*, or 'gesture', of touching the earth recalls a legendary incident in the life of the Buddha Śākyamuni. He was meditating on the very verge of Enlightenment under the bodhi tree, we are told, when Māra, the Evil One, saw what was about to happen and used all the weapons in his armoury to launch an assault on the sage. His demonic army caused boulders, arrows, and spears to rain down on the Buddha-to-be, but when these encountered the peace-filled aura of his concentration they turned to flowers and fell as offerings at his feet. Māra then sent his daughters to seduce the Buddha, but he never even looked at them. Eventually, near to despair, Māra tried his last and most subtle trick. He approached the Buddha-to-be and said, 'You are sitting on the *vajrāsana*, the very axis of the world. Upon this spot all the Buddhas of old gained their Enlightenment. By what right do you dare to sit upon it?'

Siddhārtha replied, 'I have practised generosity, ethics, and the other perfections for aeons. I have earned my right to be here.'

'Hah! You may say that. But who is your witness?' Māra

responded. If his armies couldn't dislodge the Buddha-to-be, if his daughters could not distract him, perhaps self-doubt might put an end to his quest. Siddhārtha, however, was emphatic. He said nothing, but just touched the earth with the fingertips of his right hand. In response the Earth Goddess, Vasundharā, arose out of the ground. 'I will be his witness,' she said. 'For aeons I have seen him purifying himself through his spiritual practices.' And Māra was discomfited.

This gesture of touching the earth represents complete rootedness and total assurance. It represents the unshakeable confidence of the ethically upright.

Akṣobhya embodies the Mirror-Like Wisdom. Like a mirror, this wisdom reflects impartially whatever is presented to it. It makes no judgements, never qualifies nor distorts, but simply reflects with complete truthfulness. Like the mirror, the mind imbued with wisdom reflects but is unaffected by what is presented to it. Like a still lake, nothing ruffles its composure.

Ratnasambhava

Ratnasambhava, the 'Jewel-Born One', or 'Producer of Jewels', sits on a yellow lotus throne, supported by four beautiful horses. He is made entirely of golden yellow light. His left hand, which rests in his lap, holds a magnificent jewel, the wish-fulfilling gem, symbol of the bodhicitta, while his right rests on his right knee, palm outwards, in the gesture of supreme giving. Golden light radiates from his body, illuminating his pure land, 'the Glorious', which resounds with the sound of his mantra – *oṃ ratnasambhava tram.*

Ratnasambhava embodies the Wisdom of Equality, which sees every aspect of life in all its myriad forms as equally marked by emptiness. Everything is equally devoid of inherent existence, and all beings whatsoever are equally worthy of love and compassion. All are equally precious, and all are worthy of every gift. The Wisdom of Equality is a great antidote to pride, the misplaced view that we are, in certain respects at least, somehow special and more worthy than others.

Ratnasambhava is the Buddha of abundance and generosity. He is associated with wealth and riches, and from his own vast abundance he gives freely to all. Among his retinue in the Ratna, or 'Jewel', family is Ratnapāṇi, the family protector, as well as Jambhala, the Bodhisattva of Wealth. Jambhala is a large, portly figure, somewhat like a rich merchant from ancient India. In his left hand he cradles a mongoose, which he squeezes gently. As he does so, jewels pour from the animal's mouth. In the East, Jambhala is regarded as a kind of god of wealth and people propitiate him for the sake of material gain. But Jambhala is a Bodhisattva, and it is unlikely that he would help anyone gain anything that did not help them to develop selflessness.

Ratnasambhava has everything in abundance because he actually owns nothing. In giving up the idea of ownership, which separates off 'mine' from 'yours', one inherits everything. Beauty, nature, the feel of the breeze, the colour of flowers, the sonnets of Shakespeare, and the treasury of the Dharma – these are not owned by anyone and belong to all who approach them with appreciation. For that reason, Ratnasambhava is also associated with the arts and culture. He is the supreme patron of aesthetic appreciation and is particularly allied with the human realm. The appreciation of art and culture is one of the factors that separate the human realm from that of the animals, the hells, the pretas, and the āsuras. The faculty of aesthetic appreciation is a major constituent of our humanity.

The wish-fulfilling gem that Ratnasambhava holds in his palm is the key to all riches. Being unenlightened, we all – to some extent – cherish the vain hope that somehow or other greater wealth, or more access to mundane goods of one sort or another, can put an end, for a while, to our experience of unsatisfactoriness. The bodhicitta represents the complete transformation of that inane desire. When the bodhicitta arises, our desire to bolster our ego-identity through the appropriation of the empty symbols of success, or by surrounding it with transient comforts, gives way to the deeply fulfilling desire to help all beings, in whatever way. Our aching need to take from the world in order to fill our inner emptiness changes into the desire to give to others from our inner wealth and abundance. The wish-fulfilling gem represents the desire to share everything with all. Seeing that – ultimately – the very notion of ownership is utterly empty, the Bodhisattva shares everything and tries always to help others to enter the world of ownerless aesthetic appreciation, where the beauty of this world is available equally to all.

Amitābha

The Buddha Amitābha sits in full lotus posture on a red lotus throne, supported by four glorious peacocks. His body is a warm, glowing red, the colour of rubies or the setting sun. His hands are in the gesture of meditation, resting one upon the other, thumbs lightly touching. He wears richly embroidered robes. Around his head flickers an aura of green light. Another of red surrounds his body. Both are edged with rainbows. His resounding mantra, *oṃ amideva hrīḥ*, spreads love and warmth throughout the universe.

As head of the Lotus family, Amitābha is associated with the qualities of the lotus: openness, receptivity, and spiritual growth, and he reaches out to the world of the pretas or 'hungry ghosts', giving them unconditional love, helping them to overcome their narrow and neurotic preoccupations and open themselves up instead to all that lives.

Avalokiteśvara, the Bodhisattva of Compassion, is the protector of the Lotus family, which contains some of the most famous figures in the Buddhist pantheon: White Tārā, Hayagrīva, Padmasambhava, and Śākyamuni.

Amitābha is the most popular of all the Jinas, perhaps because the unconditional love he manifests towards all beings is what we most desire. He appears in many sūtras and plays a central part in the three Pure Land sūtras: the *Larger Sukhāvatī-vyūha Sūtra*, the *Smaller Sukhāvatī-vyūha Sūtra*, and the *Amitāyur Dhyāna Sūtra*.

In the first of these we hear about a young man called Dharmākara, who lived many aeons ago. One day he approached the Buddha of that era, Lokeśvararāja, and made a series of forty-eight great vows. All these vows had as their subject Dharmākara's intention to benefit living beings, and the eighteenth vow has come to be seen as especially important:

If, O lord, after I have [once] attained enlightenment, beings in the immeasurable, numberless buddha-fields through hearing my name should direct their thought to rebirth in [my] buddha-field and should thus bring the root of karmic merit to ripeness – if they should not be reborn in my buddha-field even if they had directed their thought only ten times [toward me and my buddha-paradise], may I then not reach supreme perfect enlightenment.[25]

In making this vow, Dharmākara made it a condition of his attaining Enlightenment that he would create a pure land in which everyone who had been even slightly devoted to him should be reborn. In the same sūtra, the Buddha tells Ānanda that Dharmākara later became the Buddha Amitābha. Since Dharmākara *did* become a Buddha, it follows that he must have fulfilled his vow and have created his pure land – Sukhāvatī, the Land of Bliss.

The Pure Land schools of Buddhism maintain that there is no need to engage in arduous Dharma practice. According to some, all the efforts we make to attain Enlightenment only strengthen our own ego-based clinging. Instead, we should manifest Great Faith; we should just accept that through the great efforts of the Buddha Amitābha we will be reborn in Sukhāvatī. All we need to do is call on him and recite, with gratitude, his praises: *oṃ namo amitābhāya buddhāya* or, in Japanese, *namu amida butsu* – 'Homage to the Buddha Amitābha!'

If only we do that for a little time, we will be reborn in Sukhāvatī. There, a vast plain of lapis lazuli intersected by cords of gold stretches away in all directions. The land is covered with forests of jewel-trees that grant every wish. In these trees sit colourful birds, singing the songs of impermanence and insubstantiality. Great rivers, bearing jewel flowers in their currents, murmur the sound of the Dharma. Gentle winds cause rains of flowers to fall from the sky, and everything one could desire appears immediately upon being wished for. In all directions there are vast lotus flowers, upon which sit golden Buddhas teaching the Dharma, and in the middle of this vast, radiant scene sits the Buddha Amitābha, flanked by his two chief disciples, Avalokiteśvara and Mahāsthāmaprāpta. In this world conditions for Dharma practice are ideal. Those born here make continuous spiritual progress until they attain Enlightenment.

When he was still a 'freelance wanderer' it was an unusual vision of the Buddha Amitābha that convinced Sangharakshita that his 'spiritual apprenticeship' was over and that it was time for him to seek formal Buddhist ordination. He and a friend were staying in Virupaksha Cave on the slope of Mount Arunachala, the sacred 'Hill of Light' that rose behind Ramana Maharshi's ashram in South India. There they devoted themselves to meditation. Amitābha is sometimes thought of as the Buddha of meditation, and one night he appeared to the young Sangharakshita:

> I found myself as it were out of the body and in the presence of Amitābha, the Buddha of Infinite Light, who presides over the western quarter of the universe. The colour of the Buddha was a deep, rich, luminous red, like that of rubies, though at the same time soft and glowing, like the light of the setting sun. While his left hand rested on his lap, the fingers of his right hand held up by the stalk a single red lotus in full bloom and he sat, in the usual cross-legged posture, on an enormous red lotus that floated on the surface of the sea. To the left, immediately beneath the raised right arm of the Buddha, was the red hemisphere of the setting sun, its reflection glittering golden across the waters. How long the experience lasted I do not know, for I seemed to be out of time as well as out of the body, but I saw the Buddha as clearly as I had ever seen anything under the ordinary circumstances of my life, indeed far more clearly and vividly. The rich red colour of Amitābha himself, as well as of the two lotuses, and the setting sun, made a particularly deep impression on me. It was more wonderful, more appealing, than any earthly red: it was like red light, but so soft and, at the same time, so vivid, as to be altogether without parallel....[26]

Amitābha is associated above all with the qualities of boundless love and compassion. The poison with which he is associated is passion, and the peacocks who support his throne live on snakes, whose venom they transmute into the glorious colours in their plumes. In the same way, by the power of love, Amitābha transforms the venom of passion into Discriminating Wisdom, which sees the unique, utterly distinctive characteristics of every passing phenomenon. Although marked with emptiness, no two events are ever completely alike. In the endless flux of conditions every fleeting condition is unique. Out of his boundless love, Amitābha appreciates the complete significance of every minute event.

Amoghasiddhi

Amoghasiddhi, 'Infallible Success', is the Buddha of the dark, mysterious northern sky. His deep-green lotus throne is supported by two pairs of *shang-shang* birds, mythical beasts whose heads, arms, and torsos are human and who have the wings, feet, talons, and tails of eagles. In their hands they each hold an enormous pair of cymbals which they clash as they fly. Dark green in colour and clad in scarlet robes, his right arm is raised, palm outwards, in the gesture which bestows complete fearlessness, while his left hand, resting in his lap, supports a double vajra. His mantra, *oṃ amoghasiddhi āḥ hūṃ*, resounds throughout the universe, bestowing courage and the will to act wherever it is heard.

The double vajra, according to Indian Buddhist cosmology, is the ground upon which the entire universe stands. Inconceivably vast, this giant symbol of total integration is the foundation on which all change and transformation takes place. As the aeons unfold, universes come and go, radiating out from and collapsing back into the primal store of energy, the double vajra, within which all opposites are united and all levels of existence enfolded.

This symbolism of unification continues in the image of the *shang-shang* birds – also known as *garuḍas*. Amoghasiddhi is lord of the great transformation: the two-way transformation in which the spiritual takes bodily form, and the embodied human becomes a Buddha. Garuḍas can be seen as part animal, part human, and part divine, ascending ever upwards towards new dimensions of consciousness.

As Amoghasiddhi's consort, Green Tārā is the most famous member of the Action family. (She was – as it were – born into the Lotus family, so she is a member of both families.) The Bodhisattva Viśvapāṇi, 'Holder of All', is the Action family protector, and

Maitreya, the Buddha-to-be, is also associated with this family.

Amoghasiddhi is imbued with the All-Accomplishing Wisdom. The Enlightened mind spontaneously devotes itself to the welfare of all living beings. In doing so, it devises many ways of helping people. The Enlightened mind helps living beings naturally and spontaneously. Buddhas and Bodhisattvas do not need to sit down and think, 'How can I go and help people today? Is this person more in need of help, or that? Maybe I will go and help so-and-so.' The Enlightened mind functions freely, spontaneously, and naturally. Helpfulness pours forth in a spontaneous flood.

The All-Accomplishing Wisdom transmutes the poison of envy. Envy is one of the main emotions in the āsura world, which is in Amoghasiddhi's special care. The āsuras worship success, so from time to time they are able to hear Amoghasiddhi's mantra. He shows them the way to the infallible success they so deeply desire. Envy comes from the thwarted wish to succeed. Amoghasiddhi teaches us to look within and find the resources our desire for success demands. Through the profound introspection of meditation we come in time to perceive the ultimate emptiness of all phenomena. When we see this, we see that all apparent obstacles are empty too. With that insight we become unstoppable – envy turns into unstoppability.

In the *Bardo Thödol*, known in the West as the *Tibetan Book of the Dead*, we read how all the different Jinas and their families appear on successive days to the newly deceased in the *bardo*, the state intermediate between death and the next rebirth. If we are receptive to them, they can lead us to more fortuitous rebirths. This is how Amoghasiddhi appears in the *bardo*:

> O son of noble family, listen without distraction. On the fifth day a green light, the purified element of air, will shine, and at the same time Blessed Amoghasiddhi, lord of the circle, will appear before you from the green northern Realm, Accumulated Actions. His body is green in colour, he holds a double vajra in his hand and sits on a throne of shang-shang birds soaring in the sky, embracing his consort Samaya-Tārā. He is accompanied by the two male bodhisattvas Vajrapāṇi and Sarvanīvaraṇaviṣkambhin and the two female

bodhisattvas Gandhā and Naivedyā, so that six buddha forms appear out of the space of rainbow light.

The green light of the skandha of concept in its basic purity, the action-accomplishing wisdom, brilliant green, luminous and clear, sharp and terrifying, adorned with discs of light, will come from the heart of Amoghasiddhi and his consort and pierce your heart so that your eyes cannot bear to look at it. Do not be afraid of it. It is the spontaneous play of your own mind, so rest in the supreme state free from activity and care, in which there is no near or far, love or hate. At the same time, together with the wisdom light, the soft red light of the jealous gods, caused by envy, will also shine on you. Meditate so that there is no difference between love and hate.

But if your intelligence is weak, then simply do not take pleasure in it.

At that time, under the influence of intense envy, you will be terrified and escape from the sharp, brilliant green light, but you will feel pleasure and attraction towards the soft red light of the jealous gods. At that moment do not be afraid of the green light, sharp and brilliant, luminous and clear, but recognise it as wisdom. Let your mind rest in it, relaxed, in a state of non-action, and supplicate It with devotion, thinking, 'it is the light-ray of Blessed Amoghasiddhi's compassion, I take refuge in it.' It is the light-ray hook of Blessed Amoghasiddhi's compassion, called the action-accomplishing wisdom, so long for it and do not escape. Even if you escape it will stay with you inseparably.

Do not be afraid of it, do not be attracted to the soft red light of the jealous gods. That is the inviting path of karma accumulated by your intense envy. If you are attracted to it you will fall into the realm of the jealous gods and experience unbearable misery from fighting and quarrelling. It is an obstacle blocking the path of liberation, so do not be attracted to it, but give up your unconscious tendencies. Feel longing for the luminous, brilliant green light, and say this inspiration-prayer with intense one-pointed concentration on Blessed Amoghasiddhi and his consort:

When through intense envy I wander in saṃsāra,
on the luminous light-path of action-accomplishing wisdom,
may Blessed Amoghasiddhi go before me,
his consort Samaya-Tārā behind me;
help me to cross the bardo's dangerous pathway
and bring me to the perfect buddha state.

By saying this inspiration-prayer with deep devotion, [you]
will dissolve into rainbow light in the heart of Blessed
Amoghasiddhi and his consort, and become a sambhogakāya
buddha in the northern Realm, Perfected Actions.[27]

Vairocana

Vairocana inhabits the centre of the mandala. His white lotus
throne is supported by four golden lions, and he sits on a
white moon-mat, himself brilliant white in colour, blazing like
sunshine on snow. He has black hair and wears white robes,
deeply embroidered with white thread. His hands, held in front
of his heart, make the finely balanced gesture of teaching the
Dharma. His mantra, *oṃ vairocana hūṃ*, illuminates the whole
universe with the light of the truth.

His emblem is the dharmacakra, the golden eight-spoked wheel
of the Dharma. In ancient Indian mythology, the golden wheel was
associated with sovereignty. The *cakravartī-rāja*, or 'wheel-turning
king', was a monarch who ruled in accordance with the Dharma,
using his position to influence society for the good. The emperor
Aśoka is widely regarded as having been a *cakravartī-rāja*, as was
King Trisong Detsen in Tibet. The association of kingship and
the wheel comes from an ancient Indian tradition in which the
boundaries of a kingdom were established by setting loose a horse
with a wheel on its back. Wherever the horse went unchallenged
the king's rule held sway. The Buddha's dominion is the area
where his wheel, the dharmacakra, goes unchallenged. This is
where the Dharma holds sway and, since the principles of the
Dharma are true everywhere, the Buddha's domain includes all
of time and space. Vairocana's dominion is therefore the entire
universe.

Once, the Buddha Śākyamuni accepted an invitation from his father, King Śuddhodana, to visit Kapilavastu, the capital of the Śākyans. Hearing that his son had been seen begging in the streets and seeing him dressed in his rag robes, Śuddhodana reproached him for not living up to his royal birth. 'I come from the noblest lineage of all,' replied the Buddha, 'the lineage of the Enlightened ones. My rag robes are the traditional garb of my lineage; begging is our time-honoured custom.' Vairocana's golden wheel, his monarchic symbol, stands for the intrinsic nobility of a complete commitment to spiritual life.

The golden wheel is also the symbol of the Dharma. The Buddha Śākyamuni's first attempts to communicate his experience of Enlightenment to his former companions in asceticism is known as his first turning of the wheel of the Dharma – the *dharmacakrapravartana* – and Vairocana's teaching gesture is also called the gesture of turning the wheel of the Dharma.

Vairocana means 'illuminator' and the golden wheel is clearly a solar symbol. It illuminates and nourishes all living things, bringing light and warmth where there was cold and darkness, and it is the centre about which all else revolves. In Japan, where the cult of Vairocana spread, he is known as the Sun Buddha, and he is a central figure in the Shingon tradition, a form of Japanese Vajrayāna.

His animal, the lion, is also associated with the proclamation of the Truth. In the scriptures the Buddha's utterance is sometimes referred to as his *siṃhanāda*, or 'lion's roar'. The lion roars in the jungle at night, without fear of others. Lesser animals are afraid to make a sound, lest they be pounced on by their enemies, but according to myth and legend the lion roars to proclaim his kingship of the whole jungle. The Buddha's fearless proclamation of the Dharma, his proclamation of his sovereignty over the whole spiritual universe, is like the roaring of a lion.

Vairocana is head of the Tathāgata – or Buddha – family, whose protector is Mañjuśrī, the Bodhisattva of Wisdom.

Vairocana himself embodies the Wisdom of the Dharmadhātu, the 'sphere of truth'. This is the totality of all wisdoms. Just as the white light of the sun may be fragmented by a prism into many different colours, so the sun-like Wisdom of the Dharmadhātu is refracted throughout the mandala, manifesting its many different aspects. But wisdom is holographic – ultimately, every aspect of it contains all other aspects – so although the Dharmadhātu Wisdom is central it is, like the light of the sun, all-pervasive. From Vairocana's pure land the Dharmadhātu wisdom streams out as white light, transforming the poison of ignorance. Vairocana is particularly associated with the realm of the gods, who live in ignorance of the truth of impermanence.

The image of the all-pervasive, interpenetrating nature of the realm of the Dharmadhātu is graphically described in the *Gaṇḍvyūha Sūtra*, in which the pilgrim Sudhana encounters the bodhisattva Maitreya outside Vairocana's Tower:

> Then Sudhana respectfully circumambulated the enlightening being Maitreya and said, 'Please open the door of the tower, and I will enter.' Then Maitreya went up to the door of the tower containing the adornments of Vairocana, and with his right hand snapped his fingers; the door of the tower opened, and Maitreya bade Sudhana enter. Then Sudhana, in greatest wonder, went into the tower. As soon as he had entered, the door shut.
>
> He saw the tower immensely vast and wide, hundreds of thousands of leagues wide, as measureless as the sky, as vast as all of space, adorned with countless attributes; countless canopies, banners, pennants, jewels, garlands of pearls and gems, moons and half moons, multicolored streamers, jewel nets, gold nets, strings of jewels, jewels on golden threads, sweetly ringing bells and nets of chimes, flowers showering, celestial garlands and streamers,... Also, inside the tower he saw hundreds of thousands of other towers similarly arrayed; he saw those towers as infinitely vast as space, evenly arrayed in all directions, yet these towers were not mixed up with one another, being each mutually distinct, while appearing mutually reflected in each and every object of all the other towers.
>
> Then Sudhana, seeing this miraculous manifestation of the inconceivable realm of the great tower containing the adornments of Vairocana, was flooded with joy and bliss;

his mind was cleared of all conceptions and freed from all obstructions. Stripped of all delusion, he became clairvoyant without distortion and could hear all sounds with unimpeded mindfulness. He was freed from all scattering of attention, and his intellect followed the unobstructed eye of liberation. With physical tranquillity, seeing all objects without hindrance, by the power of production everywhere he bowed in all directions with his whole body.

The moment he bowed, by the power of Maitreya, Sudhana perceived himself in all of those towers; and in all of those towers he saw various diverse inconceivable miraculous scenes.[28]

In the realm of the Dharmadhātu we see that in reality everything contains everything else and everything interpenetrates everything else. The mind suffused with wisdom sees the ultimate translucency of all phenomena.

Śāriputra, lower left, holds a mālā or rosary. His friend Maudgalyāyana is above him, next to Ānanda, the faithful companion of the Buddha. On the lower right is Mahākāśyapa and in the centre is Dhammadinnā. They are all making the teaching gesture.

Chapter Seven

The Arhants

An Arhant is one who has attained nirvāṇa, and although the Buddha had many lay-followers, and several of these achieved high levels of spiritual development, the Buddha's main Arhant disciples were monks or nuns. But we must not think of these great beings as bhikkhus and bhikkhunīs living in the same way in which we encounter them today in South-east Asia, or even in the West. The Buddha's main disciples were chiefly forest renunciants: tough men and women who took the Going Forth very seriously indeed. Many of them, before or after they met the Buddha, walked out of lives of privilege and comfort and went into the forest to meditate.

Some time after the Buddha, as the sangha began to settle down in monasteries and the canonical record began to develop, the lives of the early Arhants came to be shown to conform to the archetype of settled monasticism, more or less as we know it today, with shaven-headed monks and nuns wearing spotless cotton (or even silk) robes, patched in a particular way and worn just so. They were often lavishly supported by a devoted laity and ministered mainly to their religious needs.[29]

According to the earliest texts, however, we see that the Buddha's early monastic followers conformed more to the wandering ascetic traditions of their day. They were a ragged and unkempt bunch (the Vinaya prohibits shaving the head or face more than once a fortnight), they wore robes made of roughly stitched pieces of discarded cloth or even old, and sometimes charred, cemetery shrouds. They lived on what scraps the villagers offered them, making a point of not begging only from the wealthy. Above all, they were devoted to meditation.

The Buddha had many such disciples. Besides the five we find on our Tree there was also Anuruddha, Master of the Divine Eye, who developed supernormal powers through meditation; Mahā-Kaccāna, Master of Doctrinal Exposition; Aṅgulimāla, the serial killer who converted to the Dharma; Ambapālī, the former courtesan; Kisā Gotamī, the mother of a child who died, and many, many others. Each had their own particular personality and their own particular strengths.

The five Arhants on the Tree each tell us something distinctive about the Dharma life. By learning their stories and meditating on their qualities we can learn a great deal about how the spiritual life, in its fullness, can be lived. They are true exemplars of the life devoted to Enlightenment.

Śāriputra

Because of his deep knowledge and skill in analytical discourse, Śāriputra was known as the Marshal of the Dharma. He was also renowned for his kindness to his fellow monks, especially the very young and the old. He was pre-eminent among the Buddha's chief disciples, but very modest, and his loyalty and deep connection with his childhood friend, Maudgalyāyana, has long been an archetype of 'horizontal' spiritual friendship.

Śāriputra was born into a Brahmin family in the village of Upatissa near Rājagṛha. From his earliest childhood he demonstrated exceptional intelligence. He began formal studies with a teacher at an early age, and soon became thoroughly versed in Brahminic knowledge and able to recite the Vedas. His fame spread throughout the region.

Near Upatissa lay the village of Kolita, where Maudgalyāyana, another gifted child, was born. He and Śāriputra were firm friends throughout their childhood. On one occasion the two friends went along to an annual festival in Rājagṛha. Watching everybody's hollow attempts at festivity, Śāriputra was filled with a sense of the sad futility of it all. 'Sooner or later,' he said to his friend, 'all these people will be dead. That includes you and me. Every one of us. With death hard on our heels, what is the point of wasting time with such distractions?' There and then, he and Maudgalyāyana decided to go forth and seek a path of liberation.

At that time, philosophers and men of religion were gravitating towards Rājagṛha, then the capital of Magadha, one of the largest of the Indian kingdoms. These men were freethinkers who had placed themselves outside the formalistic Brahminical religion of the day. Many of them claimed to teach a path of personal liberation by one means or another. The two friends visited several of these teachers. They were most impressed by the ascetic Sañjaya, who taught an agnostic scepticism and had a following of several hundred disciples, so they decided to follow him. They soon became Sañjaya's leading disciples, owing to their outstanding qualities, but having soon mastered all he had to teach, they realized they had not yet found the path to liberation and continued to yearn for a true teacher.

One day, the Buddha's disciple Aśvajit went to beg in Rājagṛha. Respectfully holding out his alms-bowl, comporting himself with a quiet, energetic, modest, and dignified mindfulness, this monk made an enormous impression on Śāriputra when he happened to see him pass by. 'Perhaps this man has attained the Enlightenment I seek,' he thought, 'or perhaps his teacher has.' So he followed Aśvajit, hoping for an opportunity to engage him in conversation.

When Aśvajit had finished his alms round and eaten his meal, Śāriputra went up to him and made the usual salutations. 'Friend,' he said, 'I am really struck by your appearance. Who are you? And who is your teacher?'

'I am Aśvajit,' the monk replied, 'and I have left home and gone forth to follow the Tathāgata, the great Enlightened teacher who comes from the land of the Śākyas.'

'And what is the doctrine of this great Enlightened teacher?' Śāriputra asked, beginning to tremble with excitement.

'I cannot say in detail,' Aśvajit replied, 'I myself have only quite recently become one of his followers and I still have a lot to learn.'

'But please, the main points will be enough,' Śāriputra responded.

Aśvajit pondered for a while and then, looking straight at the youth, he came out with what was to become one of the most famous utterances in the whole body of Buddhist teaching:

Of those things that arise from a cause,
The Tathāgata has told the cause,
And also what their cessation is:
This is the doctrine of the Great Recluse.[30]

Śāriputra shook when he heard this. In a flash, the truth of the doctrine of dependent origination pervaded his being, and liberating insight flooded his mind. At that moment he became a Stream Entrant.

Some time previously, Śāriputra and Maudgalyāyana had each vowed that if one of them discovered the way to Enlightenment before the other, he would seek out his companion to share the teaching with him. True to his word, Śāriputra immediately set out to find Maudgalyāyana. Seeing him trembling with inspiration as he approached, Maudgalyāyana realized that Śāriputra had discovered the Truth. They spoke for a while, and Maudgalyāyana also gained insight. They decided to seek out the Buddha and become his disciples.

'But what about all our fellow disciples?' Maudgalyāyana asked, 'We can't just leave them here.' So they decided to tell Sañjaya's other disciples about what they had discovered, and to leave it to them to decide how best to act.

Sañjaya, when he heard this, was distraught. 'Please stay,' he said, 'the three of us can lead this group together.' But the friends were adamant, and tried to persuade Sañjaya to accompany them. 'I couldn't do that,' he said, 'I'm a great teacher. For me to revert to the state of being a disciple would be as if a huge water tank were to change into a small pitcher.'

'But a Buddha has appeared in the world,' they replied, 'thousands will flock to him for teachings. What will happen to your following then?

'What do you think? Are there more fools in this world or wise people?' Sañjaya asked.

'Fools are many, the wise are few,' the friends replied.

'Let the wise go to the recluse Gotama, the fools will come to me.' So, together with 500 of Sañjaya's former disciples, the two friends sought out the Buddha to ask to join his sangha. Seeing them approach, the Buddha instantly recognized their great capacity. 'These two friends will become the two great jewels, supreme among my disciples,' he said.

Śāriputra was forever grateful to Aśvajit for having shown him the Way, and for the rest of his life, before he lay down to sleep each night, he made three deep prostrations in Aśvajit's direction.

The two friends often worked together in the service of the Buddha and the sangha. After the Buddha's ambitious cousin Devadatta had created a schism, and led 500 young monks away with him to the Vulture's Peak, the Buddha sent Śāriputra and Maudgalyāyana to win them back. When Devadatta saw them approaching, he assumed they had decided to join his faction and welcomed them as his own chief disciples. That evening, while he was resting, the two elders spoke to the assembled monks, led them to Stream Entry, and persuaded them to return to the Buddha.[31]

With his acute intelligence Śāriputra soon developed the reputation of having a highly developed analytical capacity. Indeed, he is credited as the founding father of the Abhidharma approach to spiritual training. But his teaching could also be very simple and direct.

An ascetic once came to see him to discuss the spiritual life. 'Nirvāṇa!' he said, 'You followers of the Buddha always go on about nirvāṇa. What exactly *is* this nirvāṇa?'

'The end of craving, aversion, and delusion. *That* is nirvāṇa', he replied simply.[32]

Perhaps because of his association with the later Abhidharma tradition, the Mahāyāna scriptures often use Śāriputra as an icon of a narrow, restricted approach to Dharma practice. The *Heart Sūtra*, for example, in which the fundamental categories of the Abhidharma are shown to have no enduring essence but are instead ultimately empty, is addressed to Śāriputra. But this is a rhetorical device. The real Śāriputra was never simply a narrow-minded Hīnayānist, nor was he merely a monkish scholar. Once, when he and Maudgalyāyana were staying together at Kapotakandara, Śāriputra was meditating in the open air on a full-moon night, his head freshly shaven. A malicious demon, passing by in a spiteful mood, gave him a severe blow on the head, but Śāriputra was so absorbed in meditation that he hardly noticed. Maudgalyāyana, with his supernormal powers, observed the whole incident.

'Friend, are you comfortable, are you all right? Does anything trouble you?' he asked.

'I am comfortable,' Śāriputra replied, 'but, since you ask, I have a slight headache.'

'That is wonderful!' Maudgalyāyana exclaimed, 'A passing demon dealt you a blow that would have felled an elephant or split a mountain peak, and all you say is that you have a slight headache!'

'Even more wonderful,' replied Śāriputra, 'that you should have seen any demon at all. What great psychic power! I've not even seen as much as a mud-sprite.'

The Buddha, who had been listening to this discussion with his divine ear, then spoke this 'inspired utterance' in praise of Śāriputra:

> Whose mind stands unmoving as a rock,
> Unattached to things that arouse attachment,
> Unangered by things that provoke anger.
> How can suffering come to one
> Whose mind has been cultivated thus?[33]

Śāriputra was renowned for his generosity and helpfulness. When the other monks made their early morning alms round, he remained behind to tidy up, disposing of refuse and neatly arranging whatever possessions they held in common. Then he would call on any who were sick and make sure they had whatever they needed. When the Buddha went about on foot with a company of monks, Śāriputra never walked at the head of the procession, as surely befitted him. Instead he first attended to the old, the very young, or the unwell, applying oil to any sores they might have on their bodies, before leaving together with them.

It is said that Śāriputra taught with infinite patience. He would admonish, advise, and instruct up to a hundred or a thousand times until his students attained Stream Entry. The Buddha often praised him for his mastery of the Dharma and his skill in exposition:

> The essence of the Dhamma (*dhammadhātu*) has been so well penetrated by Sāriputta, O monks, that if I were to question

him about it for one day in different words and phrases, Sāriputta would reply for one day in various words and phrases. And if I were to question him for one night, or a day and night, or for two days and nights, even up to seven days and nights, Sāriputta would expound the matter for the same period of time, in various words and phrases.[34]

Towards the end of his life the Buddha was staying in the Jeta Grove in Śrāvastī when Śāriputra arrived there with a company of followers. After saluting the Buddha, Śāriputra told him that the last day of his life on earth had arrived. Would the Buddha permit him to die? The Buddha asked Śāriputra whether he had selected any place for his death.

'I was born in the village Upatissa in Magadha,' Śāriputra replied, 'The house in which I was born still stands. I would like to die there.' 'Dear friend, you must do what pleases you,' the Lord replied. 'Let the Buddha forgive me my faults,' said Śāriputra. 'There is nothing to forgive,' said the Buddha, and Śāriputra walked away without showing his back to the Buddha.

Maudgalyāyana

Maudgalyāyana was known as the disciple foremost in psychic powers. He was deeply devoted to meditation and to the life of the mind, but he did not confine himself to solitary introspection. He happily shared his Dharmic understandings with others and undertook many valuable services for the Buddha and the sangha.

His family had, for generations, been Brahminical teachers in the service of noble families. They enjoyed wealth and high social status, and when their beloved son – who had already won great renown locally for his outstanding abilities – decided to adopt the wandering life, they objected fiercely. They had high hopes for the young Maudgalyāyana but, being aware of his powerful strength of will and unusual depth of thought, they realized he must have given the matter profound consideration and that his decision was not likely to be revoked. Regretfully, they gave their permission, and Maudgalyāyana went forth with Śāriputra.

After joining the sangha, Maudgalyāyana left the Bamboo Grove for a time and went to stay at the nearby Vulture's Peak. There he took to a cave for meditation. The verses ascribed to him in the *Theragāthā* open with his song in praise of solitary meditation:

> Let us, living in the forest, living on alms-food, delighting in whatever scraps come into our alms-bowls, tear apart the army of death, being well-concentrated inwardly.
>
> Let us, living in the forest, living on alms-food, delighting in whatever scraps come into our alms-bowls, knock down the army of death, as an elephant knocks down a reed-hut.
>
> Let us, living at the foot of a tree, persevering, delighting in whatever scraps come into our alms-bowls, tear apart the army of death, being well-concentrated inwardly.
>
> Let us, living at the foot of a tree, persevering, delighting in whatever scraps come into our alms-bowls, knock down the army of death, as an elephant knocks down a reed-hut.[35]

By exerting great discipline, Maudgalyāyana finally attained to the *samādhi* where neither thought nor perception occurs. During this period, whenever he became discouraged Śākyamuni himself would appear in a vision and encourage him to persevere. When Maudgalyāyana's efforts finally brought him to complete Enlightenment, he said, 'I have become Enlightened because of my Master's teaching and encouragement. I have, therefore, been born of my Master.' From then on, he was able to establish communication with the Buddha no matter what distance separated them. Once, when the Buddha went off to the Jeta Grove at Śrāvastī, and while Śāriputra and Maudgalyāyana were staying at the Bamboo Grove in Rājagṛha, Maudgalyāyana turned to Śāriputra and reported a conversation he had just had with the Buddha.

'But how could you have spoken with him when he was so far away, beyond many mountains and rivers?' asked Śāriputra. 'It's not that I miraculously transported myself to his side,' replied Maudgalyāyana, 'or that he came to mine. But somehow, using supernormal senses, I spoke to him and he replied, urging me to be diligent.'

'All the followers of the Dharma should respect you,' said Śāriputra. 'We should remain close to you and make every effort to become like you, just as the small stone nearby resembles the great Himalaya mountains.'

Maudgalyāyana, for his part, often praised Śāriputra. 'Your teachings are like food to the hungry and water to the thirsty,' he once told him, after Śāriputra had given teachings on the four ways to liberation.

Śākyamuni himself was unstinting in his praises of the two:

Cultivate the friendship of Sāriputta and Moggallāna, bhikkhus; associate with Sāriputta and Moggallāna. They are wise and helpful to their companions in the holy life. Sāriputta is like a mother; Moggallāna is like a nurse. Sāriputta trains others for the fruit of stream-entry, Moggallāna for the supreme goal.[36]

Śāriputra often brought beginners to the point of Stream Entry. He then 'handed them over' to Maudgalyāyana who trained them for Arhantship.

Maudgalyāyana always put his supernormal powers at the service of the Dharma. He visited various *devalokas* for the sake of teaching, and the Buddha sometimes called upon his peculiar gifts. Once, when the Buddha was staying on the upper storey of a building in Śrāvastī, and a crowd of monks were talking loosely and loudly on the ground floor, he asked Maudgalyāyana to shake the building with his big toe to quieten them down.

Maudgalyāyana was always very outspoken, and as he proclaimed the Buddha's Dharma he fearlessly exposed wrong views whenever he encountered them. This earned him the enmity of followers of rival teachers, especially of a group of naked ascetics who believed he had won their followers over with reports of his celestial travels, in which he apparently related that he had seen the Buddha's followers enjoying rebirth in divine realms while the followers of other sects, owing to their lack of moral conduct, suffered in miserable subhuman realms. They decided to eliminate him.

Having acquired a thousand gold coins from their followers, they offered them to a band of thugs in exchange for Maudgalyāyana's life. Using his psychic powers, Maudgalyāyana evaded the hired killers for seven days. Seeing them coming, he would slip through the keyhole of his hut, or escape through the roof. Although he had no fear of death, he did not want them to suffer the karmic consequences of killing him. But the killers were both greedy and persistent and, one day, because of the ripening of a karma from a past life, Maudgalyāyana's psychic powers suddenly deserted him. The killers entered his hut and 'pounded his bones until they were as small as grains of rice'.[37]

Thinking he was dead, they fled to claim their reward. But they had not reckoned with Maudgalyāyana's formidable psychic powers, which had now returned. By the power of his meditation he soared through the air and came to the Buddha. There he announced that the time had come for him to die. The Buddha asked him to give a final discourse to the assembled monks, which he did, displaying many wonders and marvels. Then he returned to his abode and passed into nirvāṇa.

Ānanda

For the last twenty-five years of the Buddha's life, his cousin Ānanda was his close companion. According to the Buddha, Ānanda was pre-eminent in five qualities. He was the best of the Buddha's attendants, he was foremost among those who had 'heard much', he had the best memory, the greatest mastery of the sequential structure of the teachings, and he was most steadfast in study. He was much loved in the sangha, to whom he had devoted most of his life.

Ānanda and his brother Anuruddha were Śākyan aristocrats, born in the town of Kapilavastu. Amṛtodana, their father, was the brother of the Buddha's father, Śuddhodana, although they probably had different mothers. When Ānanda was 37, the two brothers, together with several other Śākyan nobles, went forth and joined the Buddha's sangha.

During Ānanda's first rains retreat the Venerable Puṇṇa Mantānīputta gave the assembled novices a teaching on the relationship between the notion 'I am' and the five skandhas. Hearing this, Ānanda gained Stream Entry. For the next eighteen years he happily passed his time in the sangha, purifying his mind, strengthening his practice, and getting on with his fellow monks: Ānanda was renowned for his sweet, companionable nature. When he and the Buddha were both 55 years old, however, a momentous change in the pattern of his life occurred.

The Buddha called a meeting of his monk disciples. 'In my twenty years as leader of the sangha,' he said, 'I have had many different attendants, but none of them has really filled the post perfectly; again and again some wilfulness has become apparent. Now I am old and I need a trustworthy, reliable attendant.' At once all the leading disciples offered their services, but the Buddha accepted none of them. Ānanda alone held back. 'Why are you holding back?' they asked, 'Shouldn't you also volunteer?' Although he would liked to have been his revered cousin's attendant he was too modest to put himself forward. In any case, he was confident the Buddha would know whom to choose. The Buddha was aware what Ānanda was thinking. 'Ānanda would be pleasing to me,' he said, and so began a close companionship that lasted until the death of the Buddha.

Realizing that some of the disciples were likely to accord him special status because he was always at the Buddha's side, Ānanda saw that he would have to be discreet if he was to avoid jealousy, and that he would have to take special care to avoid pride. He also realized he would have to be sure never to stray from the Dharma if he was to live up to his new task. He therefore asked the Buddha to allow certain conditions to be met if he were to undertake his new duty.

Because he did not want people to think he was serving the Buddha out of desire for material gain, he asked that the Buddha should never give him any of the food he received, nor any of the robes. He insisted that he should never be given any special accommodation, nor should he be included in the personal invitations to hospitality that the Buddha received. On the other hand, he asked that if he himself was invited to a meal he could transfer the invitation to the Buddha. If people from outlying areas came to see the Buddha, he wanted the privilege of introducing them. And if he had any doubts about the Dharma, he asked that he should be able to talk to the Buddha about them at any time.

Finally, if the Buddha gave a discourse in his absence, he would agree to repeat it later in his presence. The Buddha gladly agreed to these conditions.

Ānanda was a very popular man, much loved by everybody who got to know him, and he had many spiritual friends, including, of course, the Buddha himself. He was once staying with the Buddha at Sakkhara, a Śākyan village, and reflecting on the joy and efficacy of spiritual friendship.

'Lord, I've been thinking,' he told the Buddha, 'you know, spiritual friendship seems to me to be half the spiritual life!' 'Don't say that, Ānanda, don't say that,' the Buddha replied, 'Spiritual friendship is the *whole* of the spiritual life!'[38]

Ānanda, who had a prodigious memory, and spent much of his time with the Buddha, was consequently very learned in the Dharma. A lay disciple once asked the Buddha how, after he had honoured the Buddha and the sangha, he might honour the Dharma. This was in an age when the Buddha's teachings had not yet been written down.

'If you wish to honour the Dharma,' replied the Buddha, 'go and honour Ānanda, the guardian of the Dharma.' So this disciple invited Ānanda to a meal and gave him some valuable cloth. Ānanda offered this to Śāriputra, who in turn gave it to the Buddha, for he alone was the cause of all bliss.[39]

On another occasion, after Ānanda had answered a question from some monks and then left the assembly, the Buddha turned to the monks and said, ' Ānanda is still on the path of higher training, yet it is not easy to find one who equals him fully in wisdom.'[40]

Ānanda's qualities fitted him for the special role of Guardian of the Dharma, or *dhammabhaṇḍāgārika*. Within a political state the *bhaṇḍāgārika* is the treasurer, with responsibility for storing, protecting, and dispensing the national wealth. If he is inept or irresponsible, revenue will decline and the state may become bankrupt. If he is astute, national wealth will be used wisely and there will be peace and prosperity. In the Buddha's Dispensation, wealth is the Dharma, and, especially after the Buddha's death, the life and health of the Buddha's Dispensation required that the Dharma be carefully preserved and faithfully passed on for posterity. The post of treasurer of the Dharma was therefore of

Teachers of Enlightenment

immense importance – to the extent that one who held it could rightly call himself 'the eye of the entire world', as Ānanda does in his *Theragāthā* verses:

> If one wishes to understand the Dhamma,
> One should resort to such a one,
> Who is of great learning, a bearer of the Dhamma,
> A wise disciple of the Buddha.

> Of great learning, bearer of the Dhamma,
> The guardian of the Great Seer's treasure,
> He is the eye of the entire world,
> Deserving worship, of great learning.[41]

As a child, the Buddha had been brought up by his aunt, Mahāprajāpatī. After her brother, Śuddhodana, died, Mahāprajāpatī decided she wanted to join the sangha, and since the Buddha was then visiting Kapilavastu, his former home town, Mahāprajāpatī approached him and requested three times that she be allowed to join the sangha. But each time the Buddha refused, because she was a woman. He then left Kapilavastu and made for Vaiśālī, several hundred miles away. Mahāprajāpatī and several other Śākyan women decided that they *would* Go Forth, and followed close behind. Arriving at the Hall of the Peaked Gable, where the Buddha was staying, Mahāprajāpatī stood outside the porch, 'her feet swollen, her limbs covered with dust, with tearful face and crying'.[42]

Seeing her piteous state, Ānanda decided to intercede on her behalf. He went to the Buddha and repeated Mahāprajāpatī's request three times, but each time the Buddha discouraged him. Ānanda then decided to use an indirect method.

'Suppose women *were* to go forth from home into the homeless life under the Dhamma Vinaya set forth by the Tathāgata,' he asked, 'would they be capable of attaining the fruits of Stream Entry, or the fruit of Once Returning, or the Fruit of Non-Returning, or the Fruit of Arahantship?'[43]

The Buddha admitted that women were indeed so capable, and Ānanda seized his chance. Mahāprajāpatī was of great service to the Buddha when he was an infant, he told him. She actually suckled him after the death of his mother. This alone would be a good reason for him now to help her gain final liberation. Unable to resist this argument, the Buddha agreed to the establishment of the nuns' order, providing certain rules were followed. From that time, Ānanda has always held a special place in the affections of the nuns' sangha.

Ānanda's relationship to the Buddha was not just that of servant. He was a friend, companion, and secretary, and there was great warmth and intimacy between them. He brought the Buddha water for washing his face and a tooth-stick for cleaning his teeth. He arranged his seat, washed his feet, massaged his back, fanned him, swept his cell, and repaired his robes. He slept by him, always to be on hand in case anything was needed. He accompanied the Buddha on his rounds of the monks' precincts, and always checked to see whether monks had left anything behind after meetings. He carried the Buddha's messages and called the monks together if the Buddha wanted to talk with them (sometimes even at midnight). When the Buddha was sick he got medicine for him, and once, when a monk had fallen ill with dysentery and was neglected by his fellows, the Buddha and Ānanda washed him and carried him to a resting place.

Ānanda played a large part in facilitating the Buddha's communication with the growing sangha. When there was a quarrel between the monks at Kosambī, and when Devadatta brought about a schism, Ānanda helped people clarify their doubts and renew their communication with one another. He was often the go-between for the monks, arranging their interviews with the Buddha, and he took the Buddha's words to the leaders of other sects. Refusing no one, Ānanda thought of himself as a bridge rather than a barrier:

> For twenty-five years I served the Blessed One,
> I served him well with loving deeds
> Like a shadow that does not depart.

> For twenty-five years I served the Blessed One,
> I served him well with loving speech
> Like a shadow that does not depart.

For twenty-five years I served the Blessed One,
I served him well with loving thoughts
Like a shadow that does not depart.[44]

When the Buddha was preparing to die, Ānanda became deeply distressed. He went to his lodging and stood lamenting, leaning on the door-post: 'Alas, I am still a learner with much to do! And the Teacher is passing away, who was so compassionate to me!'[45] The Buddha noticed Ānanda was missing, and sent a monk to call him. When Ānanda arrived, the Buddha consoled him, telling him that since all compounded things are subject to decay, how could he *not* die? Then he encouraged and praised him: 'For a long time, Ānanda, you have been in the Tathāgata's presence, showing loving kindness in acts of body, speech and mind, beneficially, blessedly, wholeheartedly and unstintingly. You have achieved much merit Ānanda. Make the effort, and in a short time you will be free of the corruptions.'[46] Then the Buddha addressed the monks. He told them that all the Buddhas of the past had an attendant like Ānanda, as would Buddhas of the future. And, he told them, Ānanda was always wise. He knew the right time for monks, nuns, and lay-followers to come and see the Buddha, and for kings, royal ministers, for leaders of other schools, and their pupils. Moreover, he told them, ' Ānanda has four remarkable and wonderful qualities. What are they? If a company of monks comes to see Ānanda, they are pleased at the sight of him, and when Ānanda talks Dhamma to them they are pleased, and when he is silent they are disappointed. And so it is, too, with nuns, [and] with male and female lay-followers.'[47]

After the Buddha's *parinirvāṇa*, Ānanda went off to the forest to meditate, but when it became known to the villagers that the Buddha's personal attendant was nearby, he was inundated with visitors. The Buddha, Śāriputra, Maudgalyāyana, and the just king Pasenadi had all died that year. People felt a strong need for consolation, and Ānanda, characteristically, responded to their need. In consequence he was rarely alone. Then a deva who lived in the forest appeared and spoke to him:

Having entered the thicket at the foot of a tree,
Having placed Nibbāna in your heart,

Meditate, Gotama, and be not negligent!
What will this hullabaloo do for you?[48]

Ānanda responded to this exhortation with a renewed sense of urgency. In the meantime, Mahākāśyapa had decided to call a council to regularize the contents of the Buddha's Dharma. Since Ānanda knew most of the discourses, he was indispensable to the council – yet, of all the 500 monks invited, he was the only one who was not yet an arhant. As the date of the council drew near, Anuruddha suggested that Ānanda should be admitted only if he could overcome the last of the defilements and attain arhantship. Anuruddha clearly knew what he was doing, for Ānanda now applied all his effort to spiritual practice. He practised the four foundations of mindfulness throughout the night and, in the early hours, just as he was lying down to sleep, his mind was finally released from all the cankers. The council was about to begin; no sooner were all the monks seated than Ānanda arrived, flying through the air by his psychic power, and took his seat. On the basis of Ānanda's recollections, the anthologies that make up the Sutta Piṭaka were settled.

When Ānanda was 120 years old he realized his end was near, so he planned a journey from Rājagṛha to Vaiśālī, just as the Buddha had done. When the king of Magadha and the princes of Vaiśālī heard of this, they hurried from both directions to bid him farewell. In order to do justice to both sides, Ānanda raised himself into the air by his psychic powers and allowed the fire element to consume his body. His relics were then divided and stupas erected. It was typical of Ānanda's gentle skilfulness that any quarrel over his funeral rites and remains was thus avoided.

Kāśyapa

Kāśyapa was a formidable ascetic, devoted to solitary meditation, but his early life did little to prepare him for the hardships he willingly embraced after meeting the Buddha.

Born into a wealthy Brahmin family in Magadha, Kāśyapa led a pampered early life. Observing how little joy he took in secular life, fearful that he would soon Go Forth, and anxiously desiring

Teachers of Enlightenment

an heir, his parents continually pressed him to marry. In the end, to escape their constant importunity, he had a goldsmith make an exquisitely beautiful and noble female form from pure gold. 'I'll marry when you can find me a girl like this,' he told them.

His parents searched the land and, in due course, actually found a maiden, Bhaddhā Kapilānī, who resembled the statue. She and Kāśyapa were duly wed, but she also harboured strong spiritual desires, and they both remained celibate.

After the death of Kāśyapa's parents, he and his wife put on ochre robes, cut off each other's hair, and, taking up their begging-bowls, abandoned the household life together. At the first crossroads they came to, Kāśyapa took the right turn and she the left, and so they parted.

Bhaddhā made her way to Śrāvastī, where she joined the bhikkhunī sangha, became an arhant, and devoted herself to the education of the younger nuns.

When Kāśyapa and Bhaddhā parted, the earth trembled through the force of their renunciation. Perceiving this, the Buddha realized that it meant an outstanding disciple was on his way and he set out to meet his future pupil. Some way along the road he took his seat beneath a banyan tree and waited – his aura lighting up the area. When Kāśyapa saw the Buddha sitting there in his glory, he realized at once that this man was the teacher for him and he fell prostrate at his feet. 'The Blessed One, Lord, is my teacher and I am his disciple! The Blessed One, Lord, is my teacher and I am his disciple!' he exclaimed. The Buddha accepted him as a disciple, and gave him three rules of training:

> You should train yourself thus, Kassapa: 'A keen sense of shame and fear of wrongdoing (*hiri-ottappa*) shall be present in me towards seniors, novices, and those of middle status in the Order.
>
> 'Whatever teaching I hear that is conducive to something wholesome, I shall listen with an attentive ear, examining it, reflecting on it, absorbing it with all my heart.
>
> 'Mindfulness of the body linked with gladness shall not be neglected by me!' Thus should you train yourself.[49]

Kāśyapa then took off his fine robe and made a seat for the Buddha. The Buddha commented on the softness of the fine cloth. 'Please take it. You must have it,' Kāśyapa replied. 'But what will you wear?' asked the Buddha. 'May I be so bold as to beg my master's robe?' asked Kāśyapa. 'But it is old and worn, and made of nothing but old scraps of cloth. Can you *really* wear it?' asked the Buddha. 'I will prize it beyond all things,' said Kāśyapa. And so they exchanged robes.

Conscious of the great honour the Buddha had bestowed upon him, Kāśyapa took upon himself the *dhūtaguṇas*, a set of particularly austere ascetic practices, which he followed for the rest of his life. Thus he undertook only to wear patched robes and never to own more than three of them; to live only on alms; not to omit any house on his almsround, no matter how poor or abusive its occupants; to eat only at one sitting and only from the alms-bowl, refusing all other food; to live in a forest, or under a tree, or in the open air, or in a charnel ground; to be satisfied with whatever dwelling he found; and to sleep always in an upright position instead of lying down.

Not long after his ordination Kāśyapa gained Enlightenment, but he continued to practise the *dhūtaguṇas*, not only for his own sake, he said, but also as an example to others.

In the *Theragāthā* he tells this story: One day he came down from the mountain to make an almsround. In the street he saw a leper eating his meal and courteously stopped at his side. The leper, with his leprous hand, put a morsel into Kāśyapa's bowl, but as he threw it in, one of his fingers broke off and fell into the food. In accordance with his vows, Kāśyapa sat at a wall nearby and ate his meal. 'And I felt no disgust – then or after. For those who take things as they come – living on scraps and using only cow's urine for medicine, taking rags from refuse heaps for their robes and living at the foot of a tree – truly, they are contented everywhere.'[50]

Kāśyapa is also regarded as the second patriarch of all the Chan and Zen schools. Once, when the Buddha was staying at the Vulture's Peak, he sat with a large gathering of disciples waiting for him to teach. In complete silence, the Buddha simply held up a golden flower and sat there quietly, not saying a word. Kāśyapa alone understood the meaning of this, and quietly smiled at the Buddha. 'I have the most precious spiritual treasure, Kāśyapa, which at this moment I hand over to you!' said the Buddha. Thus began the 'special transmission outside the scriptures'.

Kāśyapa lived to a great age, eventually presiding over the First Council that was held after the Buddha's death. By the time he died, it is said, he had not lain on a bed for 120 years. Despite his great asceticism, his life was filled with joy and aesthetic delight. In the *Theragāthā* he sang in praise of solitary meditation:

Spread over with *kareri* garlands,
These regions are delightful to my heart;
Resounding with elephants, so lovely,
Those rocky mountains give me delight.

The splendid hue of dark-blue clouds,
Where streams are flowing, cool and clear,
Covered with indagopaka insects:
Those rocky mountains give me delight.

Like towering peaks of dark-blue clouds,
Like lofty houses with gabled roofs,
Resounding with elephants, so lovely:
Those rocky mountains give me delight.

Their lovely surfaces lashed by rain,
The mountains are resorted to by seers.
Echoing with the cries of peacocks,
Those rocky mountains give me delight.

There is enough for me, desiring to meditate,
Enough for me, resolute and mindful;
There is enough for me, a bhikkhu,
Resolute, desirous of the goal.

This is enough for me, desiring comfort,
A bhikkhu with a resolute mind.
This is enough for me, desiring exertion,
A stable one of resolute mind.

They are like the blue blossoms of flax,
Like autumn sky covered with clouds,
With flocks of many kinds of birds:
Those rocky mountains give me delight.

No crowds of lay folk visit these hills,
But they are inhabited by herds of deer,
With flocks of many kinds of birds:
Those rocky mountains give me delight.

Wide gorges are there where clear water flows,
Haunted by monkeys and by deer,
Covered by wet carpets of moss:
Those rocky mountains give me delight.

The music of a five-piece ensemble
Can never give me so much delight
As I derive when with one-pointed mind
I gain proper insight into the Dhamma.[51]

Dhammadinnā

The Buddha thought of Dhammadinnā as the foremost teacher of
the Dharma among the nuns. We do not know much about her life,
but her teaching, particularly on the spiral and cyclical nature of
conditioned existence, has played a large part in the development
of Sangharakshita's thought.

Before Going Forth she had been the wife of Visākha, a
wealthy citizen of Rājagṛha and a close friend of King Bimbisāra.
One day her husband went to visit the new teacher, Śākyamuni,
who was then staying at the Bamboo Grove, and after listening
to his discourse he became a 'non-returner'. On hearing this,
Dhammadinnā decided that she too wished to renounce the
world and strive for Enlightenment. Respecting her intentions,
Visākha sent her to join the community of nuns in a golden
palanquin provided by his friend the king. There she resolved
to take up the spiritual life in earnest and took herself off to
the remote countryside where she practised intensively, soon
to become an arhant.

When Dhammadinnā returned to the Bamboo Grove to spend time with the Buddha, Visākha went to see her, curious to find out what his former wife had made of her intensive practice. The *Cūḷavedalla Sutta* of the *Majjhima-Nikāya* recounts the story of their meeting.

Visākha questioned Dhammadinnā very closely. To begin with, perhaps, he did not take her very seriously. Maybe he was just testing her to see if she had really learned anything. Very soon, however, it became clear that she was in fact instructing him, and he followed her words intently.

He began by asking her about the nature of the self – what does it comprise and how does it come to be? She told him that it comprises the five skandhas, that it comes into being as a result of our craving, and that it ceases when we stop craving:

'Lady, "personality, personality" is said. What is called personality by the Blessed One?'

'Friend Visākha, these five aggregates affected by clinging are called personality by the Blessed One; that is, the material form aggregate affected by clinging, the feeling aggregate affected by clinging, the perception aggregate affected by clinging, the formations aggregate affected by clinging, and the consciousness aggregate affected by clinging. These five aggregates affected by clinging are called personality by the Blessed One.'

Saying, 'Good, lady,' the lay follower Visākha delighted and rejoiced in the bhikkhunī Dhammadinnā's words. Then he asked her a further question:

'Lady, "origin of personality, origin of personality" is said. What is called the origin of personality by the Blessed One?'

'Friend Visākha, it is craving, which brings renewal of being, is accompanied by delight and lust, and delights in this and that; that is, craving for sensual pleasures, craving for being, and craving for non-being. This is called the origin of personality by the Blessed One.'[52]

She then expounded the Eightfold Path as the means to bring about the cessation of craving, and – in passing – showed how the eight limbs of the path correspond to the threefold way.

The path of ethics, she explained, corresponds to the practices of right speech, right action, and right livelihood. The path of meditation corresponds to right effort, right mindfulness, and right concentration. The path of wisdom corresponds to right vision and right emotion. Their discussion covered many abstruse topics. Eventually, and perhaps most importantly, it concluded with Dhammadinnā outlining two fundamental tendencies within conditioned existence.

There is a cyclical tendency, she told him, in which pleasant feelings simply give way to painful ones, painful feelings give way to pleasant ones, and neutral feelings give way to ignorance. And there is a spiral tendency in which ignorance instead gives way to true knowledge, true knowledge gives way to liberation, and liberation gives way to nirvāṇa:

> 'Lady, what is the counterpart of pleasant feeling?'
> 'Friend Visākha, painful feeling is the counterpart of pleasant feeling.'
> 'What is the counterpart of painful feeling?'
> 'Pleasant feeling is the counterpart of painful feeling.'
> 'What is the counterpart of neither-painful-nor-pleasant feeling?'
> 'Ignorance is the counterpart of neither-painful-nor-pleasant feeling'.
> 'What is the counterpart of ignorance?'
> 'True knowledge is the counterpart of ignorance.'
> 'What is the counterpart of true knowledge?'
> 'Deliverance is the counterpart of true knowledge.'
> 'What is the counterpart of deliverance?'
> 'Nibbāna is the counterpart of deliverance.'[53]

There is, in other words, a *saṃsāric*, cyclic, or reactive tendency within conditioned existence, where states simply pass over into their opposites, and there is also a *nirvāṇic*, creative, or spiral tendency, in which positive mental states can increasingly be augmented.

'And what does nirvāṇa give way to?' asked Visākha. 'You have pushed this line of questioning too far,' replied Dhammadinnā,

Teachers of Enlightenment

'You have not seen that there is a limit to such questions. The spiritual life culminates in nirvāṇa and that is its end. If you like, go to the Buddha and ask him. Then remember what he tells you!'

Pleased with what he had heard from his former wife, Visākha went to the Buddha and recounted their conversation. 'Dhammadinnā is truly wise, Visākha,' the Buddha told him, 'If you had asked me any of those questions I should have explained it all to you in the same way. You should remember what she has said.'

This is a rare example of a female disciple's teaching being given the status of *Buddhavacana* – the 'word of the Buddha'. By stating that he would have taught things in exactly the same way, the Buddha gave Dhammadinnā's teaching the stamp of canonical authenticity.

Dhammadinnā's verses in the *Therīgāthā* also echo those of the Buddha. She took his verses, which appear in the *Dhammapada*, and transposed them into the feminine gender:

Eager for the end of suffering,
full of awareness,
that's the way.

When one's heart is not
attached to pleasure, we say,
'That woman has entered the stream.'[54]

At the lower left, Avalokiteśvara holds a rosary and a flowering lotus while clasping the wish-granting jewel, the bodhicitta, to his heart. Above him, Mañjuśrī wields the Sword of Wisdom, while clasping to his heart the text of the Perfection of Wisdom in 8,000 lines. In his right hand Vajrapāṇi holds up the vajra, and with his left he makes the gesture warding off demons. Kṣitigarbha clasps the mendicant's staff and holds the wish-granting jewel in his lap. Green Tārā, clasping the stems of flowering lotuses, makes the gestures of giving and fearlessness.

Chapter Eight

The Bodhisattvas

The Bodhisattvas who appear on the lotus to the left of the Buddhas of the Three Times dwell in the realm of the archetypal imagination, the *sambhogakāya*. Each has their place in the vast mandala that forms around the five Buddhas, playing their own particular part in one of the Buddha 'families', which they enrich with their own distinctive qualities.

Each of the Bodhisattvas on our Tree has, at one time or another, been the centre of a devotional cult – using that term in its traditional sense: a system of worship expressed in ceremonies, rituals, and so on. Over time, a whole array of myths and legends grew up around these Bodhisattvas, especially the more popular ones, and we will look at some of these below.

Generalizing somewhat, we might say that the Bodhisattvas all represent more specific dimensions of the qualities of the particular Buddha at the head of their family, as these are enacted in the world. Thus, Amitābha stands for the principle of love and Avalokiteśvara stands for that love as an active force in the world – in other words, for compassion – and Tārā stands for the quintessence of love, a mother's love, all-embracing, all-accepting.

The Bodhisattva ideal, the ideal of continual self-transcendence for the benefit of all, stands at the very heart of the Triratna Buddhist Order, and these five glorious figures stand for the altruistic dimension of Going for Refuge – a dimension without which no Going for Refuge is complete.

Radiant in their beauty, each of these figures embodies one or another of the chief facets of Enlightenment. Between them, the three family protectors – Mañjuśrī, Avalokiteśvara, and Vajrapāṇi – stand for the cognitive, the affective, and the volitional dimensions of the Enlightenment experience: understanding, emotion, and action transformed into wisdom, compassion, and skilful means. Tārā stands for the heart-essence of the Bodhisattva's compassion and Kṣitigarbha for the unrelenting urge to save living beings, however dire the circumstances one must encounter to reach them. In approaching any one of these great figures, learning their stories, and becoming more deeply acquainted with them, our appreciation of the inner dimensions of the Bodhisattva ideal may come to be immeasurably enriched.

Avalokiteśvara

Avalokiteśvara's primary quality is *mahākaruṇā* – great compassion. For this reason he is often spoken of as the quintessential Bodhisattva, because compassion, above all, is what makes one a Bodhisattva. As the family protector of Amitābha's Lotus family, he represents Amitābha's infinite love at work in the world.

Rich in skilful means, Avalokiteśvara adopts whatever form or gender best facilitates helping others: peaceful or wrathful, male or female. As he moved towards the east, for example, her sex became ambiguous. In China she is known as Guanyin (and Kannon or Kwannon in Japan) – 'one who hearkens to the sound of the world', and he appears sometimes as a majestic male form, sitting in the posture of royal ease, but also as a beautiful and gentle female Bodhisattva, best known in her graceful 'white-robed' form.

On the Refuge Tree Avalokiteśvara appears in a four-armed form: on a fully open, pure white lotus flower is a radiant white moon-mat, symbol of complete purity. A sixteen-year-old prince is seated here in lotus posture. He is snow white in colour, like a conch-shell, and adorned in ravishing silks and priceless gems. Upon his head he wears the Bodhisattva's five-jewelled crown. Beneath his top-knot long blue-black hair flows down. He has four arms. The inner pair gently clasp the *cintāmaṇi* – the wish-fulfilling jewel – to his heart. This is the bodhicitta – or 'will to Enlightenment' – that alone can satisfy the heart's deepest yearnings. His outer pair of arms hold up a white lotus flower and a crystal rosary. His gently smiling eyes express profound compassion for all beings everywhere:

O you, whose eyes are clear, whose eyes are friendly,
Whose eyes betray distinguished wisdom-knowledge;
Whose eyes are pitiful, whose eyes are pure,
O you, so loveable, with beautiful face, with beautiful eyes!

Your lustre is spotless and immaculate,
Your knowledge without darkness, your splendour like the sun,
Radiant like the blaze of a fire not disturbed by the wind,
Warming the world you shine splendidly.

Eminent in your pity, friendly in your words,
One great mass of fine virtues and friendly thoughts,
You appease the fire of the defilements which burn beings,
And you rain down the rain of the deathless Dharma.

In quarrels, disputes, and in strife,
In the battles of men, and in any great danger,
To recollect the name of Avalokiteśvara
Will appease the troops of evil foes.

His voice is like that of a cloud or drum;
Like a rain-cloud he thunders, sweet in voice like Brahma.
His voice is the most perfect that can be.
So one should recall Avalokiteśvara.

Think of him, think of him, without hesitation,
Of Avalokiteśvara, that pure being.
In death, disaster, and calamity
He is the saviour, refuge and recourse.

As he who has reached perfection in all virtucs,
Who looks on all beings with pity and friendliness,
Who is virtue itself, a great ocean of virtues,
As such Avalokiteśvara is worthy of adoration.

He who is now so compassionate to the world,
He will a Buddha be in future ages.
Humbly I bow to Avalokiteśvara
Who destroys all sorrow, fear and suffering.[55]

These lines, from the Bodhisattva Akṣayamati's hymn of praise to Avalokiteśvara, as recounted in the *Lotus Sūtra (Saddharma Puṇḍarīka)*, derive part of their meaning from one rendering of Avalokiteśvara's name. 'Avalokita' can mean 'one who looks down' and 'Īśvara' means 'Lord'. Avalokiteśvara is therefore the 'Lord Who Looks Down' – in compassion.

Avalokiteśvara is to be found in many parts of the Mahāyāna literature. He is the central figure in the famous *Heart Sūtra (Hṛdaya Prajñāpāramitā Sūtra)*; the *Kāraṇḍa-vyūha Sūtra*, which is devoted entirely to him, recounts many of his legends; and in the *Śūraṅgama Sūtra* we read how he gained Enlightenment through reflecting on sound. Universal, primordial sound, according to the Sūtra, is his very essence:

> How sweetly mysterious is the Transcendental Sound
> of Avalokiteśvara. It is the pure Brahman Sound. It is
> the subdued murmur of the sea-tide setting inward. Its
> mysterious Sound brings liberation and peace to all sentient
> beings, who in their distress are calling for aid; it brings
> a sense of permanency to those who are truly seeking the
> attainment of Nirvana's Peace.[56]

As Chenrezig, Avalokiteśvara is the guardian and patron deity of Tibet. Pious Tibetans believe that the Dalai Lama is Avalokiteśvara in human form. Images of Chenrezig are found everywhere in Tibet, where most villages are approached by way of a 'maṇi-wall', a wall made of stones inscribed with the mantra *oṃ maṇi padme hūṃ*. This six syllable mantra is recited with great devotion by Tibetans (who pronounce it *oṃ maṇi peme hūṃ*). Some translate it '*oṃ*, the Jewel in the Lotus, *hūṃ*', but its meaning is far deeper and more mysterious than that, and it has grown rich with association over time. It has come to be associated particularly with certain aspects of the Wheel of Life, a rich symbolic image that depicts how beings move from life to life, or mental state to mental state. The Wheel of Life distinguishes six main states of being, or 'realms' – that of the gods, the āsuras or jealous gods, the humans, the animals, the pretas or hungry ghosts, and the hells. In each of these realms Avalokiteśvara appears as a differently coloured Buddha, holding out to the beings in that realm whatever they need in order to change themselves for the better.

So, it is said, the syllable *oṃ* is white in colour, and when it is recited, white light streams out to the realm of the gods. Avalokiteśvara appears in the realm of the gods as a white Buddha called 'the Powerful One of the Hundred Blessings', playing the music of impermanence on a lute, striving to arouse the gods from their complacency.

The syllable *ma* is green, and green light streams from it into the world of the āsuras, where he appears as the green Buddha Vīrabhadra, brandishing the flaming sword of wisdom.

From the yellow syllable *ṇi*, yellow light streams out to the human realm, where Avalokiteśvara manifests as the Buddha Śākyamuni, holding out the prospect of Going Forth.

Blue light streams from the blue syllable *pa* into the animal realm, where he appears as the Buddha 'Steadfast Lion', holding the book that symbolizes reflexive consciousness.

The red syllable *dme* emits red light, which streams into the world of the pretas where Avalokiteśvara appears as the red Buddha 'Flaming Mouth', dispensing nectar to assuage their blazing hunger and thirst, transforming desire for sense pleasures into desire for the good.

From the smoky-blue *hum*, light streams out to the hells, where Avalokiteśvara appears twice – once as Yāma, the Lord of Death, holding up a mirror in which beings see the karma that brought them to this plight, and once as a smoke-coloured Buddha, holding out the flame that purifies karma.

One of the strangest of Avalokiteśvara's many forms is that with a thousand arms and eleven heads, which has become the symbol of the Triratna Buddhist Order. Just as each of Avalokiteśvara's thousand arms holds a particular implement to be used in saving living beings, so each member of the Order, in their own unique way, reaches out to others. And just as the heads of Avalokiteśvara look out towards each of the cardinal and intermediate points, so the Order looks out to beings everywhere.

Tibetans tell a story of how Avalokiteśvara came to have a thousand arms. Many aeons ago, the Bodhisattva Avalokiteśvara made a vow in the presence of his teacher, the Buddha Amitābha.

'May I have the opportunity to establish all living beings in happiness. Until I relieve all living beings, may I never, even for a moment, feel like giving up my efforts for the sake of others in exchange for my own peace and happiness. If ever I should think only of my own happiness, may my head be cracked in ten pieces and may my body be split, like the petals of a lotus, into a thousand pieces.'

He then went among the people and taught them the mantra *am maṇi padme hum* – pronouncing the Dharma with infinite compassion. After that he entered a deep meditation. Making an intense effort to dispel the sufferings of beings, he meditated for a long time. Eventually emerging from meditation, he looked about him and saw that he had not helped even one hundredth of the people to achieve liberation. Seized by bitter sorrow, just for an instant the thought arose in him 'What is the use? I can do nothing for them. It is better for me to be happy and peaceful myself.'

At that moment his head cracked into ten pieces and his body split into a thousand parts. In agony he cried out to the Buddha Amitābha, who came instantly to his aid, transfiguring the ten pieces of his head into ten faces, one for each of the Ten Perfections, and making his torn flesh into a thousand arms, all the better to work for the benefit of living beings. On the crown of the ten-faced head Amitābha placed his own head, and radiated boundless, inconceivable light in all directions.

And so Avalokiteśvara continues to function in the world. Whatever the circumstances, however bleak, wherever an act of love or compassion is performed, there Avalokiteśvara shows himself, urging living beings ever onwards to greater and greater heights of altruism and self-transcendence, for the sake of all. And whenever we ourselves perform a kind act – of body, speech, or mind – Avalokiteśvara is there working through us. What could be better than to make ourselves, ever more effectively, a channel for his skilful means?

Mañjuśrī

Mañjuśrī is the Bodhisattva of wisdom, the perfect complement to compassion. Where there is wisdom there too will be compassion; without compassion there can be no wisdom.

Most commonly known as Mañjuśrī, 'gently auspicious', but also as Mañjughoṣa, the 'gentle-voiced one', he is the patron of all arts and sciences, the supreme master of eloquence, and it is said that through performing his *sādhana* (visualization meditation) one develops one's knowledge and intelligence – and even one's memory.

He is the family protector of Vairocana's Tathāgata family, and his animal is the lion, which is also associated with Vairocana. He is sometimes said to be the colour of a lion's eye.

In the clear blue sky appears a pale blue lotus throne, upon which is a radiant white moon-mat. Here sits a beautiful sixteen-year-old prince, made entirely of golden-yellow light. In lotus pose, effortlessly at ease, he inclines gracefully to the right. His right arm lightly grasps the flaming sword of wisdom, which cuts off all wrong views at their root. His left hand holds a text to his heart – the *Perfection of Wisdom in 8,000 Lines*. Five blue lotuses are wound into the long blue-black hair beneath his five-peaked jewelled crown. His beautiful body is adorned with fine silks and precious jewels, and his blue eyes radiate a calm sense of perfect understanding and complete appreciation:

> Your speech is pleasant, gentle, charming, heart-stirring,
> Harmonious, its sweetness is pure, stainless clear light,
> Worth hearing, taming the wild with sweetness,
> Not rough, not coarse, very calm, it pleases the ear.
> Satisfying body, mind, and heart; it generates delight,
> Painless, all-informing, it is to be understood.
> Brilliantly delightful, intensely delightful,
> Totally illuminating, enlightening,
> Rational, relevant, free of all redundancy,
> Its tone is sweet as a lion, elephant, lord of serpents,
> Dragon, gandharva, kalavinka, Brahma,
> Crane, lord of swans.
> Its drumbeat is not high, not low, penetrating all appropriately,
> Your phrases are expressive, not incomplete,
> Not disheartened, not feeble, pervaded with joy and insight,
> Cohesive, relevant, and all conclusive
> Satisfying all senses, not contemptuous, not vacillating,
> Renowned throughout the whole thoughtless samsara.

It dispels the three times, punishes the demon hosts,
Emerging with supremacy in all its forms.
Such a voice with sixty-four qualities,
All are present even in a single statement,
It gives happiness to the hearing of the lucky
As far as space can reach.
It does not seem too loud when near, nor faint when far,
But accords with the language of each of countless disciples like
    a crystal prisming various colors,
Manifests as coming from all parts of your body, such as crown,
    urna-hair, and throat,
And yet it pacifies all the notions of all those hearers, just as the
    Brahma-voice can manifest from sky.
Like the deep thunder within the rain-cloud
Girt with its belt of beautiful red lightning.
By this merit of praising the speech of Manjughosha,
May I never be parted from the hearing of your speech![57]

Mañjuśrī's mantra is *oṃ a ra pa ca na dhīḥ*. *Dhīḥ* is the seed syllable associated with Perfect Wisdom, and the five syllables *a ra pa ca na* are the first five letters of the 'alphabet of Perfect Wisdom' in which each letter of the Sanskrit alphabet is associated with an epithet of the Perfection of Wisdom. He appears in many Mahāyāna sūtras, where he is often shown teaching the Dharma, especially in its more abstruse forms, and homage is often paid to him at the beginning of philosophical texts, particularly those of the Madhyamaka, such as the *Perfection of Wisdom in 700 Lines*, in which he plays a significant part. In the *Gaṇḍavyūha*, it is his advice to the young aspirant Sudhana – that he seek out a *kalyāṇa mitra* – that caused him to set out on his epic pilgrimage.

According to the Indo-Tibetan tradition, there are thirteen main forms of Mañjuśrī. He is usually golden-yellow or orange, but he can also be white or, less commonly, black. Sometimes he holds the sword and the book. At other times he hold the stems of lotus flowers, which bloom at his shoulders, supporting the sword and the book upon their petals.

In Nepal, Mañjuśrī is believed to have created the Kathmandu Valley by draining the waters of a lake, and in China, it is said, he still turns the wheel of the Dharma on Mount Wutai in Shanxi Province. Wutai Shan is a chain of five mountain peaks, and in the Indian tradition Mañjuśrī is sometimes known as Pañcacīra, 'Five Crests'. Known as Monju in Japanese Zen, he is one of the two principal attendants of the Buddha Śākyamuni, and his figure is found in virtually every temple and monastery.

In the *Vimalakīrti Nirdeśa* only Mañjuśrī, of all the Buddha's followers, has the courage to visit the ailing Vimalakīrti, who has trounced them all in debate on different occasions. One by one, Vimalakīrti asks Mañjuśrī's retinue how one enters 'the Dharma door of nonduality'. Each does his best to answer, but Mañjuśrī shows them all that their explanations are caught up in subtle dualities. He then gives his own view:

> To know no one teaching, to express nothing, to say
> nothing, to explain nothing, to announce nothing, to indicate
> nothing, and to designate nothing – that is the entrance into
> nonduality.[58]

Turning to Vimalakīrti, Mañjuśrī then asked *him* to elucidate the entrance into the principle of non-duality. Thereupon, Vimalakīrti kept his silence, saying nothing at all. 'Excellent! Excellent, noble sir!' said Mañjuśrī. 'This is indeed the entrance into the nonduality of the bodhisattvas. Here there is no use for syllables, sounds, and ideas.'[59]

With his sword of wisdom, Mañjuśrī cuts through all dualistic concepts. How might we apply this in our own lives? Sangharakshita gives us some useful hints in one of his lectures on the *Vimalakīrti Nirdeśa*:

> Duality itself is the means to non-duality, because the duality
> between duality and non-duality is not ultimate.
>
> This is still, it must be admitted, very much in the realm of
> the metaphysical. But we can apply the same principle on a
> much more down-to-earth level, and come up with our own
> dualities. Here are a few to begin with. They are certainly not
> so sublime as those of the *Vimalakīrti Nirdeśa*, but no doubt
> they come somewhat closer to our own experience and as such

they may be more useful. They may not carry us as far into the depths of non-duality, but at least they will help us move in that direction from where we are now.

Masculine and feminine are two; individuality is the entrance into non-duality.

Organizer and organized are two; co-operation is the entrance into non-duality.

Teacher and taught are two; communication is the entrance into non-duality.

God and man are two; blasphemy is the entrance into non-duality.

Male and female are two; celibacy is the entrance into non-duality.

Individual and group are two; the spiritual community is the entrance into non-duality.[60]

From these hints it should be possible for us to derive many more of our own practical 'entrances into non-duality'.

The Wisdom of Mañjuśrī is further from our normal intellectual understanding than the Sun from the Earth, but by contemplating him in all his subtlety and grandeur, by developing increasingly strong feelings for his overwhelming beauty, and by delving deeper and deeper into the Wisdom traditions over which he presides – perhaps above all by applying the Dharma to our daily lives – we can come in time to make his Wisdom more and more our own. In time we too may enter and pass through one or another of those Dharma doors to non-duality.

Vajrapāṇi

Vajrapāṇi stands for will, action, or energy. He is perhaps most often associated, in the Triratna Buddhist Community at least, with his wrathful form. Here he appears as a gigantic deep-blue figure, with enormous muscles and a swollen belly, bursting with energy. Standing on a sun disc, with a tiger skin about his loins and a garland of human skulls hung about his neck, he stamps to the right. He is wreathed in snakes, and his huge three-eyed head is surmounted by a diadem of five skulls. His left hand makes the gesture of warding off demons and the enemies of the Dharma, while his right is raised, brandishing a golden vajra which he is about to hurl. He is trampling on writhing human forms, demonstrating his conquest of greed and hatred, and his whole body is surrounded by a blazing aura of flames.

The peaceful form of Vajrapāṇi which appears on the Refuge Tree presents an altogether different, but no less heroic, aspect. His lotus throne is royal blue in colour. Upon it appears a luminous white moon-mat, and here he sits in the gracious posture of royal ease. Young, handsome, smiling gently, bedecked in silks and jewels, he is made entirely of royal blue light. His left hand rests gently on the moon-mat, and on his right palm stands a perfectly balanced golden vajra. In his heart, the deep-blue syllable *hum* radiates energy and spiritual power.

Vajrapāṇi is the chief protector of Akṣobhya's Vajra family, thus he is associated with transcendental wisdom, and the power, strength, and untiring energy of his animal, the elephant. Like the elephant, the Enlightened mind is unstoppable – it cannot be turned back by any of the hindrances. Vajrapāṇi may also be known as Vajradhara, 'Holder of the Vajra', or as Guhyapati, 'Lord of Mystic Teaching'. His mantra, *oṃ vajrapāṇi hūṃ*, expresses the energy that shatters delusion.

Over the centuries, Vajrapāṇi has undergone continuous change and evolution. We first encounter him in the Pāli scriptures, where he appears as Vajirapāṇi ('vajira' being the Pāli form of 'vajra'). Vajirapāṇi is one of Śākyamuni's protective deities.

In the *Ambaṭṭha Sutta* of the *Dīgha-Nikāya* we read about a young Brahmin called Ambaṭṭha who, puffed up with caste prejudice and his own self-importance, repeatedly insults the Buddha, saying that the Buddha's Śākyan clan are menials who ought to defer to Brahmins such as himself. In order to take him down a peg or two, the Buddha asks Ambaṭṭha whether he has heard the story that his own people, the Kaṇhāyan clan, were in fact descended from a Śākyan slave-girl. Embarrassed, Ambaṭṭha keeps silent. The Buddha asks a second time, and again Ambaṭṭha will not answer. Then the Buddha says, 'You'd better answer me now Ambaṭṭha. Whoever does not answer a fundamental question put to him three times by a Buddha, at the third asking his head will split in seven pieces!'

And at that moment Vajrapāṇi the yakkha, holding a huge
iron club, flaming, ablaze and glowing, up in the sky just
above Ambaṭṭha, was thinking: 'If this young man Ambaṭṭha
does not answer a proper question put to him by the Blessed
Lord by the third time of asking, I'll split his head into seven
pieces!' The Lord saw Vajrapāṇi, and so did Ambaṭṭha. And
at the sight, Ambaṭṭha was terrified and unnerved, his hairs
stood on end, and he sought protection, shelter and safety
from the Lord. Crouching down close to the Lord, he said:
'What did the Reverend Gotama say? May the Reverend
Gotama repeat what he said!' 'What do you think, Ambaṭṭha?
Have you heard who was the ancestor of the Kaṇhāyans?'
'Yes, I have heard it just as the Reverend Gotama said, that is
where the Kaṇhāyans came from, [she] was their ancestor.'[61]

Buddhaghosa identified Vajirapāṇi as the god Indra, the god of the
storm who wields a thunderbolt and is known as the Thunderer.
The early Buddhist scriptures show Indra, the great god of the
Vedas, attending the Buddha. With the passing of time, Indra
appeared less and less in the Buddhist texts, and Vajrapāṇi's
stature grew steadily.

In the early Mahāyāna scriptures he continued to appear as a
yakṣa (in the *Sūtra of Golden Light* he is Lord of the Yakṣas) but he
gradually became more and more prominent. In the *Lotus Sūtra*
he is mentioned as one of the forms Avalokiteśvara may adopt
in order to convert living beings. By the time of the tantras he
appears as a great Bodhisattva, even – in some of them – the chief
Bodhisattva. He finally reached the very heights and, as Vajradhara,
he is revered as the supreme Buddha of several Tantric traditions.
In China and Japan he is known simply as Vajra (Japanese, *Kongō*),
and he plays a significant role in Shingon.

There is a popular Mahāyāna legend which tells how
Vajrapāṇi gained his deep-blue colour. Once upon a time the
Buddhas all met together on top of Mount Meru to discuss
the best means of procuring *amṛta*, the elixir of life, which lay
concealed at the bottom of the ocean. Evil demons were in
possession of a powerful poison and were using it to bring
destruction to humankind. In order to acquire the antidote, the

Buddhas decided to churn the ocean with Mount Meru. When the *amṛta* had risen to the surface, they gave it to Vajrapāṇi to keep hold of until they could decide on the best means of using it. But Vajrapāṇi left the elixir unguarded for a moment, and it was stolen by Rāhu the demon. There followed a terrible struggle for the possession of the *amṛta*. Rāhu was conquered in the end, but the elixir had been defiled, and the Buddhas, to punish Vajrapāṇi, forced him to drink it, whereupon he became dark blue from the poison in the *amṛta*.

Vajrapāṇi, as he appears on the Refuge Tree, would never let his attention slip even for a moment. As the protector of the Vajra family, his wisdom is supreme and he continuously perceives the whole universe in its ultimate, vajra nature.

Kṣitigarbha

Kṣitigarbha, whose name means 'Earth Store' or 'Womb of the Earth', appears on the Refuge Tree in the robes of a monk in the Sarvāstivādin tradition. Shaven-headed, with a tuft of hair between his eyebrows, in his right hand he holds the *khakkhara*, or mendicant's staff, with which he forces open the gates of hell. The *khakkhara* is surmounted by six rings, which symbolize his willingness to stand by the beings in all six realms. His left hand holds to his heart the blazing wish-fulfilling gem, the bodhicitta, which lightens the darkness. His face is calm and peaceful, and his eyes gaze out at the world with unwavering compassion. His mantra is *oṃ kṣitigarbha bodhisattva yaḥ*.

Kṣitigarbha makes a speciality of helping those who suffer, not from the kind of *dukkha* that we encounter daily but from profound pain and torment. Time after time he plunges into the deepest hells to rescue beings caught up in misery. He never holds back, but enters deep into their world to meet them and gives them what they really need.

The willingness of Kṣitigarbha to enter the hells has two aspects. Subjectively, it represents the penetration of the Dharma into all the shadowy, untransformed aspects of our psyche, bringing light where once there was only darkness. Objectively, it represents the Bodhisattva's willingness to take the Dharma wherever it is needed, however difficult and painful the conditions.

Kṣitigarbha is hardly known in the Indo-Tibetan Buddhist world, but in eastern Asia he is extremely important. In China he is known as Dizang and in Japan as Jizō, where he is frequently depicted in six different aspects – one for each of the six realms. Mount Jiuhua in eastern China is held sacred to him.

The story of how he came to be a great Bodhisattva is told in one of the most popular sūtras in Chinese Buddhism, the *Sūtra of the Past Vows of Kṣitigarbha Bodhisattva*.[62] Many aeons ago, in the time of a previous Buddha, there lived a Brahmin woman who had gained much merit from her former lives and was respected by everyone. Whether walking, standing, sitting, or lying down she was always surrounded by protective devas. Her mother, on the other hand, held damaging views, and often disparaged the Three Jewels. The wise woman tried in all sorts of ways to convince her mother of right views, but without success. Eventually, the mother died and was reborn in a hell realm.

Knowing that when her mother was alive she had not understood the nature of conditionality, the Brahmin woman realized that, in accordance with her karma, she would be reborn in a state of woe. So she sold the family house, bought incense, flowers, and other items, and performed a great offering in the Buddha's temple.

Suddenly, the voice of the Buddha was heard in space, saying, 'O weeping holy woman, do not be so sorrowful. I shall show you where your mother has gone. After your offering is complete, return home quickly. Sit upright thinking of my name and you will certainly know your mother's place of rebirth.' So after she had finished worshipping the Buddha, the Brahmin woman returned home where, mindful of her mother, she sat upright recollecting the Buddha.

A day passed, then she suddenly saw herself beside a sea of seething and bubbling water. Many horrible beasts with iron bodies flew about in all directions, but she remained calm and fearless because of the power of recollecting the Buddha. A demon king bowed and came to welcome the holy woman, saying, 'Excellent, O Bodhisattva. Welcome! And why have you come here?'

The Brahmin woman asked the demon king, 'What is this place?'

'This is the first sea of the western face of the Great Iron Ring Mountain,' he replied.

The holy woman asked, 'Why is this water seething and why are there so many criminals and evil beasts?'

'These are the newly dead of your world who have done evil deeds and who, during the first forty-nine days after their death, had no survivors to perform acts of merit on their behalf to rescue them from difficulty. Moreover, during their lives they created no skilful karma. In accordance with their own deeds the hells appear, and they must first fathom this sea.'

The holy woman again spoke to the ghost king: 'My mother has not been dead long, and I do not know on what path she has gone.'

The demon king placed his palms together respectfully and told the Bodhisattva, 'Please, Holy One, return to your home. Do not be worried or sorrowful, for your mother was born in the heavens three days ago. It is said she was succeeded by a filial child who made offerings and cultivated merit for her sake in the temple.'

The Brahmin woman quickly returned as if from a dream, understood what had happened, and swore a deep vow before the image of the Buddha in the temple, saying, 'I vow to establish many skilful means in response to living beings who are suffering due to their bad karma. Until the end of future aeons, I shall cause those beings to obtain liberation.'

That Brahmin woman is now the Bodhisattva Kṣitigarbha.

According to the sūtra, contemplating Kṣitigarbha and reciting his name overcomes poverty and protects one's travels, and his worship can increase intelligence and improve the memory. He not only helps the dead but offers practical solutions to our day-to-day problems. In Japan, Kṣitigarbha is a protector of travellers and children, as well as being the patron deity of warriors (who may well need him most).

The sūtra also tells how Kṣitigarbha works in all kinds of guises, adopting different manifestations according to the needs of his task. A vast host of transformations of the Bodhisattva Kṣitigarbha, together with an uncountable number of beings, once came to pay homage to the Buddha. All those beings, who themselves had suffered in the hells for aeons, had been saved and attained Buddhahood because of Kṣitigarbha's strong vows and great compassion.

Śākyamuni blessed all the transformations of Kṣitigarbha, commending them for their work, and went on to explain that he himself had adopted innumerable transformations in order to save living beings. And yet,

'Although I have tried my utmost to convert the erring ones from this world of sufferings, I could see that there might be one or two out of every ten who are still sinful. I ask you to seek transformations of other Buddhas to convert them in all possible ways and means. There are, without doubt, intelligent ones who are likely to be converted after my preaching and attain Buddhahood by my persuasion to practise good deeds, but unintelligent wrong-doers can only be converted after a lengthy period of preaching. For the stubborn ones, it is useless to expect any respect or faith from them. In spite of all the obstacles, I had endeavoured to convert these miserable creatures and lead them to real Salvation by performing different transformations. I performed transformation as males, females, devas, spirits, devils, mountains, forests, streams, rivers, pools or anything to bring benefit upon human beings and to convert them all without any exception....

'You should recollect how strenuously I have lived from kalpas to kalpas with unremitting toil to convert even stubborn beings to Salvation. Stubborn ones can still be found, and if they are cast into Hell for punishment, you should remember how I requested you to work earnestly to lift them to Buddhahood and Enlightenment, till the next Buddha, by the name of Maitreya Buddha, will be born to this world.'

Just at that moment, the various transformations of the Kṣitigarbha Bodhisattva from different universes were seen consolidated into one form and, with tears in his eyes, he said to the Buddha, 'You have been kind enough to bestow upon me supernatural power and transcendental wisdom for kalpas and kalpas. May my innumerable transformations of different forms be successful in pervading various universes to lead mankind to real Salvation. Though human beings have not the slightest interest in reaping good deeds, I shall strive to convert them gradually and bring great benefit and happiness to all. Pray, do not be disheartened over the evils of these beings, as I shall bear the full responsibility to convert them to the supreme state of Buddhahood.' … Kṣitigarbha Bodhisattva requested the Honoured of the World not to feel distressed over the evils of human beings in the generations to come by repeating his vow three times.

Śākyamuni Buddha was thus highly delighted and said, 'My blessings. I appreciate your strong vows and may you be praised for your efforts to heal the human world, and that your aim for Buddhahood after your firm resolution to convert them be achieved.'[63]

There are 'hells within', and 'hells without'. Sometimes we have to descend to a hell within to confront our own pain and darkness, and to shed light on it and transform it. And there are people living in hell without, to whom we need to take the Dharma. In doing that we 'descend to them' – figuratively speaking. We do not join them in hell, but we must be willing to be confronted by the reality of their pain if we want to help them.

Kṣitigarbha's attitude to suffering beings tells us that no one is beyond the help of the Dharma and that people can make enormous spiritual progress even when they start from the most difficult position. He dives right in and engages with them where he finds them, reaching out especially to those in painful circumstances. Whether their privations are physical, psychological, economic, or political, Kṣitigarbha never hesitates. In all circumstances, however anguished, he always embodies the true Bodhisattva attitude.

Following Kṣitigarbha's example, we learn to stretch ourselves, going beyond our usual limits both for our own sake and for the sake of others.

Tārā

'Tārā' can mean 'star', but it is more often taken to mean 'saviour-ess', or 'one who ferries across' – from saṃsāra to nirvāṇa. There are many forms of Tārā, including an important set of twenty-one forms. On the Refuge Tree she appears in her green form, as Āryatārā.

On a pale blue lotus flower rests a white moon-mat. Here sits Āryatārā, jade green in colour, made entirely of soft, glowing light. She is sixteen years old, full-breasted and exquisitely beautiful, with long blue-black hair. She has a meditation sash tied about her body and wears a silken rainbow skirt. Bracelets, armlets, anklets, necklaces, and a Bodhisattva crown, all made of the finest gems, adorn her beautiful form. Her left foot rests upon her right thigh, in meditation posture, while her right foot, supported by a small pale blue lotus, steps gracefully forwards to enter the world of suffering beings. Her right arm reaches down in the open palm mudrā of supreme giving. Her left hand is held in front of her heart, palm outwards, the thumb and ring finger lightly grasping the stem of a spray of pale blue lotus flowers at her left shoulder: a bud, a half-open flower, and one in full bloom. The other fingers of her left hand point upwards, forming the mudrā that bestows protection and fearlessness through invoking the Three Jewels. Her eyes, of the finest sapphire blue, gaze out with intense compassion and she smiles with gentle tenderness.

Her mantra, *Oṃ tāre tuttāre ture svāhā*, is turquoise or jade green in colour. When it is recited, rays of rainbow light flow out in all directions, alleviating the suffering of living beings.

There are many stories that tell how Tārā came to be. One day the great Bodhisattva Avalokiteśvara gazed upon the world with his gentle blue eyes, and everywhere he looked he saw beings in states of woe. There was no time or place ever free from war, sickness, poverty, and cruelty. Nor was there anywhere where beings were free from the suffering they continuously inflicted upon themselves by their deluded acts of body, speech, and mind. Overcome with immense pity for this suffering world, tears rolled down the beautiful face of Avalokiteśvara in two broad streams. Falling to earth, they gradually accumulated, forming a great lake of tears. Out of this lake emerged a pale blue lotus, which slowly opened to reveal the exquisite form of Āryatārā, the quintessence of compassion, born of the compassionate tears of Avalokiteśvara.

According to another story, in the world-system Manifold Light, many kalpas ago, there lived a princess called Moon of Knowledge. She was greatly devoted to the Buddha of that world and continually made splendid offerings to him and his retinue. Eventually, out of the power of her faith and devotion, she developed the bodhicitta. Then some of the monk disciples of that Buddha urged her to pray to be reborn in a male body, so that she could follow the Bodhisattva's career. The princess, however, saw that 'male' and 'female' were both simply concepts imputed on to experience, and had no existence in reality. She made a great vow, saying, 'There are many who seek Enlightenment in a man's body, but none who work for the sake of living beings in the body of a woman. Therefore, until saṃsāra is empty, I shall work for the benefit of living beings in the body of woman.' She remained in her palace, practising meditation, until she had perfected a *samādhi* called 'saving all sentient beings', and by that means, morning and evening, she rescued countless beings from saṃsāra. That is how she came by the name of Saviouress.

Āryatārā is especially associated with fearlessness and spontaneous helpfulness. Just as a mother responds unhesitatingly whenever her children are threatened, so Green Tārā instantly steps down into the world to help any living being who calls upon her. Traditionally, she is said to protect from 'the eight great terrors': lions, elephants, fire, snakes, robbers, captivity, shipwreck, and demons. Sometimes this list is understood symbolically to represent the spiritual dangers of pride, delusion, anger, wrong views, avarice, attachment, and doubt, but it has also been taken very literally, and the sixteenth-century Tibetan scholar, Tāranātha, opens his *Golden Rosary: a History Illuminating the Origin of the Tantra of Tārā* by recounting some stories of Tārā's assistance which are taken from the oral tradition. For example, there is the story of how she protects from the fear of lions:

> A wood-gatherer went to the forest, and met a hungry lioness who set about eating him. Carrying him in her jaws, she returned near her den. Frightened and terrified, he implored Tārā, and there appeared before him a woman clad in leaves, who took him out of the lioness's mouth and set him down in the marketplace of the town.[64]

There is a vast literature of poems and praises to Tārā, including the beautiful Sanskrit poem 'The Hundred and Eight Names of

Venerable Āryatārā', which opens at the Potalaka, Avalokiteśvara's pure land, where he is giving teachings to his retinue. The great Vajrapāṇi approaches Avalokiteśvara and asks how beings may be saved from the terrors that arise from greed, hatred, and delusion. Avalokiteśvara replies:

> Of Amitābha, the Protector,
>   were born to me the Mothers of
> The World, wise, having great compassion,
>   raised up for the world's saving;
>
> Like unto the risen sun,
>   their faces radiant as full moons,
> The Tārās illuminate the trees,
>   with the gods, men and āsuras,
>
> They cause the triple world to shake,
>   and terrify yakṣas and rākṣasas.
> The Goddess holding a blue lotus
>   in Her hand says, 'Fear not, fear not!'
>
> 'It is to protect the world
>   that I was produced by the Conquerors.
> In the wilderness, in clashes of arms,
>   where one is troubled by diverse dangers,
>
> 'When but my names are remembered,
>   I protect all beings perpetually.
> I, O Lord, shall lead them across
>   the great flood of their diverse fears;
>
> 'Therefore the eminent Seers sing
>   of me in the world by the name of Tārā,
> Raising their hands in supplication,
>   full of reverence and awe.'[65]

At Vajrapāṇi's further request, Avalokiteśvara then goes on to expound the 108 names of Tārā.

It is sometimes said that Tārā is like a virgin, a mother, and a queen. Like a virgin, she is completely pure, unstained by the world. Even as she steps out into the world her foot comes to rest on a white moon-mat. She acts in the world but it never defiles her. Like a mother, she cares for all beings as though each were her only child, and like a mother she is completely accepting. If one of her devotees neglects, for some reason, to perform her sādhana, Tārā will always understand and forgive. Finally, like a queen she exercises spiritual sovereignty. Dignified and fearless, she assumes responsibility for the whole universe and lays down the law of the Dharma to bring an end to suffering everywhere.

Vajrasattva, pure white in colour and wearing the regal ornaments of a Bodhisattva, holds a vajra and bell, the masculine and feminine principles united.

Chapter Nine

Vajrasattva

Vajrasattva occupies a special place, right at the top of the Tree, above the five Jinas. In fact, he is not really *on* the Tree at all, but simply appears in the clear blue sky, hovering at the highest point of the Tree. His position is important, for Vajrasattva appears here as an ādi-buddha. *Ādi* means beginning, or primordial, and Vajrasattva stands here not as the Buddha who has existed since the start of time, but rather as the Buddha who exists entirely *beyond* space and time. He represents the *dharmakāya*, the True Nature of Buddhahood, which exists beyond space, time, and all conceptual and symbolic constructs. His true nature is beyond the very furthest reaches of the expressible; he is a symbol of that which cannot be symbolized.

As a Buddha appearing in Bodhisattva form, Vajrasattva is white in colour, signifying purification, and here the purification consists in the realization that ultimately we have never been impure. We are all pure from the beginningless beginning, pure by our very nature – essentially, in the depths of our being. We are pure of all conditionality, pure – even – of the very distinction between conditioned and unconditioned. Our true nature is no-nature and we are, in our very essence, completely unstained. For anyone brought up in a guilt-ridden culture like ours, this statement can come as a great relief. When we recognize our essential, pure, Vajrasattva nature, all irrational guilt is completely destroyed.

Vajrasattva does not appear in any of the Mahāyāna scriptures. He is an exclusively Tantric figure, and plays a number of important roles in Tantric practice. In particular, the visualization of Vajrasattva occurs in all the traditional sets of the four foundation yogas, where one visualizes him and recites his mantra 100,000 times as an aid to the complete purification of one's body, speech, and mind.

To begin with, everything around us dissolves into a vast blue sky, stretching away in all directions. All our hopes and fears – our rounds of thought – vanish into the sky, and all is still.

Above our heads, out of the clear, blue emptiness, a perfect white lotus blooms. Above it is a circle of white light, a moon-mat. On this spotless throne appears a figure made of white light, seated serenely in full-lotus posture, wearing dazzling silks and jewels made only of light.

His right hand is held to his heart, palm upwards. Balanced perfectly upright upon it is a vajra, the diamond sceptre of the Buddhas. The vajra may appear to be gold or crystal, but it is made of light, of Mind, of Reality itself.

His left hand is by his side, holding a vajra-bell – a silver bell with a vajra handle. His head is crowned with five jewels and his body is surrounded by an aura of five-coloured light: white, yellow, red, blue, and green, for Vajrasattva is the union of the mandala of the five Buddhas, the complete embodiment of their wisdoms. He has long black hair flowing over his shoulders and looks down at us with a smile of total acceptance.

At his heart's core is another small white lotus and moon-mat. Upon this, standing upright, is the deep-blue seed syllable *hūṃ*. Around it is a circle of white letters, like a string of pure white pearls. These are the letters of the 'hundred-syllable' mantra of Vajrasattva.

As we deepen our concentration on the radiant figure above us, dewdrops of white light-nectar form on the *hūṃ* and the white mantra garland. These drops become heavier, fuller, and slowly begin to fall. They flow down through the body of Vajrasattva and touch the crown of our head. The nectar drops are cool, soothing, and healing. They flow into our body, drop by glistening drop, and we feel deeply refreshed.

The rhythm of the falling nectar quickens. The drops are no longer distinguishable. They become a flowing, healing stream, pouring from Vajrasattva's heart into our body and mind. The stream of light begins to wash away all our unskilful karma, all our foolish actions, all our selfishness. Even physical diseases are washed away. Clouds of darkness fall from us.

The purification is reinforced by the turning of the letters in Vajrasattva's heart. They circle gently around the *hūṃ*, chanting the sound of the mantra. One by one the hundred syllables restore us to our true home, our true nature.

The glistening light-nectar cleanses us of even our flesh-and-blood nature, born to die. Our body becomes like a perfect crystal vase. This body-shaped vase of light is completely filled with the white nectar. We feel light, pure, and free as the blue sky.

In their deepest nature mantras are essentially untranslatable. Nonetheless, Sangharakshita has made a rendering that gives us some sense of it. The transliteration given here is based on the form of the mantra as he received it from his teacher, Dudjom Rimpoche. It begins '*oṃ vajrasatva samaya*.' (When you take up a sādhana you make a *samaya* – a bond or vow with the figure you are going to visualize – that you will keep up the practice regularly. If you do this faithfully, the figure you are going to visualize will, for its part, present you with the fruits of the practice.)

Oṃ vajrasatva samaya	Om. Bond of Vajrasattva
Manupālaya	Defender of human beings
Vajrasatva 'tvenopatiṣṭha	With thy Vajrasattvahood, stand beside me:
Dṛdho me bhava	Be firm for me
Sutoṣyo me bhava	Be glad for me
Supoṣyo me bhava	Be pleased for me
Anurakto me bhava	Love me deeply
Sarva siddhim me prayaccha	Accord me all perfections
Sarva karma suca me	Purify all my karma
Cittam śreyaḥ kuru hūṃ	Make me a better mind
Ha ha ha ha hoḥ	(laughter)
Bhagavān sarva tathāgata	Blessed all ye Buddhas!
Vajrama me muñca	Liberate me, Vajra-like ones
Vajrī bhava	Be truly Vajric
Mahāsamayasatva	Great Hero of the bond
Āḥ hūṃ phat	Away with evil!

(*Phat!* is the sound used for subduing demons.)

Vajrasattva has a special relationship with death, and his mantra is often chanted to help the newly deceased. The approach of death is the time when our past actions, skilful and unskilful, are brought most closely home to us, and it is the time when our future rebirth may be determined. It is therefore a time when we most need to call on the essential purity of Vajrasattva to help us to purify our karma. In the same way, Vajrasattva has a relationship to the act of confession. When we confess we are trying to let go of the unskilful act, we are confessing. If we confess wholeheartedly, we may come to experience at least something of our own true Vajrasattva nature.

All the canonical texts of the Buddhist tradition

Chapter Ten

The Dharma Texts

The lotus flower directly behind the Buddha on the Refuge Tree supports a stack of Dharma texts. These are the sacred texts of Buddhism – the *Tripiṭaka* – and it is to the teachings which these embody that all Buddhists go for Refuge:

> Well communicated is the Teaching of the Richly Endowed
>   One,
> Immediately Apparent, Perennial, of the Nature of a Personal
> Invitation, Progressive, to be understood individually, by the
>   wise.

> All my life I go for Refuge to the Truth.

> To all the Truth-Teachings of the past,
> To all the Truth-Teachings yet to be,
> To all the Truth-Teachings that now are,
> My worship flows unceasingly.
> No other refuge than the Truth,
> Refuge supreme, is there for me.
> Oh by the virtue of this truth,
> May grace abound, and victory![66]

The Buddha's Dharma is 'well communicated' – the Buddha knew the Truth from his own direct experience, and whatever he said, whatever he did, was a direct expression of that. Being himself supremely sensitive and empathetic, he was a master communicator, and for that reason his teachings were 'immediately apparent'. Those to whom he spoke did not need a degree in philosophy or theology to understand him. He spoke directly to their immediate experience.

And what the Buddha taught was 'perennial'; it made complete sense 2,500 years ago and it makes the same sense today. When, through the various layers of translation, we come to what the Buddha was actually getting at, its meaning is completely clear and completely relevant. The Buddha addressed the essential human condition, the fact of suffering and the way to overcome it. This does not change over time.

But the utterance of the Enlightened mind, for all its grandeur, standing as it does outside space and time, is nonetheless addressed always to individuals – it has 'the nature of a personal invitation'. The Buddha always teaches conditionally: 'If you want to escape from suffering, do this.' There are no imperatives here, and there is never any room for dogma, much less for the use of force in the application of the Buddha's teaching.

The Dharma is also 'progressive'. As we apply it to our lives, so we change for the better and grow in wisdom and understanding. With this greater clarity we return to the Dharma and our new understandings take us further still along the path. The path to Enlightenment is gradual. This is the first of eight 'amazing and astounding' facts that the Buddha attributed to his Dharma in the *Udāna*:

> Just as, monks, the mighty ocean flows down, slides and
> tends downward gradually, and there is no abrupt precipice,
> so also in this dhamma-discipline the training is gradual, the
> action is gradual, the procedure is gradual; there is no abrupt
> penetration of knowledge. Since this is so (monks) this is the
> first strange and wonderful thing, seeing which monks take
> delight in this dhamma-discipline.[67]

Finally, the Dharma is to be 'understood individually, by the wise'. When we become Enlightened, we will do so in our own unique way. The Enlightenment of Nāgārjuna expressed itself differently from the Enlightenment of Vasubandhu. Tārā and Mañjuśrī, Śāriputra and Maudgalyāyana – all express their own individual understanding of the Dharma. And yet, paradoxically, the more we apprehend it individually, for ourselves, the closer we come to understanding the insights of others. The more we participate in the Dharma life ourselves, the more deeply we enter the one great ocean that has but one taste – the taste of freedom. As the Buddha put it in the text previously cited:

> Just as, monks, the mighty ocean is of one flavour, the flavour of salt, even so, monks, this dhamma is of one flavour, the flavour of release. Since this is so (monks) this is the sixth strange and wonderful thing (seeing which monks take delight in this dhamma-discipline).[68]

The texts of the Dharma, appearing on the lotus behind the Buddha, have one purpose only: to free living beings. Their value is beyond price. They are more than mere books, and perhaps when we visualize them we should see them written in words of flame on pages of gold and jewels. But exactly which texts are they? And what is the *Tripiṭaka*?

The term itself means simply 'three baskets', and its derivation is uncertain. Perhaps it refers to the three baskets in which the ancient manuscripts were originally stored and classified. As the different texts of Buddhism were classified, a distinction arose between the Sūtra, Vinaya, and Abhidharma Piṭakas. The first comprises the different discourses of the Buddha (or other Enlightened persons), the second is the collection based on the code of monastic discipline, and the third is the vast project of analysis that Buddhist scholars undertook in their attempt to plumb the inner mechanisms of the mind and its apprehension (or misapprehension) of the world. But perhaps *Tripiṭaka* simply refers to the process of transmission from person to person. In India, baskets of earth are often passed down a line of hands on a building site. Or possibly the term *piṭaka* originally derived from the root *pitṛ*, 'father', and means 'that which belongs to the Father', i.e. the Buddha. But whatever its derivation and whatever it means, the term *Tripiṭaka* has been sanctified by millennia of use and it always refers to the canonical texts of Buddhism.

The English term 'canon' is more simply understood. It refers to a list of texts, especially sacred texts, that are held to be genuine. In the Buddhist tradition, canonicity is given only to texts that are regarded as being *Buddhavacana* – that is, the actual word of the Buddha.

The Buddhist tradition as a whole has taken this term in two ways. For some, it is taken literally to mean the actual historical record of the teachings of the Buddha Śākyamuni, although they generally allow as *Buddhavacana* those teachings that were given by leading disciples and which the Buddha explicitly approved. For others, the term connotes any verbal expression of the state of Enlightened consciousness, be it by Śākyamuni, subsequent Enlightened masters, or even archetypal Buddhas and Bodhisattvas. That said, there is a central core of tradition running through the canon which, even for the Mahāyāna, in principle maintains that 'Whatever is well said is the Word of the Buddha', and hesitates to accept as such any teaching that conflicts with traditional scriptural sources.

Whatever its provenance, we must never forget that Buddhist canonical literature *is* literature. It is not a repository of authoritative texts where it is possible to find the final and definitive word on every subject as, for example, the Bible, Torah, or Koran are held to be by fundamentalist followers of their faiths. One may sometimes find a kind of quasi-fundamentalism in some Buddhist circles, but that attitude goes against the very nature of the texts upon which it claims to depend and cannot be justified by a reading of Buddhist canonical literature as a whole. When the Kālāmas of Kesaputta went to see the Buddha and asked for his advice, telling him they were confused by the different claims to truth of the many different teachers and traditions they encountered, the Buddha acknowledged their doubts:

Yes, Kālāmas, you may well doubt, you may well waver. In a doubtful matter wavering does arise.

Come, Kālāmas. Do not go upon what has been acquired by repeated hearing; nor upon tradition; nor upon rumor; nor upon what is in a scripture; nor upon surmise; nor upon an axiom; nor upon specious reasoning; nor upon a bias towards a notion that has been pondered over; nor upon another's seeming ability; nor upon the consideration, 'The monk is our teacher.' Kālāmas, when you yourselves know: 'These things are good; these things are not blamable; these things are praised by the wise; undertaken and observed, these things lead to benefit and happiness,' enter on and abide in them.[69]

We need always to test whatever claims to be *Buddhavacana* against our own experience. At the same time we must beware of drawing premature conclusions. We should know that, when it comes to transcendental truth, there is much that we do not know, and our ordinary sense of the truth is deeply rooted in our unenlightened, conditioned, attitudes.

Buddhavacana is the communication from an Enlightened heart or mind to the heart or mind of those as yet unenlightened. It exists to serve the benefits of living beings. It is, therefore, literature of the highest possible standing, and that is how we should read it.

In a paper entitled *The Glory of the Literary World*,[70] Sangharakshita sought to convey a sense of what that might mean. He quoted from the *Essay on Literature* by the third-century Chinese writer Lu Ji:

Writing is in itself a joy,
Yet saints and sages have long since held it in awe.
For it is Being, created by tasking the Great Void,
And 'tis sound rung out of Profound Silence.
In a sheet of paper is contained the Infinite,
And, evolved from an inch-sized heart, an endless panorama.
The words, as they expand, become all-evocative,
The thought, still further pursued, will run the deeper,
Till flowers in full blossom exhale all-pervading fragrance,
And tender boughs, their saps running, grow to a whole jungle
  of splendour.
Bright winds spread luminous wings, quick breezes soar from
  the earth,
And, nimbus-like amidst all these, rises the glory of the literary
  world.[71]

Lu Ji's conception of the uses of literature is equally valuable and evocative:

The use of literature
Lies in its conveyance of every truth.
It expands the horizon to make space infinite,
And serves as a bridge that spans a myriad years.
It maps all roads and paths for posterity,

And mirrors the images of worthy ancients,
That the tottering Edifices of the sage kings of antiquity may be
     reared again,
And their admonishing voices, wind-borne since of yore, may
     resume full expression.
No regions are too remote but it pervades,
No truth too subtle to be woven into its vast web.
Like mist and rain, it permeates and nourishes,
And manifests all the powers of transformation in which gods
     and spirits share.
Virtue it makes endure and radiate on brass and stone,
And resound in an eternal stream of melodies ever renewed on
     pipes and strings.[72]

The qualities that Lu Ji ascribes to literature are the qualities of
Buddhavacana. There are resonances between what he says of
literature and what the Buddha says of his own teaching in the
Lotus Sūtra:

It is like a great cloud
that rises up in the world
and covers it all over.

This beneficent cloud is laden with moisture,
the lightning gleams and flashes,
and the sound of thunder reverberates afar,
causing the multitude to rejoice.
The sun's rays are veiled and hidden,
a clear coolness comes over the land;
masses of darkness descend and spread –
you can almost touch them.
The rain falls everywhere,
coming down on all four sides.
Its flow and saturation are measureless,
reaching to every area of the earth,
to the ravines and valleys of the mountains and streams,
to the remote and secluded places where grow
plants, bushes, medicinal herbs,

trees large and small,
a hundred grains, rice seedlings,
sugar cane, grape vines.
The rain moistens them all,
none fails to receive its full share.
The parched ground is everywhere watered,
herbs and trees alike grow lush.
What falls from the cloud is
water of a single flavor,
but the plants and trees, thickets and groves,
each accept the moisture that is appropriate to its portion.[73]

There are several different versions of the *Tripiṭaka*; schools and traditions differ considerably in what they allow as canonical. In the Triratna Buddhist Order we take an inclusive approach. We revere the *Tripiṭaka* as a whole, although none of us could ever hope to master it, least of all in its expanded, Mahāyāna, forms.

For most of us the Buddhist tradition is like a vast undiscovered continent. When we venture into it we need a reliable guide and translator, someone who, through their own experience, knows the lie of the land and understands the many different dialects. And such translation is not merely a linguistic matter – it is not enough just to know what the Chinese, Sanskrit, Tibetan, or Pāli words mean. There is also the question of translating between cultures, from East to West, and translating between dimensions, from more or less transcendental to more or less mundane contexts.

In the Triratna Buddhist Order we take Sangharakshita – and, increasingly, his more senior disciples – as our guides. Under their guidance we approach the tradition as a whole, and with their help we learn ever more clearly to hear the voice of the Buddha and the great teachers of the past, speaking to us down the ages, urging us ever onwards and upwards, towards Enlightenment, for the sake of all.

Chapter Eleven

The Teachers of the Past

Introduction

The Refuge Tree of the Triratna Buddhist Order has enormous historical significance. For the first time in Buddhist history many of the great schools and traditions – Madhyamaka, Yogācāra, Theravāda; Kagyu, Nyingma, and Gelug; Chan, Faxiang, and Tiantai; Sōtō Zen, Rinzai Zen, Jōdo Shin, and Shingon – some of which grew up in complete ignorance of each other – have been brought together and united within one symbolic whole. The teachers of the past represent, each in their own way, a significant strand in the history of the Buddhist world.

The fact that Sangharakshita has made such a diverse choice in his selection of the teachers of the past says something in itself. In the Triratna Buddhist Order we draw on the whole Buddhist tradition for our inspiration. There is something we can learn from every aspect of it. This principle of ecumenicity recognizes that Buddhism as a whole is a single tree with many branches, and that the same vital juice of spiritual practice that sustains and vitalizes the younger and smaller branch that is the FWBO circulates through all the older branches as well.

Nonetheless, Sangharakshita *did* make a selection. He chose some teachers and not others. His choices were made based on his personal understanding and on the wider understanding of the Buddhist tradition at the time in which he made those choices. Since then, Buddhists have come to question why, for example, female teachers and mythic figures are not given more prominence by the tradition. That is a valid question, and one which Buddhists in the future will no doubt address.

For now, though, we must understand that in creating a new Refuge Tree, Sangharakshita's decision, informed by his Dharmic and historical knowledge, and the culture that formed him, were highly personal and rooted in his own spiritual intuitions.

As we contemplate these figures for ourselves, as we find out more about them, we can begin to get some feeling for what it is that each of them has contributed to Sangharakshita's approach to the Dharma and what we can learn from them.

But what does the fact of a certain teacher's inclusion on the Tree mean for us individually? Does it mean, for example, that as members (or aspiring members) of the Triratna Buddhist Order we trace our spiritual lineage back to the great masters who founded these schools, regarding them as our spiritual ancestors?

We have to be careful here, for there are certain approaches to the notion of spiritual lineage that can lead to a kind of spiritual snobbery, wherein you may think you have attained to a certain spiritual significance because you think of yourself as belonging to a particular spiritual lineage, either by way of Tantric initiation or Zen 'Dharma transmission', or because you have taken a particular teacher as your own, or simply because you regularly attend a particular Buddhist centre or temple. In other words, the tendencies towards vanity that are often associated with ancestry in the more literal sense can easily be transposed to a spiritual context.

The idea of spiritual lineage can also become caught up with ideas of 'transmission' in an almost materialistic way, as if spiritual insight were something that could be passed literally from teacher to disciple, in a single convenient package. But that is not how spiritual life actually works. The great teachers of the past point out the way. It is up to us to follow. Spiritual experience is not something you can be 'given'; on this side of Real Going for Refuge it is always, and only, the fruit of dedicated spiritual practice.

We cannot get anything from the teachers of the past apart from knowledge and inspiration, but *that* we can get in abundance, for all of them were, above all else perhaps, great spiritual teachers, and their abundant writings and accounts of their lectures and teachings amount to a great treasure-house of spiritual understanding and inspiration. Reading these and studying them more deeply, especially with the help of those who have a little more understanding than ourselves, they can continue to lead us forward on the path.

But more than that, perhaps. The great teachers of the past each led exemplary spiritual lives. They dedicated themselves wholeheartedly to the Dharma. Each of them made strenuous efforts in pursuit of the Goal, and then, each having attained to whatever degree of transcendental insight, they dedicated their lives to helping others. By contemplating their lives and teachings we ourselves can be inspired to follow in their footsteps and make stronger, more inspired efforts. In that way we open ourselves to their continuing spiritual influence, and thus the great teachers of the past continue to teach, living on, as great spiritual presences, even today.

Nāgārjuna, at the back on the left, is in front of the Arjuna tree under which
he was born, entwined by two snakes. Asaṅga is accompanied by a small dog.
Vasubandhu teaches and debates wearing his pandit cap. Śāntideva has his hands
together in prayer and Buddhaghosa holds the text of the Visuddhimagga.

India

Nāgārjuna

Nāgārjuna's is the first great name to occur in the development of Buddhist thought. In the face of an emerging pedantic and dogmatic Buddhist scholasticism, which had begun to reify the categories into which it analysed phenomena, treating them as if they somehow described ultimately existing entities, Nāgārjuna's incisive reassertion of the Buddha's Middle Way was electrifying, and it has resounded through all later Mahāyāna developments.

Sometimes referred to as a 'second Buddha', we know less about him than we do about the Buddha himself, and numerous works attributed to him were probably written by others. Although there is some disagreement among scholars as to which of the works attributed to Nāgārjuna were actually written by him, the *Mūla-madhyamaka-kārikā*, 'Root Verses on the Middle Way', is agreed to be the defining standard. Whoever wrote that is the person now considered to be Nāgārjuna.

Analysing the textual tradition, some scholars think there were two major and several minor Nāgārjunas, all of whom were somehow conflated as the tradition developed. There was the second-century author of the *Mūla-madhyamaka-kārikā*, Ārya Nāgārjuna, who was born in South India and came to be known as the second Buddha. And there was the ninth-century master of the *Guhyasamāja Tantra*, the *siddhācārya* Nāgārjuna, a disciple of Saraha, who is regarded as one of the *mahāsiddhas* of the Tantric tradition.

The biographical and mythical accounts of ārya Nāgārjuna vary, but they tend to agree that he was born to a Brahmin family in South India. According to one popular account, the brilliantly learned young Nāgārjuna used the art of invisibility to seduce women in the royal court, and narrowly escaped death at the hands of the guards. Seeing that his passions inevitably gave rise to suffering, he renounced his privileged status, entered the sangha, and soon became proficient in all the texts available to him.

Still dissatisfied, he went in quest of more. His travels brought him to the *Mahānāga*, the king of the Nāgas, who led him down into the great ocean, there revealing to him a great store of texts including the whole corpus of the *Prajñāpāramitā* or *Perfection of Wisdom*. These he mastered within ninety days, and then he discovered a further, inexhaustible store. There is no end, he saw, to what can be written, and no end to what can be intellectually understood. He realized that an experiential realization of the contents of the sūtras was needed – not just greater learning. Thus he entered a period of deep meditation, from which he emerged with profound realization, and he went on to expound the *Perfection of Wisdom* teachings and compose texts of his own.

The Madhyamaka tradition – the tradition of the 'Middle Way' which Nāgārjuna is said to have founded – taught a way to liberation through the realization of the ultimate emptiness of all phenomena. From the point of view of the Middle Way, one neither affirms nor negates the existence of phenomena, but seeing that they arise always and only in dependence upon conditions, one recognizes their ultimately empty nature. Thus in the *Mūla-madhyamaka-kārikā* Nāgārjuna asserts:

We declare that whatever is conditioned arising is emptiness.
It is a provisional name for the mutuality of being and, indeed,
it is the middle way.[74]

Taking any claim that something exists – sometimes using logic, sometimes rhetoric – Nāgārjuna showed that such could not be the case: all claims to existence, upon analysis, pass into their own contradictions. Between the twin claims of existence and non-existence lies the truth of dependent origination or 'mutuality of being', which, being entirely without any fixed, final, and irreducible essence, is itself 'empty'.

The *Mūla-madhyamaka-kārikā* begins with eight famous negations:

I pay homage to the Fully Awakened One,
the supreme teacher who has taught
the doctrine of relational origination,
the blissful cessation of phenomenal thought-constructions.
  Therein, every event is marked by:
non-origination, non-extinction,
non-destruction, non-permanence,
non-identity, non-differentiation,
non-coming into being, non-going out of being.[75]

These negations are an attempt to overcome our innate tendency to grasp a static view of reality and to help us to apprehend the ultimately illimitable dynamic flux which is dependent origination.

The world of phenomena, according to Nāgārjuna, exists and is possessed of meaning only in a conventional (or relative) sense. The conventional world is 'real'; though it is not a figment of our imagination, it is radically impermanent. Phenomena lack inherent existence, everything depends upon passing conditions. It *is* meaningful, at the relative level, to ascribe truth or falsity to any given proposition, and at this level the phenomenal world, including all the teachings of the Buddha, has validity. That is the world of relative truth. The absolute truth, on the other hand, is the truth of the complete absence anywhere of any form of inherent existence. To realize this is to let go of all deluding attachments and to achieve nirvāṇa – complete liberation. This is not merely an intellectual matter, however, and can only be brought about through strenuous spiritual practice. Such practice takes place within the context of the conventional world. We approach the absolute, therefore, by way of the relative, whose value is consequently inestimable:

Those who do not know the distinction between the two
truths cannot understand the profound nature of the Buddha's
teaching.
  Without relying upon everyday common practices (i.e.
relative truths), the absolute truth cannot be expressed.

Without approaching the absolute truth, Nirvāṇa cannot be attained.

A wrongly conceived śūnyatā can ruin a slow-witted person. It is like a badly seized snake or a wrongly executed incantation.[76]

Asaṅga

Asaṅga and his brother Vasubandhu stand out among the founding fathers of the Yogācāra tradition of Mahāyāna Buddhism. Their impact upon all later developments of Mahāyāna Buddhism – some of which followed, some of which opposed, the Yogācāra – was enormous.

In the *Saṃdhinirmocana Sūtra*, a definitive Yogācāra sūtra, the Buddha explains that externally perceived objects and the images perceived in meditation are both merely the product of ideas. They are simply the activity of the mind. This 'mind only' doctrine is the central Yogācāra teaching. It does not imply that everything is 'made' of mind (which would simply reduce mind to a kind of universal 'matter') but that all our experience depends upon our mind. Everything we sense, feel, or think is inextricably part of a mental process, and the things we experience, at whatever level, cannot be fundamentally different from the mind that experiences them; if they were, they would be completely inaccessible to each other.

Through intense meditation practice one gains a living conviction of the ultimate identity of the world of experience and the world of mental processes. Both come to be seen as *vijñaptimātra*, 'mere ideation', and then, when there is nothing to grasp, there is no more grasping, and all delusory duality is overcome.

The Yogācāra claimed that the Mādhyamikas, the followers of the school of Nāgārjuna, went too far in denying the possibility of anything having inherent existence. There *was* something that really existed, they said, and that was the mind. The Mādhyamikas were concerned to eliminate the ontological claims that had crept into Buddhism via the Abhidharma tradition. Ontology is that part of metaphysics that relates to the nature of existence, or being as such. The *dharmas* of the ābhidharmikas, the constituent elements of the world and mental events, were said to be ontological entities; they had, in other words, an essential existence. The Mādhyamikas countered this by reasserting the Buddha's teaching of the Middle Way between existence and non-existence. 'All *dharmas* are śūnyatā', they asserted, and for them Śūnyatā came to mean the complete absence of inherent existence.

The Yogācārins took another approach. 'Yogācāra' can be translated as 'the way, or application, of yoga' and their approach focused on profound insight experiences that arise in the course of meditation. In the context of such experiences they analysed the flow of mental events and applied the teaching of dependent origination psychologically, rather than ontologically. 'Emptiness', for them, meant not the ultimate non-existence of the mind – that, they thought, shaded too far into nihilism. Instead, they took it to mean the absence of any dualism between the perceiving subject and the perceived object, experiential realization of which yielded the experience of *tathatā*, or 'suchness', which in time came to be identified with the Buddha-nature. The Mādhyamikas were very suspicious of this approach, seeing it as allowing for a kind of 'substantialism' and the readmittance of an 'essence' that it had been so keen to excise.

The apparent tension between these two approaches continues even today, with different Mahāyāna schools and traditions disputing around the Middle Way. But perhaps the truth is that such disputes are inevitable. The exact Middle Way is, after all, inexpressible, and any claims about how things really are will inevitably veer, however slightly, towards existence or non-existence.

Asaṅga, who is thought to have lived between about 310 and 390 CE, was the eldest of three brothers who were the sons of a Brahmin, a court priest at Puruṣapura (now known as Peshawar), in what was then the kingdom of Gāndhāra. All the brothers became monks in the Sarvāstivāda order.

The Sarvāstivādins, the 'asserters that everything exists', believed in the reality of external objects of consciousness, and at that time their ancient scholastic tradition was prominent in Gāndhāra. During his studies, however, Asaṅga came upon the *Prajñāpāramitā* sūtras of the Mahāyāna, which was then overturning the old established scholastic schools of Buddhism in favour of a life dedicated to active compassion. Unable to understand these, and not receiving any help from his teachers, he retired to the forest to meditate.

There, according to legend, he withdrew to a cave, resolving not to give up his meditation until the Buddha Maitreya manifested before him, but after three years without result, he left his cave, discouraged. Nearby, he met a man making a needle from an iron spike by rubbing it with a piece of cotton. Seeing this, his resolution returned and he went back to the cave and meditated unremittingly for six more years. Still Maitreya did not appear. Disheartened, Asaṅga again left his cave. Outside he saw how a rock had been completely worn down by single drops of water and the beating wings of passing birds. Again his patience returned and he resumed his meditation, this time for another three years. But finally, after twelve years without result, he despaired completely and set out to return to his monastery.

On the outskirts of a town he saw an old she-dog whose hind-quarters were crawling with maggots. Feeling great pity for her, and wanting to relieve her suffering, he was plunged into conflict, for neither could he bear to destroy the maggots. Instead, he cut a piece of flesh from his thigh and placed it near the dog. Then, putting out his tongue, he prepared to transfer the larvae one by one. The sight of the wound was so disgusting that he had to close his eyes. Suddenly there was a great ringing in his ears and he opened his eyes. Standing before him, arrayed in splendour, was Maitreya. Despite his joy, Asaṅga exclaimed without thinking, 'Why did you never come to me during the twelve years I was meditating?'

Maitreya answered, 'I was with you all the time, but you could not see me, because you did not yet have great compassion. Try carrying me through the town on your shoulders to show me to the people.' So Asaṅga lifted Maitreya on to his shoulders and carried him through the town, hoping to let everyone see the Buddha. But no one in the town saw Maitreya, and only one old woman saw even the dog. Then Maitreya transported Asaṅga to the Tusita heaven, where he studied the Dharma for fifty years. When he eventually returned to India he brought with him a number of key Yogācāra texts.

Perhaps this legend points to significant elements in the Yogācāra's origins. The Tusita heaven, like all the heavens in Buddhism, is the objective counterpart of the higher mental states experienced in meditation. Maitreya lives in the Tusita heaven, so perhaps Asaṅga met him in meditation. Alternatively, it is also said that Asaṅga's teacher in the Yogācāra doctrine was Maitreyanātha, who lived around 275–350. Perhaps Asaṅga encountered him as a kind of hermit-philosopher during his long retreat.

Asaṅga's *Yogācārabhūmi* is a key text of the Yogācāra. Essentially a meditation and practice manual, it begins by introducing the practitioner to mindfulness meditation, focusing on one's body, feeling, and thoughts as well as *dharmas*, both in oneself and in others. Through this, a preliminary insight into the non-difference between self and others arises, and further meditations deepen this insight at increasingly subtle levels. Gradually eliminating the mental activity that gives rise to the perception of duality, the practitioner passes through the various stages of the Bodhisattva path, eventually to experience a 'turning about in the deepest seat of consciousness', after which one dwells in pure, undifferentiated *tathatā*, or 'suchness'. This approach freely adapted the Abhidharma analysis of self and the world into *dharmas*, incorporating it into the Mahāyāna world-view.

As we shall see in the next section, Asaṅga went on to convert his brother Vasubandhu to the Mahāyāna and particularly to the Yogācāra approach. Between them the two brothers exerted an enormous influence on the Buddhist thought and practice of their time.

Vasubandhu

Vasubandhu was a man of immensely deep and diverse learning. Works attributed to him include religious poetry, fables, commentaries on sūtras, and independent treatises, in both prose and verse. He deals with logic, psychology, the history of the Buddhist canon, medicine, and meditation. Given the enormous breadth of his approach, it is no wonder he is found in the mythical lineage of teachers in approaches as apparently diverse as Zen and Pure Land Buddhism.

One day his mother admonished him, 'Son, you were not born to do mundane tasks or to bring up a family, but to propagate the Buddha-Dharma. I beg you to become a monk and study the *Tripiṭaka*. Exert yourself for the Buddha-Dharma.'

So Vasubandhu took ordination and studied the Sarvāstivādin *Tripiṭaka*, amazing his teachers with the brilliance and quickness of his mind. After a time, however, he decided to go to Kashmir – then a more orthodox seat of learning than his birthplace, Puruṣapura, in the Gāndhāran kingdom – to further his studies. Here he debated fiercely with learned Kashmiri masters, refuting many of their points and developing a considerable reputation.

In due course, however, frustrated by the over-intellectual dogmatics of the Kashmiri masters, he returned to Puruṣapura where he lived in a small private house, supporting himself by lecturing on the Dharma before the general public, lectures which in time were published as his *Abhidharmakośa*.

Around this time, he came upon some of his brother Asaṅga's works, but he did not believe these could have been heard from the Buddha Maitreya. 'Poor Asaṅga!' he thought, 'For twelve years he practised meditation in a cave, but because he did not attain *samādhi*, he concocted enough fantastic writings to weigh down the back of an elephant.' News of this soon reached Asaṅga who, deciding the time had come to try to open up his gifted brother to the Mahāyāna, asked one of his disciples to memorize the *Akṣayamati-nirdeśa-sūtra* and another to memorize the *Daśabhūmika Sūtra*. He then told them to go and recite these scriptures near his younger brother's house, the first at midnight and the second at dawn. This they did.

That night Vasubandhu heard the *Akṣayamati-nirdeśa-sūtra*, in which a transcendental Bodhisattva teaches worldlings about the absence of own-being, the absence of existing and ceasing, and the absence of any detriment or excellence in all *dharmas*. Vasubandhu was greatly impressed. The logical principles of the Mahāyāna seemed to be well-founded, but it seemed to have no practice, 'like a fruit that melts in the mouth but gives no substance to the stomach'. But when at dawn the *Daśabhūmika Sūtra*, which outlines the path of the Bodhisattva, was recited, he saw that the Mahāyāna was well-founded in practice too, and he was overwhelmed with

Teachers of Enlightenment

faith. 'The Mahāyāna is indeed sublime in both motive and effect. But my tongue has insulted it! I must cut it out!' and he began searching for a knife. Asaṅga's two disciples quickly intervened and begged him, 'Please, come to your brother who holds the method for purifying unskilful acts. How can your unskilful action be eliminated by cutting off your tongue?'

So Vasubandhu went to Asaṅga and they discussed the Dharma. Again and again Vasubandhu expressed his doubts, but Asaṅga did not lose confidence and continued to answer his questions. Eventually, overwhelmed by his brother's clarity and patience, Vasubandhu asked Asaṅga for the secret of his knowledge. 'I approach my *yidam* with all my questions,' Asaṅga replied, 'It is his answers that I transmit.'

Vasubandhu's *Trisvabhāva Nirdeśa* expounds the Yogācāra doctrine of 'three natures'. Everything that can be known, all objects of cognition, can be classified under these three natures. The primary aspect – the 'way things really are' – is the *paratantra-svabhāva*, the 'dependent, or conditioned, nature', and it is this that really exists. But it is essentially a mental process – it is the continual flow of mutually conditioned and conditioning mental events that make up consciousness. In other words, it is dependent origination viewed from the mind-only perspective. All the elements within it 'depend' on each other for their existence.

The unenlightened mind, however, cannot grasp this. Instead, it creates the duality of the false, 'imagined' nature. This *parikalpita-svabhāva* is the kind of existence we normally ascribe to the everyday world. It is unreal and has only the conventional existence that we project from the activity of our unenlightened minds. It is the product of the falsifying activity of language, which imputes duality on to the mutually dependent flow of mental events. Seeing ourselves as independent subjects, apprehending an objective, external world, we 'imagine' a world of dualistic phenomena. The Enlightened mind, however, sees things as they really are. It apprehends the *pariniṣpanna-svabhāva* – the 'perfected' or 'absolute' nature. This is the truth that all things are completely lacking in duality.

Vasubandhu illustrates these three natures using the metaphor of an illusionist's trick:

When by means of a spell (*mantra*) something is made to appear in the illusory form of an elephant (e.g., out of a piece of wood), there is only the appearance in the form of an elephant, but it (elephant) is really non-existent there in all respects.

Here the Imaginary aspect is the elephant, the Relative or Conditioned aspect is its form, and the absence of a real elephant there is admitted to be the Absolute aspect.

Similarly does 'that which has in it unreal conception' (*asatkalpa*) appear in dual form out of the basic consciousness (*mūlavijñāna*). (But) the duality does not really exist there at all; there is only the semblance of it.[77]

Vasubandhu's various works have had a profound impact on the development of Mahāyāna Buddhist thought, especially in China and Japan, where he is regarded as a patriarch in the Chan, Zen, and Pure Land Schools and where Xuanzang established his Faxiang School around Vasubandhu's central teachings.

Śāntideva

Śāntideva lived at the great monastic university of Nālandā, probably between 685 and 763 CE. He is the author of two great works, the splendidly poetic *Bodhicaryāvatāra*, 'Guide to the Bodhisattva's Way of Life', and the *Śikṣā-Samuccaya*, 'Compendium of Instruction', which consists mainly of quotations from nearly a hundred Mahāyāna sūtras, many of which are no longer recoverable from any other source.

Although he was an advanced practitioner who had visions of the Bodhisattva Mañjuśrī, from whom he received teachings directly, he appeared to his fellow monks to be a layabout, good at only three things: eating, sleeping, and defecating. One day, in order to humiliate him, the other monks invited him to recite from the scriptures before the whole monastery. At that time Nālandā was the pre-eminent educational institution in southern Asia, housing several thousand students, and Śāntideva modestly refused so grand an invitation. The monks insisted, however, and eventually Śāntideva agreed. To add to his humiliation, they built a very high

Teachers of Enlightenment

teaching seat for him, one that he could not reach, to ironically imply a recognition of his elevated reputation. Reaching out his hand, however, Śāntideva miraculously lowered the seat, took his place upon it, and asked whether he should present something known or something original. Sardonically, the gathering opted for the latter and, to their amazement, Śāntideva proceeded to expound the magnificent thousand-verse poem which we now know as the *Bodhicaryāvatāra*. Upon reciting the lines

> When neither something nor nothing remains before the mind,
> There are no other alternatives.
> Grasping no object,
> The mind attains peace.[78]

he ascended far into the sky, his words remaining clearly audible even after he completely vanished. Eventually rediscovered in a far corner of India, he refused to return to the monastery, and according to later Tantric tradition he disrobed, lived for twelve years as a palace guard (armed only with a gold-painted wooden sword), married a low-caste woman, and ended his days as a hermit in a remote mountain cave.

According to legend, the *Śikṣā-Samuccaya* was first discovered sitting on the shelf of the room that Śāntideva had used at Nālandā, implying that it was a text which Śāntideva had compiled simply for his own use and perhaps that of a few friends. Such was his unassuming nature.

The *Bodhicaryāvatāra* is remarkable for being at one and the same time a work of fervent devotional poetry, a practical guide to Mahāyāna spiritual training, and an abstruse philosophical treatise. Intended to help aspiring Bodhisattvas to orient themselves towards other beings and to act from that basis, it teaches two basic methods for so doing: the practice of the recognition of the equality of self and other, and that of exchanging self and other:

> May I be a protector for those without one,
> A guide for all travellers on the way;
> May I be a bridge, a boat and a ship
> For all who wish to cross (the water).

May I be an island for those who seek one
And a lamp for those desiring light,
May I be a bed for all who wish to rest
And a slave for all who want a slave.[79]

and

Whatever joy there is in this world
All comes from desiring others to be happy,
And whatever suffering there is in this world
All comes from desiring myself to be happy.

But what need is there to say much more?
The childish work for their own benefit,
The Buddhas work for the benefit of others.
Just look at the difference between them ![80]

As well as being an exhortation to practise the Six Perfections of the Bodhisattva Path (the perfection of generosity, ethics, forbearance, vigour, meditation, and wisdom) the *Bodhicaryāvatāra* (in its first three chapters) contains all the elements of the traditional Mahāyāna *anuttarapūjā* or 'Supreme Worship', the sevenfold pūjā, which consists of worship, salutation, going for refuge, confession, rejoicing in merits, supplication, and transference of merits.

The text moves from the exuberantly devotional:

In those sweet-smelling bath-houses, where canopies gleam
with pearls, over delightful pillars, brilliant with gems, rising
up from mosaic floors of clear, brilliant crystal,
From many pots, encrusted with enormous gems, filled
with exquisitely fragrant water and flowers, see, I bathe the
Tathāgatas and their sons, to the accompaniment of songs and
music.[81]

to the pragmatic:

There is nothing which remains difficult if it is practised. So, through practice with minor discomforts, even major discomfort becomes bearable.

The irritation of bugs, gnats, and mosquitoes, of hunger and thirst, and suffering such as an enormous itch: why do you not see them as insignificant?[82]

to the philosophically abstruse:

If illusion is the same as the mind it is false to claim that it is also different. If it exists as a thing in its own right, how is it the same? If it is the same, then it does not exist in its own right.[83]

It is not clear exactly how much of the *Bodhicaryāvatāra* that has come down to us was actually written by Śāntideva. The second, ninth, and tenth chapters have all been variously disputed and the various life-stories of Śāntideva disagree as to the length of the work. Nevertheless, what we actually have today is more than enough to work with, and the text, which is one of the greatest works of spiritual literature ever composed, continues to inspire and guide spiritual practitioners 1,200 years after it was first committed to writing.

Buddhaghosa

Buddhaghosa is the most famous commentator of the Theravāda and is credited with establishing Pāli as the lingua franca of that tradition. He was born in Maghada, near Bodh Gaya, at the end of the fourth century, and brought up in a Brahmin family, but after encountering Buddhist texts for the first time, he converted to Buddhism and went to Sri Lanka to further his training. There he entered the Mahāvihāra Monastery, where he studied Theravādin teachings under the tutelage of the renowned Saṅghapāla Thera. At that time the Mahāvihāra was reputed to be the most 'ultraorthodox' of the three chief Sinhalese monasteries and, enjoying royal patronage, was closely linked to Sinhalese matters of state. The leading scholars there were men of considerable influence.

Establishing himself in the Mahāvihāra approach to practice, Buddhaghosa produced the most outstanding commentarial and exegetical literature of his time. Chief among these was the *Visuddhimagga*, or 'Path of Purification', an exhaustive guide to the path of ethics, meditation, and wisdom. One of the great masterpieces of Buddhist commentarial literature, it describes in great detail the principal practices of basic Buddhism as understood at the Mahāvihāra at that time. He summarized the available commentarial material of the Vinaya and much of the Sutta Piṭaka commentary. Many of the characteristics of the mainstream 'orthodox' Theravāda that we know today are the result of Buddhaghosa's synthesis.

Legend has it that on coming to Sri Lanka Buddhaghosa first learned all the Sinhalese commentaries on the Theravāda by heart. Convinced of the veracity of their approach, he asked his brother monks to supply him with the *Tipiṭaka*, so that he could write a commentary. To test him, his brother monks gave him but two stanzas, saying, 'Show your ability with these; when we have seen that you have it, we will give you all the books.'

On that text alone, he summarized the *Tipiṭaka* together with its commentary. Thus was born the *Path of Purification*. Then he assembled all the monks who were proficient in the Dharma and began to read it out. In order to demonstrate his skill to the multitude, deities hid the book and he was obliged to prepare it a second and a third time. When the book was finally brought out to be read, the gods returned the other two copies, and when the assembled bhikkhus read out the three copies together, it was found there was no difference between the three in either the chapters, the order of the material, the phrases, or the syllables of the original texts.

In the *Visuddhimagga* Buddhaghosa gave concise expression to the notion of the ultimate emptiness of all *dharmas*:

No doer of the deeds is found;
No one who ever reaps their fruits:
Just bare phenomena roll on –
This view alone is right and true.

Teachers of Enlightenment

No god, no Brahmā, can be found,
No maker of this wheel of life:
Just bare phenomena roll on,
Dependent on conditions all.[84]

and the volume on wisdom pays particular attention to the issue
of dependent origination. But he is, perhaps, most useful to us for
the precise instruction he gives on the many varieties of meditation
practice used at the Mahāvihāra at that time:

> A meditator who wants to develop [loving-kindness] ...
> should seat himself comfortably on a well-prepared seat in a
> secluded place. To start with he should review the danger in
> hate and the advantage in patience. Why? Because hate has
> to be abandoned and patience attained in the development of
> this meditation subject....
>
> But when he begins, he must know that some persons
> are of the wrong sort at the very beginning and that
> lovingkindness should be developed towards certain kinds
> of persons and not towards certain other kinds at first. For
> lovingkindness should not be developed at first ... specifically
> towards the opposite sex, or towards a dead person.... If he
> develops it specifically towards the opposite sex, lust inspired
> by that person springs up in him. An Elder supported by a
> family was asked, it seems, by a friend's son, 'Venerable Sir,
> towards whom should lovingkindness be developed?' The
> elder told him, 'Towards a person one loves.' He loved his
> own wife. Through developing lovingkindness towards her
> he was fighting against the wall all the night (blinded by
> lust arisen under cover of the lovingkindness). That is why it
> should not be developed specifically towards the opposite sex.
>
> But if he develops it towards a dead person, he reaches
> neither absorption nor access. A young bhikkhu, it seems, had
> started developing lovingkindness inspired by his teacher.
> His lovingkindness made no headway at all. He went to a
> senior elder and told him, 'Venerable Sir, I am quite familiar
> with attaining jhāna through lovingkindness, and yet I cannot
> attain it. What is the matter?' The elder said, 'Seek the sign,

friend (the object of your meditation).' He did so. Finding that his teacher had died, he proceeded with developing lovingkindness inspired by another and attained absorption. That is why it should not be developed towards one who is dead.

First of all it should be developed only towards oneself, doing it repeatedly thus: 'May I be happy and free from suffering' or 'May I keep myself free from enmity, affliction and anxiety and live happily'....

So he should first, as example, pervade himself with lovingkindness. Next after that, in order to proceed easily, he can recollect such gifts, kind words, etc., as inspire love and endearment, such virtue, learning, etc., as inspire respect and reverence met with in a teacher or his equivalent or a preceptor or his equivalent, developing lovingkindness towards him in the way beginning 'May this good man be happy and free from suffering'. With such a person, of course, he attains absorption.

But if this bhikkhu does not rest content with just that much and wants to break down the barriers, he should next, after that, develop lovingkindness towards a very dearly loved friend, then towards a neutral person as a very dearly loved friend, then towards a hostile person as neutral. And while he does so, he should make his mind malleable and wieldy in each instance before passing on to the next.[85]

[Thus he dwells] pervading one direction with his heart endued with lovingkindness, likewise the second direction, likewise the third direction, likewise the fourth direction, and so above, below, and around; everywhere and equally he dwells pervading the entire world with his heart endued with lovingkindness, abundant, exalted, measureless, free from enmity, and free from affliction.[86]

Milarepa, in the posture of royal ease, sings his yogic songs. Atiśa teaches the Dharma. Padmasambhava holds a skull cup of blood and wears a pandit's cap. Tsongkhapa also makes the teaching gesture.

Tibet

Milarepa

Through the illustration of his own life, the great yogi Milarepa set an example of the perfect Bodhisattva, and a model of the incorruptible life of a genuine practitioner. Living without possessions in the high Himalayan wastes, he made it clear that poverty is not a kind of deprivation, but a necessary way of emancipating oneself from the tyranny of material possessions. He showed that Tantric practice does not imply indulgence and laxity, but hard labour, strict discipline, and steadfast perseverance, and that without resolute renunciation and uncompromising discipline, all the sublime ideas and dazzling images depicted in Mahāyāna and Tantric Buddhism are no better than magnificent illusions.

His biography, together with all the songs it contains, was put together in the fifteenth century, and remains, even today, one of the greatest sources of inspiration in Tibetan Buddhism.

Milarepa, whose name approximately translates as 'Mila who wears the cotton cloth of an ascetic', was born around 1025 in western Tibet, near to the Nepalese border. His wealthy father died when Milarepa was seven, and the family property fell into the hands of an uncle and aunt who – despite an oath sworn to his father – treated Milarepa, his mother, and his sister almost as slaves. Begged by his mother to avenge these injuries, Milarepa turned to sorcery and, having eventually mastered the destructive forces of nature, killed many people with a fierce storm.

Overcome by remorse, and learning that the only way to expunge his bad karma was by gaining Enlightenment in this very lifetime, Mila turned to the teacher Rongton, who sent him in turn to Marpa, the famous translator who had just returned from India after many years of study there. Marpa saw that Mila was a student of extraordinary potential and enormous determination. He also realized that before he could fulfil that potential Mila needed to purge himself of his bad karma, and so, for six years, he treated him as a servant and, pretending to be a harsh master, subjected him to a gruelling regime that brought Mila to the verge of suicide.

Once his karma had been purified in this way, Marpa prepared Mila for the yogi's life of solitude. He transmitted to him his principal teachings of Mahāmudrā, the effortless realization of emptiness, and the Six Yogas of Naropa, with particular emphasis on the practice of *tummo*, or 'psychic heat', which allowed him to live above the snow line dressed only in a thin cotton cloth.

By this time, however, Milarepa had been separated from his family for many years, and one day, while meditating in his cave, he fell asleep and dreamed that he returned home and saw the bones of his mother lying in the ruins of his house. He dreamed that his sister was a vagabond beggar and that his house and fields were deserted and overgrown with weeds. He awoke weeping bitterly and, stricken with grief, left Marpa and went back to his home village, where the apprehensions of his dream were confirmed. Seeing this painful human existence helplessly and futilely consumed by impermanence, an anguish of desire to renounce the world arose within him. He made a solemn vow that he would meditate uninterruptedly on a remote mountain until he reached complete Enlightenment. For twelve consecutive years he meditated alone in a cave, living on nothing but nettles, until his whole body became greenish in colour. As a consequence of this consistent effort, he finally earned his reward and realized complete Enlightenment.

After this he began to accept disciples and to teach people through his famous songs. He had many disciples and patrons, the most famous of whom was the physician Gampopa, who founded the monastic tradition of the Kagyu School.

Milarepa taught spontaneously, freely responding in song and verse to whoever asked him for teachings. One day, five young nuns came to visit him high in the mountains, at the Tiger Cave of Senge Tson. 'This place full of terror,' they said, 'it is supposed to be an ideal place to gain improvement in meditation. Can this be true? Have you found it so?' Milarepa then sang:

Obeisance to you, my Guru!
I met you through having accumulated great merits,
And now stay at the place you prophesied.

This is a delightful place, a place of hills and forests.
In the mountain-meadows, flowers bloom;
In the woods dance the swaying trees!
For monkeys it is a playground.
Birds sing tunefully,
Bees fly and buzz,
And from day until night the rainbows come and go.
In summer and winter falls the sweet rain,
And mist and fog roll up in fall and spring.
At such a pleasant place, in solitude,
I, Milarepa, happily abide,
Meditating on the void-illuminating Mind.

Oh, happy are the myriad manifestations!
The more ups-and-downs, the more joy I feel.
Happy is the body with no sinful Karma,
Happy indeed are the countless confusions!
The greater the fear the greater the happiness I feel.
Oh, happy is the death of sensations and passions!

The greater the distress and passions,
The more can one be blithe and gay!
What happiness to feel no ailment or illness;
What happiness to feel that joy and suffering are one;
What happiness to play in bodily movement
With the power aroused by Yoga.
To jump and run, to dance and leap, is more joyful still.

What happiness to sing the victorious song,
What happiness to chant and hum,
More joyful still to talk and loudly sing!
Happy is the mind, powerful and confident,
Steeped in the realm of Totality.

The most extreme happiness
Is the self-emanation of self-power;
Happy are the myriad forms, the myriad revelations.
As a welcoming gift to my faithful pupils,
I sing of yogic happiness.[87]

Atiśa

The Dharma flourished in Tibet for about sixty years after
the founding of Samye Monastery. Then, in the middle of the
ninth century, the last of the pro-Buddhist kings, Ralpachen,
was assassinated and replaced by his brother Langdarma, who
persecuted the Buddhists of his kingdom until he was assassinated
by a monk who wished to protect the Dharma. For two centuries
Tibet descended into lawlessness, and the Dharma began to
decline. By the eleventh century, however, the situation had begun
to stabilize to some extent, and the old royal family, surviving
in the west of the country, patronized the Dharma. In 1042 the
famous Indian teacher, Atiśa, accepted their invitation to come
to Tibet and teach.

Atiśa received the deputation from the kingdom of western Tibet
while he was staying at the monastic university of Vikramaśīla. The
king had been captured by bandits and they were holding him to
ransom. They would free him only if his subjects could raise his
weight in gold. After many years, his nephew, who was acting as
regent in the king's absence, had managed to raise the weight of
his body, but not his head. The king, grown old, and realizing how
oppressed his subjects had been in trying to find that much gold,
contacted his nephew from captivity. 'Don't worry about me,' he
said, 'I am old and worn out. I shall soon die. Just leave me here
in captivity and use the gold to invite the great Atiśa to Tibet. The
Dharma is what is really important.'

When Atiśa heard this story he was deeply moved and, after
consulting Tārā, his tutelary deity, who told him that doing so
would considerably reduce his remaining span of life but would
enable him to benefit many beings, he accepted the invitation.
Leaving behind all he had achieved in India, he devoted the last
twelve years of his life to spreading the Dharma in Tibet, where his

impact on the reviving Buddhist community was enormous. He is credited with starting what is known as the 'second diffusion' of the Dharma in Tibet. Unlike the first diffusion, this second phase was marked by a reliance upon Indian sources of inspiration, and Atiśa was very active in stopping the random and careless propagation of religious texts and practices, many of them highly dubious, which had by then developed.

Atiśa Dīpaṅkara Śrījñāna had been born into an aristocratic family in what is now Bangladesh. His family were Vajrayāna practitioners and Atiśa naturally followed in their footsteps. It is said that he received his first Vajrayāna initiation from his own father, a local chieftain. As he grew up, however, Atiśa came to feel that he was not getting anywhere with his Vajrayāna practice and he decided to look to the earlier Buddhist traditions for inspiration and teaching. He thus began a study of the Āgama literature, the Sanskrit recensions of those texts which we now know mainly in their Pāli form. He also studied the Vinaya and the Abhidharma. Having mastered these, he conceived the strong desire to study the Mahāyāna, but there were few texts and no Mahāyāna masters present in India at the time, and he had to travel all the way to Sumatra, a perilous journey taking thirteen months, in order to find texts and a teacher. Such was his determination. Returning in due course to India, he established himself at Vikramaśīla, where he developed a reputation as a great scholar and Buddhist practitioner. It was from here that he left for Tibet.

Atiśa's disciple Dromtön founded the first wholly Tibetan Buddhist order – the Kadam, who took as their root text Atiśa's *Bodhipathapradīpa*, 'Lamp on the Path to Bodhi'. This text systematically integrates all the teachings that Atiśa had received from his many teachers, and outlines a gradual path to Enlightenment, based upon ethics, proceeding to the development of compassion and wisdom, and culminating in Tantric practice. This 'triyāna system' sees the Hīnayāna as embodying the path of ethics, the Mahāyāna as embodying the path of compassion and wisdom, and the Tantra as leading to Supreme Enlightenment. Atiśa's teachings combined the two principal traditions of the Indian Mahāyāna, stressing Nāgārjuna's assertion of the need for a deep insight into *śūnyatā* as well as Asaṅga's view of the all-encompassing compassionate action of the enlightened mind. He is also credited with spreading the practice of devotion to Tārā throughout Tibet. Time and again Atiśa stressed the importance of Going for Refuge to the Three Jewels; so much so, in fact, that he came to be known as the Refuge Guru.

Many of Atiśa's direct teachings to his disciples have been preserved in the form of the Kadam Precepts:

'Although you keep the three vows [of the three yānas], if you do not renounce the three realms of saṃsāra, your activities will only increase your worldliness. Although you strive to perform virtuous deeds in body, speech, and mind, both day and night, if you do not dedicate this work to the Enlightenment of all, you will end up with numberless wrong concepts [views]. Though you meditate and are considered a holy and wise teacher, if you do not abandon your interest in the eight worldly concerns, whatever you do will be only for the purposes of this life and in the future you will not find the right path.'[88]

One of his disciples once asked him, 'Is it possible for one who realizes ... voidness to attain buddhahood with only the wisdom and meditation of voidness?'

Atiśa replied, 'Whatever you perceive, whatever you proclaim – there is nothing that has not come from your own mind. Understand that this realization of mind is empty. Understanding the non-duality of the realization of mind and of voidness is *wisdom*. *Meditation* is the continuous concentration on this wisdom without distraction. Deeds are the accumulation of merit and wisdom while you realize from the viewpoint of this meditation that everything is like an illusion. Once you are under the influence of these three, their practice will come even in dreams. Once it has come in dreams, it will come at the moment of death. When it comes at the moment of death, it will be present in the bardo. Once it is present in the *bardo*, there is certain to be accomplishment of the superior siddhi, and you will become a buddha.'[89]

At another time, he was asked, 'What is the final goal of the Teaching?'

Atiśa replied, 'The final goal of the teaching is possession of the essence of voidness and compassion. Just as in the world there is a panacea for all sickness called the solitary heroic medicine, there is the realization of voidness, which remedies all the fettering passions.'

'But many say they have realized voidness. Why do their anger and attachment remain?'

'They are speaking empty words, for when you fully realize the meaning of voidness, your body, speech, and mind react with pleasure, like slipping fresh butter into barley soup. The great sage Āryadeva said:

The nature of existence –
Is it empty or not?
Merely feeling this doubt
Tears saṃsāra asunder.

'Therefore, when you realize the correct meaning of voidness, it is just like the solitary heroic medicine, for all the path is included in that realization.'

'How do you include the entire path within the realization of voidness?' the disciples asked.

'All the path is included in the six transcendences (pāramitā). When you realize the correct meaning of voidness – and lose your blind lust for all things, material and spiritual – your life becomes one flowing act of transcendent giving. In the absence of attachment, you are no longer defiled by non-virtuous deeds, and you enter the ever-flowing harmony of transcendent moral practice. In this freedom from defilement, you also liberate yourself from the passionate domination of "I" and "mine", and attain the ever-flowing transcendent patience. As you take great pleasure in the realization of voidness, your life becomes one ever-flowing transcendent effort. Through this, you lose all attraction to objects and enter the ever-flowing transcendent meditation. And finally, when your mind is freed from the habit of seeing everything through the prism of three aspects (for example, the three aspects of giving are: the act of giving, the giver of the gift, and the recipient of the gift), you will attain the ever-flowing transcendent wisdom.'[90]

Padmasambhava

Around the middle of the eighth century, King Trisong Detsen invited the great sage Śāntarakṣita from Nālandā to Tibet to help spread the Dharma. Unable to make much headway among the Tibetans (local demons kept destroying Samye, the monastery he was trying to build), Śāntarakṣita suggested the king invite Padmasambhava, the great Tantric master from Urgyen, who alone had the skill to subdue the powerful animist forces that dominated the land. Profoundly skilled in the ways of the mind, Padmasambhava reached into the depths and learned the root names of the dark forces at work within the Tibetan psyche. He brought them under control and 'converted' them to the Dharma, thenceforth to function as Dharma protectors in a land where the teachings subsequently thrived.

Throughout the Himalayan region, where he is known as Guru Rimpoche, 'Greatly Precious Guru', Padmasambhava has long been widely revered, especially among the Nyingmapa, who consider him to have been a second Buddha.

One of Padmasambhava's chief disciples was his consort Yeshe Tsogyal, formerly a wife of King Trisong Detsen. She is credited with the composition of a record of his life – the *Padma bKa'i Thang Yig*, or 'Life and Liberation of Padmasambhava'.[91] Here we learn that Padmasambhava first appeared in the land of Uḍḍiyāna (Urgyen in Tibetan), a place now thought to be the Swat Valley in Pakistan.

But Uḍḍiyāna is also a mythical realm, existing beyond space and time. There, the Bodhisattva Avalokiteśvara, seeing that Uḍḍiyāna was suffering from famine and drought, appealed to the Buddha Amitābha for help. Amitābha sent out a beam of red light from his tongue. This struck a lake, where a lotus flower opened. From his heart he projected the mystical syllable *hrīḥ*, which appeared as a golden vajra in the centre of the lotus. This transformed into an eight-year-old boy enveloped in an

Teachers of Enlightenment

aura of rainbow light. Thus Padmasambhava, the 'Lotus Born', appeared. Rain poured down and the drought and famine were dispelled.

The king of Uḍḍiyāna adopted the boy, groomed him for succession, and arranged for his marriage to a royal princess, but, weary of the world, the young man renounced his home and kingdom. As he was about to leave he was accused of killing the wife and son of a minister, and banished from the kingdom to the Cemetery of Chilly Grove:

> Then having hastened to the land of Pañcāla, the Prince
> dismounted from the marvellous horse and sat down in the
> cavern where the Precepts of India are guarded.
>
> After the ritual opening of the mandala of the Diamond
> Plane, at the end of seven days of adjuration he attained the
> perfect state.
>
> The host of the gods of serenity, like the iridescent arch of
> the sky, held up to the Elect a supernatural mirror.
>
> Seeing his face, he obtained both the mighty and common
> Attainments, and became the Knowledge of Life Receptacle
> exempt from birth and death.[92]

Having attained to Awakening, Padma remained in the cemetery for five years, teaching the Dharma to the crowd of *ḍākinīs*:

> There are to be seen countless ḍākinīs:
> some of them have eyes that dart out sun rays;
> others give rise to thunderclaps and ride water buffaloes;
> others hold sabres and have eyes which inflict harm;
> others wear death's heads one above the other and ride tigers;
> others wear corpses and ride lions;
> others eat entrails and ride garuḍas;
> others have flaming lances and ride jackals;
> others, five-faced, are steeped in a lake of blood;
> others in their numberless hands
> carry many generations of living beings;
> others carry in their hands their own heads which they have
> severed;

others carry in their hands their own hearts which they have
      torn out;
there are others who have made gaping wounds in their own
      bodies
and who empty out and devour their own intestines and
      entrails;
there are others who hide and yet reveal their male or female
      sexual organs,
riding horses, bulls, elephants.[93]

Fearless in the face of death, Padma now wandered throughout
India, meditating in cremation grounds and learning all he could
of philosophy, astrology, healing, poetics, and all the other arts
and sciences. Soon mastering the Buddhist canon, he was initiated
into the secret doctrines of the Tantra and, outwardly appearing
as a shaven-headed, yellow-robed monk, he lived inwardly within
luminous Tantric mandalas, consorting with ḍākinīs.

Eventually he returned to Uḍḍiyāna with his consort, princess
Mandāravā. Recognized by the king and ministers, he was
condemned to be burned alive. For three weeks smoke billowed
from the pyre, but when the king went to inspect the site he saw,
not a smouldering pyre, but a vast lake with Padmasambhava
and Mandāravā dancing in union on a giant lotus flower. The
king begged Padmasambhava to teach him the Dharma, and
Padma stayed in Uḍḍiyāna for thirteen years before resuming
his itinerant way of life, finally settling in Bodh Gaya. It was here
that he received Trisong Detsen's invitation to help Śāntarakṣita
in Tibet. Upon Padma's arrival, the king and his courtiers went
out to meet the Guru:

Padma, the Great One from Uḍḍiyāna, reflected:
'I was not born from a womb; I was born by apparition;
the king was born from a womb and so by birth I am the
      greater.
At this instant the Law of Uḍḍiyāna lays hold on his kingdom.
This king of defiled Tibet is great through his paternal lineage.
But who are we, he and I? Plunged in darkness is his mind;
I am learned in the five realms of knowledge,

Teachers of Enlightenment

Buddha in a single lifetime, exempt from birth and death.
It is out of necessity that he invites me here.
Formerly this king bowed down before me.
Shall I or shall I not return his bow?
If yes, the majesty of the Doctrine will be slighted.
If no, since he is the king, he will be angered.
Yet, however great he be, bow down I cannot.'

And King Trisong Detsen thought to himself:
'I am sovereign over all the black heads of Tibet.
The Bodhisattva Abbot has already made obeisance to me –
the Guru must prostrate himself as well.'
So, loath to extend the first greeting, he stood there hesitant.

Now the Guru sang his greatness and nobility:
'The Buddhas of the Three Times passed through the gate of
    the womb.
Theirs are knowledge and merit, heaped up thrice
    innumerable,
but I am the Buddha Padma Jungnay, Sprung from the Lotus.
Mine are the counselings which pierce the lofty concepts of
    the Dharma;
I possess the precepts of the Tantric Scriptures;
I explain exhaustively, clearly distinguishing all the
    Vehicles....

I am Padmasambhava the Little One.
Mine are the counselings of the ecstasy of the Doctrine that
    rouses from sleep.
While in the three realms the transitory being dies,
I evoke that glorious Yoga, Receptacle of the Knowledge of Life.

I am Padmasambhava the Deathless.
Mine are the counselings for the diamond life of the Doctrine.
I am not dependent upon the four external elements,
nor do I set up a dwelling for the internal body of flesh and
    blood.

I am Padmasambhava the Unborn.
Mine are the counselings of the Great Seal of the Doctrine.

My diamond body will never wane,
for my mind, in Awakening, is perennial lucidity.

I am Padmasambhava the Ageless.
Mine are the counselings of the Dharma that assuages the
   suffering
of those whose vitality yields to sickness,
whose splendid appearance has been struck down by
   circumstance.

I am Padmasambhava Who Knows No Sickness.
The counselings of the Great Perfection of the Dharma are mine.

And you, king of barbarian Tibet,
king of the country without virtue,
uncouth men and ogres surround you.
You rely upon famine's serfs,
and neither joy nor good humor are yours.
As for your queens, they are rākṣasī in human shape.
Beautiful purple ghouls surround them,
sandalwood, turquoise, and gold adorn them;
but they have no hearts and no minds.

You are king, your lungs swell.
Great is your power, your liver is well-satisfied.
Sceptre in hand and haughty, you stand high.
But I, Sire, will not bow down before you.
And yet, in accordance with my conjoined vows,
having come to the heart of Tibet, here I stay.
Great king, witness, have I come?'

He spoke, turned his hands and, springing up from his finger
a miraculous flame seared the king's garments.
King, ministers, courtiers could not withstand him.
Bowing in unison, they prostrated themselves as though swept
   by a scythe.[94]

Padma then journeyed throughout Tibet, subduing local deities
and binding them by oath to protect and serve the Dharma. At
Samye Monastery he co-opted the local demons as night-time

labourers, and arranged that the king of the Nāgas contribute towards the cost of the monastery:

Then the Guru said....
'No oath yet binds the minds of the nāgas: the lot of them
rise up in hostility, and misunderstanding is breaking out.'
The king deplored Padma's insistence on the nāgas' submission:
'The monastery is scarcely half done
and the royal resources are at an end. What can we do?'
Then the Guru said, 'There is a way.
Let the king of men Trisong Detsen
ally himself with the king of the nāgas!
I will make the liaison between you.'

The Guru led him to the shores of the great lake of Malgro
and hid the king, ministers, and subjects in one of the two valleys.
He raised near the lake a silken tent
and stayed there three days in meditation.
In the morning a marvelous woman appeared:
'What has the Guru come to do at the lake?'
'Let the king of men Trisong Detsen
and the nāga king Nanda make an alliance.
The king's monastery is not completed.
Let the nāgas lend their assistance!'
The message having been transmitted,
a great serpent appeared in the morning two days later
and stirred up the water; gold flooded all the shores.
The sovereign hailed the subjects and asked them to collect it.[95]

The old animist culture of Tibet was not destroyed by Padma-sambhava, but transformed by linking it to a Dharmic aspiration for Enlightenment. Once Samye was completed, in 779 CE, Śāntarakṣita ordained the first seven bhikṣus in Tibet and established a monastic sangha. Then he and Padmasambhava oversaw the start of the huge task of translating the entire Buddhist canon from Sanskrit and Chinese into Tibetan.

Seeing that people were not yet ready for some of the practices and doctrines that he wished to impart, Padma inscribed esoteric texts in a terse, densely encoded script which he hid in temples, caves, and mountain crevices, predicting that his disciples would return in future lives to reveal these '*terma*' teachings when the time was ripe.

Despite occasional opposition from reform movements, the Nyingma tradition of unconventional, often non-monastic masters that Padmasambhava is credited with having established has flourished throughout the Himalayan region for twelve centuries. His devotees continue to call upon the Greatly Precious Guru:

> Hüm
> To the north-west of the land of Urgyen
> On the calyx of a lotus flower
> Oh wondrous, the highest siddhi has been attained,
> Thus Padmasambhava declares.
> Oh thou who art encircled with an entourage of ḍākinīs
> Following thy example will I work.
> Thou must come here to give me thy blessing.

Tsongkhapa

Tsongkhapa's birth, in eastern Tibet in 1357, was accompanied by auspicious portents and prophetic dreams. From an early age he was recognized as a spiritual genius, receiving the lay precepts from the fourth Karmapa at the age of three! At sixteen he left his remote homeland on the Chinese border and travelled to the spiritual heartland of central Tibet. There he spent the remaining forty-six years of his life, wandering, studying with great lamas, writing, debating, retreating to caves for prolonged meditation, and founding monasteries.

The compilation of the Tibetan Buddhist canon had just been finalized by Butön. There had been a great need to establish some order upon the enormous collection of texts that had been brought to Tibet over the previous six centuries, and the Tibetans devised an arrangement which bore little resemblance to the Indian *Tripiṭaka*. They divided the material into those works they thought to be the genuine word of the Buddha – the *kangyur* or ' translated word' – and those which were thought to be commentarial – the *tengyur* or 'translated treatises'.

In similar fashion, Tsongkhapa sought to reform the Dharma practice of Tibet. Identifying himself with the purity of Atiśa's original Kadam order, he emphasized to monks the importance of adherence to the *vinaya*, forbidding among other things the practice of father–son inheritance within monasteries, and he excluded all those practices that appeared to have no clear Indian Buddhist precedent. In his writing he stressed how the basic doctrines of the sūtra tradition were indispensable prerequisites for the more advanced practices of the Tantra. Philosophically, he criticized those who treated the relative world as a mere illusion that obscured the ultimate truth of reality. Instead, he stressed the identity of the myriad phenomena of the world with their ultimate truth:

> ... Whoever could find
> Anything even more wonderful,
> To praise You with, O Protector,
> Than the proclamation of relativity? [i.e. dependent
>   origination]
>
> 'Whatever depends on conditions,
> That is empty of intrinsic reality!'
> What method of good instruction is there,
> More marvellous than this discovery?
>
> Of course the naive can seize upon it
> As just confirming their extremist chains,
> But the wise find that very (relativity)
> The way to cut the whole net of fabrications.[96]

In other words, you miss the point of the Buddha's teaching if you imagine the relative world to be somehow separate from ultimate reality.

In the final ten years of his life, from 1409 to 1419, Tsongkhapa engaged in a continuous round of intensive activity. He established three new monasteries for the Gelug Order – which reveres him as its founder – Ganden, Drepung, and Sera, and many more were to follow. He instituted the annual Monlam prayer festival at Lhasa and threw himself into writing and teaching, and composed, among many other texts, an exhaustive *lam rim* – a text that describes the stages of the path, based on Atiśa's compendious *Bodhipathapradīpa*.

In the course of time the main Gelug monasteries grew to become the largest such institutions in the world, resembling small towns, with a combined population of over 20,000 monks. Gelug influence grew apace and, approximately 150 years after Tsongkhapa's death, the fifth Gelug Dalai Lama came to rule Tibet.

Tsongkhapa's interpretations of the teaching are among the most influential within the overall framework of Tibetan Buddhism. His root text on the *Three Principles of the Path* – renunciation, bodhicitta, and right view – is a seminal text of the Gelug School:

I bow down to the venerable lamas.

I will explain as well as I am able
The essence of all the teachings of the Conqueror,
The path praised by the Conqueror's offspring,
The entrance for the fortunate ones who desire liberation.

Listen with clear minds, you fortunate ones
Who direct your minds to the path pleasing to Buddha,
Who strive to make good use of leisure and opportunity
And are not attached to the joys of saṃsāra.

Those with bodies are bound by the craving for existence.
Without pure renunciation, there is no way to still
Attraction to the pleasures of saṃsāra.
Thus, from the outset seek renunciation.

Leisure and opportunity are difficult to find.
There is no time to waste: reverse attraction to this life.
Reverse attraction to future lives: think repeatedly
Of the infallible effects of karma and the misery of this world.

Contemplating this, when you do not for an instant
Wish the pleasures of saṃsāra,
And day and night remain intent on liberation,
You have then produced renunciation.

Renunciation without pure bodhi-mind
Does not bring forth the perfect bliss
Of unsurpassed enlightenment;
Therefore, Bodhisattvas generate excellent bodhi-mind.

Swept by the current of the four powerful rivers,
Tied by strong bonds of karma, so hard to undo,
Caught in the iron net of self-grasping,
Completely enveloped by the darkness of ignorance,

Born and reborn in boundless saṃsāra,
Carelessly tormented by the three miseries –
All beings, your mothers, are in this condition.
Think of them and generate bodhi-mind.

Though you practice renunciation and bodhi-mind,
Without wisdom, the realization of voidness,
You cannot cut the root of saṃsāra.
Therefore, strive to understand dependent origination.

One who sees the infallible cause and effect
Of all phenomena in saṃsāra and nirvāṇa,
And destroys all false perceptions,
Has entered the path that pleases the Buddha.

Appearances are infallible dependent origination;
Voidness is free of assertions (of existence or non-existence).
As long as these two understandings are seen as separate,
One has not yet realized the intent of the Buddha.

When these two realizations are simultaneous and concurrent,
From a mere sight of infallible dependent origination
Comes certain knowledge that completely destroys all modes
    of mental grasping.
At that time the analysis of the profound view is complete.

Appearances clear away the extreme of existence;
Voidness clears away the extreme of non-existence.
When you understand the arising of cause and effect from the
    viewpoint of voidness,
You are not captivated by either extreme view.

Son, when you realize the keys
Of the three principles of the path,
Depend on solitude and strong effort,
And quickly reach the final goal![97]

Huineng, on the left, is sitting beside a rice pestle and mortar. Along with Zhiyi, in the centre, he is seated in meditation. Xuanzang translates at his desk.

China

Huineng

The author of the only Chinese work ever to be included in the *Tripiṭaka* and thus designated a *sūtra* (a word traditionally reserved for the discourses of a Buddha), Huineng, who lived between 638 and 713 CE, is revered by all the Chan and Zen Buddhist schools. Known as the sixth patriarch of Chan Buddhism, he is perhaps more properly regarded as the founder of that tradition, for he was the first to give Chan, which before him had been strongly marked by traditional Indian Buddhism, a truly Chinese stamp.

The *Sūtra of Huineng*, also known as the *Platform Sūtra*, begins autobiographically. Huineng, a poor illiterate woodcutter, happened by chance to hear the *Diamond Sūtra* being recited in the local town and immediately became Enlightened. Learning that the reciter lived at the monastery of the fifth patriarch, Huineng went there and was put in the kitchen to pound rice. One day, in order to test his followers and find a successor, the fifth patriarch asked the monks to compose a verse that set out their understanding of Chan. Shenxiu, the most intellectually brilliant monk, alone rose to the challenge, writing his stanza, at first anonymously, on a wall. It began by comparing the human body to the Bodhi tree, under which the Buddha had gained Enlightenment:

> Our body is the *bodhi* tree,
> And our mind a mirror bright.
> Carefully wipe them hour by hour,
> And let no dust alight.[98]

Upon hearing the stanza recited, Huineng responded:

There is no *bodhi* tree,
Nor stand of a mirror bright.
Since all is void,
Where can the dust alight?[99]

A passing official wrote this stanza on the wall for him. Reading Huineng's stanza, the fifth patriarch saw at once that he had realized the essence of mind, but he also saw the potential dangers from jealousy should such an apparently simple young man be publicly elevated to the highest position. He rubbed Huineng's stanza off the wall and, secretly appointing him his successor, sent him away into hiding.

Fifteen years later, still in hiding and not yet ordained, Huineng came upon two monks arguing about a banner which was blowing in the wind. 'It's the banner that moves,' said one monk. 'No, it's the wind that moves,' said the other. 'It's the mind that moves,' said Huineng.

When the master of their monastery was told of this, having long heard rumours of the fugitive sixth patriarch, he recognized Huineng for who he was and asked him to be his teacher. Thus began Huineng's career as one of the greatest Chan masters.

The *Sūtra of Huineng* records a number of the Master's teachings on aspects of the path. He commented on many topics – ethics, meditation, and wisdom (of course), but also on the way in which the Dharma was regarded in his time – and made clear, practical distinctions. For example, at that time two schools – that of Huineng of the south and Shenxiu of the north – flourished side by side. These were distinguished by the names Sudden (for the south) and Gradual (for the north). The question of which sect they should follow baffled certain Buddhist scholars of the time. Seeing this, Huineng addressed the assembly as follows:

So far as the Dharma is concerned, there can be only one school. (If a distinction exists) it exists in the fact that the founder of one school is a northern man, while the other is a southerner. While there is only one Dharma, some disciples realize it more quickly than others. The reason why the names *Sudden* and *Gradual* are given is that some disciples are superior to others in mental dispositions. So far as the Dharma is concerned, the distinction of sudden and gradual does not exist.[100]

Just before his death the patriarch spoke as follows:

In parting from you, let me leave you a stanza entitled the Real Buddha of the Essence of Mind. People of future generations who understand its meaning will realize the essence of mind and attain buddhahood. It reads:

The essence of mind, or *tathatā* (suchness), is the real buddha,
While heretical views and the three poisonous elements are
   Māra.
Enlightened by right views, we call forth the buddha within us.
When our nature is dominated by the three poisonous elements
We are said to be possessed by Māra;
But when right views eliminate from our mind these poisonous
   elements
Māra will be transformed into a real buddha....
When our temperament is such that we are no longer the slaves
   of the five sense objects,
And when we have realized the essence of mind even for one
   moment only, then truth is known to us....
I have hereby left to posterity the teaching of the Sudden school
For the salvation of all sentient beings who care to practise it.
Hear me, future disciples!
Your time will have been badly wasted if you neglect to put this
   teaching into practice.

Having recited the stanza, he added, 'Take good care of yourselves. After my passing away, do not follow the worldly tradition and cry or lament. Neither should messages of condolence be accepted, nor mourning be worn. These things are contrary to the orthodox teaching, and he who does them is not my disciple. What you should do is to know your own mind and realize your own buddha-nature,...

Then he uttered another stanza:

Imperturbable and serene, the ideal man practises no virtue.
Self-possessed and dispassionate, he commits no sin.
Calm and silent, he gives up seeing and hearing.
Even and upright, his mind abides nowhere.

Having uttered the stanza, he sat reverently until the third watch of the night. Then he said abruptly to his disciples, 'I am going now,' and in a sudden passed away. A peculiar fragrance pervaded his room, and a lunar rainbow appeared, which seemed to join up earth and sky. The trees in the wood turned white, and birds and beasts cried mournfully.[101]

Zhiyi

Zhiyi was the first person in the history of Chinese Buddhism to set out a complete, systematic, and critical classification of the Buddhist teaching. He founded the Tiantai School, which grew to become the leading Buddhist sect in China. Exported to Japan in the ninth century, it thrived there as the Tendai School.

Although the Tiantai School considers Zhiyi its fourth patriarch, he was, historically speaking, their founder, because it was he who systematized the doctrines of that school and brought them to completion. He was born in 538, his father a prominent government official and his mother a devout Buddhist. When he was seven, we are told, he visited a temple and astounded the monks by memorizing the twenty-fifth chapter of the *Lotus Sūtra*, the chapter dealing with the Bodhisattva Avalokiteśvara, after hearing it only once. This was the first major turning point of his life for, even at such a tender age, he had apparently grasped, in one flash of intuition, its full meaning.

Zhiyi would have received the usual education for members of his class – a thorough grounding in the Confucian classics and the texts of Taoism, as well as the reading and writing of poetry and high literature. His writings show a wide acquaintance with secular as well as religious literature, and he was able to express himself not only to the Buddhist monks of his time, but to society in general.

Those times were highly disordered, and the Liang dynasty, beset by rebellion and turmoil, came to an end in 557. The effects of misrule were everywhere apparent. Shifts in the political situation deprived Zhiyi's family of its former power and status. Then his parents died. Finally, seeing a great library razed to the ground, he became painfully aware of the impermanence of all mundane things and resolved to leave the household life. At the age of 17 he became a monk and familiarized himself with all the prevailing Mahāyāna doctrines.

When he was 23, he finally met his master, Huisi, who was then living in seclusion. Aware of Huisi's reputation as a teacher of rare ability and understanding, Zhiyi made the dangerous journey into a remote and war-torn region to seek him out, and eventually found him living on Mount Ta-Su.

Zhiyi stayed with Huisi for seven years, studying the *Lotus Sūtra* with him and deepening his realization. Huisi, traditionally regarded as the third patriarch of the Tiantai, passed on to Zhiyi the doctrine of the 'triple truth' that had first been expounded by Huiwen, the second patriarch. This doctrine is derived from Nāgārjuna's emphasis on the emptiness of conditioned phenomena – indeed, the Tiantai regard Nāgārjuna as their first patriarch.

The first truth states that all phenomena, possessing no independent reality, are empty. The second truth maintains that phenomena nevertheless do have an apparent existence, limited in time. The third truth, which stands above the first two and includes them, is the truth of 'the middle' and is equated with *tathatā* – 'suchness', 'just this' – the true state of things that is not found outside of phenomena. The ever-changing phenomenal world is identical with the world as it really is. The whole and all its parts are one. All things are so merged with one another that each contains all the others.

In 557 Zhiyi left Huisi and Mount Dasu and made his way to Jiankang, present-day Nanjing, which then served as the capital of the Chen dynasty. Here, his reputation as a teacher grew rapidly, and he was called upon to expound the Dharma not only to his fellow monks, but also to members of the royal court as well as to ordinary men and women.

Despite these outward signs of success, Zhiyi felt that too few of his followers were able to grasp the true significance of his doctrines and, in 575, at the age of 37, he abruptly left Jiankang and made his way south to Mount Tiantai on the sea-coast of Zhejiang Province. In this remote mountain region, famed for its beautiful rugged scenery, Zhiyi settled down to practise. Here, his fame as a teacher became so great that the reigning emperor of the Chen dynasty decreed that the revenue from an entire district in the vicinity of the mountain be devoted to his upkeep and that of his community, the nascent Tiantai School, which based its teachings mainly on the *Lotus Sūtra*.

Troubled by the numerous apparent contradictions and doctrinal differences in the scriptures that had been translated into Chinese by that time, Zhiyi embarked on an immense programme of systemization. He regarded all the chief varieties of Buddhist doctrine as true and assumed they had all been present in the mind of Śākyamuni from the time of his Enlightenment. Taking up an idea from the *Lotus Sūtra*, he taught that the Buddha had unfolded his teachings gradually, in five periods, taking into account the capacity of his listeners: as they progressed spiritually, they could absorb progressively more profound doctrines. In the fifth and final period the Buddha preached the *Lotus Sūtra*, which Zhiyi helped to establish as the most popular scripture of eastern Asia. The system he developed was filled with encyclopaedic detail, its scholarship was widely respected, and it attracted much popular support.

For Zhiyi, study and meditation were *both* indispensable. He criticized those who indulged in a purely intellectualized Buddhism as well as those who practised without a basis of understanding. This attitude found expression in his developed teaching on 'calm and insight' – *zhiguan*, or *śamatha/vipaśyanā* – which remains one of the most widespread modes of meditation practice in Chinese and Japanese Buddhism.

This is the introduction to *zhiguan* from his *Tongmeng zhiguan* or 'Dhyāna for Beginners' :

'Avoid all evil, cherish all goodness, keep the mind pure. This is the teaching of Buddha.'

Teachers of Enlightenment

There are many different paths to Nirvana, but the most important one for us is the path of *Dhyāna*. Dhyāna is the practice of mind-control by which we stop all thinking and seek to realize Truth in its essence. That is, it is the practice of 'stopping and realizing'. If we cease all discriminative thought it will keep us from the further accumulation of error, while the practice of realizing will clear away delusions. Stopping is a refreshment of the lower consciousness, while realizing may be compared to a golden spade that opens up a treasury of transcendental wealth. Stopping is an entrance into the wonderful silence and peacefulness of potentiality (*dhyāna-samāpatti*); while realizing is an entrance into the riches of intuition and transcendental intelligence (*mati-prajñā*). As one advances along this path, he comes into full possession of all means for enriching himself and for benefiting others....

We may liken these two powers, *samāpatti* and *prajñā*, to the wheels of a chariot and the wings of an eagle. If a follower has only one, he is led into an unbalanced life.... Though the errors eventuating from unbalance may differ from the errors of ignorance, they alike lead a person to the same false views. This explains clearly that if one is to attain Supreme Perfect Wisdom in an immediate way, he must hold the two powers in equal balance: he must be both prepared and ready....

Those who are really seeking Truth, but are more advanced, should not look upon this book with contempt because it is written simply and for beginners. They should be humble and prudent because of the difficulties they will encounter when they come to its practice. It is possible that some will be able to digest its teachings with great ease and, in the twinkle of an eye, their hindrances will be abolished and their intelligence will be boundlessly developed and so will their supernormal understanding, also. But if you just read over the literal meaning and do not enter into its significance, you will not be able to find your way to enlightenment – the reading will be just a waste of time. Such a reader will be likened to a poor man who spends his time in counting another man's treasures and being no richer for it himself.[102]

Zhiyi was also a great organizer, builder, and fund-raiser. He is credited with having established thirty-five monasteries and to have funded the transcription into Chinese of fifteen complete volumes of the *Tripiṭaka*. He spent much of his time travelling and teaching, all the time maintaining his relations with the royal court. In 597 the emperor invited Zhiyi to visit him, but en route Zhiyi fell ill. Aware of the approach of death, he offered part of his belongings to an image of Maitreya. Soon after that he died, while invoking the Buddha Amitābha.

Xuanzang

Xuanzang, who lived from about 600 to 664 CE, is famed as a pilgrim, adventurer, scholar, translator, and teacher. In quest of teachings, he made a long and dangerous pilgrimage to India, which he recorded in great detail. Returning to China, he played an important part in the translation of Buddhist texts and terminology into Chinese, clearing up much that had previously been obscure and contradictory. His definitive commentary on one of Vasubandhu's key works became the root text of the Faxiang School that he cofounded.

The sixteenth-century Chinese novel, *The Journey to the West*, by Wu Cheng'en,[103] a version of which is known in the West as *Monkey*, is based on Xuanzang's experiences on his pilgrimage. There, he appears as the hero-monk Tripitaka.

Born into a family in which there had been scholars for generations, Xuanzang received a classical Confucian education in his youth, but under the influence of an older brother he became interested in the Buddhist scriptures and soon converted to Buddhism. He travelled with his brother to Chang'an and then to Sichuan to escape the political turmoil that gripped China at that time. While in Sichuan, he began to study Buddhist philosophy – especially the texts of the Yogācāra – but he was perplexed by apparent inconsistencies in the texts and by the fact that his various teachers interpreted these works differently. He therefore resolved to go to India, to study at the source of Buddhist knowledge.

In 629 he petitioned the court for a permit to travel, and on being refused he left the country by stealth and began his great adventure. His journey nearly ended as soon as it began. First, his guide tried to murder him – which he avoided by waking up just in time – and then he got lost in the trackless desert, escaping only after calling on Avalokiteśvara for help. His first major stop was Turfan, where the king, greatly impressed by his wisdom, would not allow him to leave. Xuanzang only managed to persuade the king to let him go by threatening a hunger strike, but once the king had consented to the pilgrim's departure, he made all the necessary arrangements to facilitate his travels through Central Asia, providing letters of introduction to various princes along the way.

He travelled north of the Taklamakan Desert, via the oasis centres of Karashar, Tashkent, and Samarkand, into Bactria. Crossing the Hindukush Mountains into Kapga, he descended from the Iranian plateau to the milder region of Nagarahāra. Then, having entered Gāndhāra, he visited Peshawar and Taxila, and proceeded to Kashmir, where he studied for two years.

In 633 he decided it was time to visit the holy land of Buddhism. Bandits captured his party as they were sailing down the Ganges, and, pleased by his exotic appearance, they wanted to offer Xuanzang as a human sacrifice. Xuanzang replied, 'If this dirty and contemptible body could fulfil your purpose, then I would not dare to begrudge it. But I have come from far away to pay my respects to the Bodhi tree, the Buddha images, and the Vulture's Peak, as well as to seek for the Dharma. These purposes have not yet been accomplished. If you kill me now, I am afraid it may not go well with you.' The bandits were completely unabashed by this, so Xuanzang asked for a few moments of calm in order to pray to Maitreya. As he was praying, he entered deeply into meditation. Suddenly a violent wind arose and terrified the bandits, and they called out desperately to Xuanzang in his meditation, begging his forgiveness.

Xuanzang then proceeded as rapidly as possible to the sacred places: Śrāvastī, Kapilavastu, Kuśinagara, Benares, Vaiśālī, Pāṭaliputra, and finally Bodh Gaya. After this he made his way to Nālandā to study the Vijñānavāda doctrines with Śīlabhadra, the famous abbot of the monastery, who was then already 106 years old. He stayed at Nālandā for fifteen months, perfecting his knowledge of Buddhist philosophy and Sanskrit, then, taking to the road again, he went down the east coast to South India, hoping to go from there to Ceylon. Civil strife on the island, however, thwarted this plan, so he started north again, up the west coast to the Gujarat peninsula. From there he returned to Nālandā for a second stay, this time concentrating on Indian philosophy.

Xuanzang's reputation was so great in India that many rulers wanted to meet and to honour him. One of these was Bhaskaravarman Kumara, the king of Assam, whom Xuanzang visited. Then they both travelled together to call on Harsha, the great emperor of northern India. The emperor, having heard of the arrival of the famous Chinese monk, hurried over to pay his respects, bowing to the ground and kissing Xuanzang's feet. He then convened a grand assembly and debate, 'to dissipate the blindness of the Hīnayāna and to shatter the pride of the Brahmins', as he put it. For eighteen days the contestants debated, but in the end Xuanzang emerged triumphant over all.

After this, Xuanzang made preparations to return to China, receiving valuable assistance from Harsha, who provided him with escorts and loaded him with gifts. This time he took the southern route across Central Asia, finally arriving back in the T 'ang capital in 645. Although he had been away for sixteen years, his great reputation had preceded him and the tumultuous welcome he received at the capital must have recalled memories of the way he had originally stolen across the border, travelling only by night for fear of detection by the imperial guards stationed at the passes.

A few days after his arrival, Xuanzang had an audience with the emperor, who questioned him about the climate, products, peoples, and manners of the countries he had visited. The emperor was so pleased with the information he received that he wanted the pilgrim to take some official post, but Xuanzang preferred to remain a monk and dedicated the remainder of his life to the task of translating the rich store of sūtras he had brought back with him.

It is said that he carried back to China 657 works packed in 520 cases. Devoting himself to literary work, Xuanzang completed 73 translations, including some of the most important Mahāyāna sūtras, to a very high level of literacy, and played a large part in the vital task of creating an adequate Buddhist terminology in Chinese.

Teachers of Enlightenment

His *Datang Xiyu Ji*, or 'Records of the Western Regions', has been of great value to historians and archaeologists for the data it contains. Here is his description of Nālandā, as he then found it:

> The priests, to the number of several thousands, are men of the highest ability and talent. Their distinction is very great at the present time, and there are many hundreds whose fame has rapidly spread through distant regions. Their conduct is pure and unblamable. They follow in sincerity the precepts of the moral law. The rules of this convent are severe, and all the priests are bound to observe them. The countries of India respect them and follow them. The day is not sufficient for asking and answering profound questions. From morning till night they engage in discussion; the old and the young mutually help one another. Those who cannot discuss questions out of the *Tripiṭaka* are little esteemed, and are obliged to hide themselves for shame. Learned men from different cities, on this account, who desire to acquire quickly a renown in discussion, come here in multitudes to settle their doubts, and then the streams (of their wisdom) spread far and wide. For this reason some persons usurp the name (of Nālandā students), and in going to and fro receive honour in consequence. If men of other quarters desire to enter and take part in the discussions, the keeper of the gate proposes some hard questions; many are unable to answer, and retire. One must have studied deeply both old and new (books) before getting admission.[104]

After praising the qualities of several of Nālandā's alumni – Dharmapāla, Candrapāla, Guṇamati, Sthiramati, Prabhāmitra, Jinamitra, Jñānacandra, Śīghrabuddha, Śīlabhadra, and others – Xuanzang continues:

> The sacred relics on the four sides of the convent are hundreds in number. For brevity's sake we will recount two or three. On the western side of the *saṅghārāma*, at no great distance, is a *vihāra*. Here the Tathāgata in old days stopped for three

months and largely expounded the excellent law for the good of the Devas.

To the south 100 paces or so is a small *stūpa*. This is the place where a Bhikṣu from a distant region saw Buddha. Formerly there was a Bhikṣu who came from a distant region. Arriving at this spot, he met the multitude of disciples accompanying Buddha, and was affected inwardly with a feeling of reverence, and so prostrated himself on the ground, at the same time uttering a strong desire that he might obtain the position of a Cakravartī monarch. Tathāgata having seen him, spoke to his followers thus: 'That Bhikṣu ought much to be pitied. The power (character) of his religious merit is deep and distant; his faith is strong. If he were to seek the fruit of Buddha, not long hence he would obtain it; but now that he has earnestly prayed to become a Cakravartī king, he will in future ages receive this reward: as many grains of dust as there are from the spot where he has thrown himself on the earth down to the very middle of the gold wheel, so many Cakravartī kings will there be for reward; but having fixed his mind on earthly joys, the fruit of holiness is far off.'

On this southern side is a standing figure of Guanzizai (Avalokiteśvara) Bodhisattva. Sometimes he is seen holding a vessel of perfume going to the *vihāra* of Buddha and turning round to the right.

To the south of this statue is a *stūpa*, in which are remains of Buddha's hair and nails cut during three months. Those persons afflicted with children's complaints, coming here and turning round religiously, are mostly healed.

To the west of this, outside the wall, and by the side of a tank, is a *stūpa*. This is where a heretic, holding a sparrow in his hand, asked Buddha questions relating to death and birth.

To the south-east about 50 paces, within the walls, is an extraordinary tree, about eight or nine feet in height, of which the trunk is twofold. When Tathāgata of old time was in the world, he flung his tooth-cleaner on the ground here, where it took root. Although many months and years have elapsed since then, the tree neither decreases nor increases.[105]

Together with his pupil Kuiji, Xuanzang founded the Faxiang, or 'Marks of Existence', School of Chinese Buddhism, which continued to develop the teachings of the Yogācāra found in the writings of Asaṅga and Vasubandhu. The root text of this school is Xuanzang's *Cheng weishi lun* – 'Proof of Nothing-But-Cognition' – a compilation, with commentary, of ten previous commentaries on Vasubandhu's *Thirty Verses*.

The Faxiang approach stresses the fact that everything is only ideation, and that the 'external world' posses no independent reality. Things exist only in so far as they are objects of consciousness.

The quotation below, taken from an early section of the *Cheng weishi lun*, may give some sense of the intricacies of the argument that follows it. Here, *ātman* is defined as assuming the form of sentient beings, living things, highly realized persons, and so on. *Dharmas*, on the other hand, appear in the form of qualities, substances, actions, skandhas, sense-spheres, planes of existence, and so on:

> Although the phenomena of Atman and dharmas lie within the consciousness, yet, because of wrong mental discrimination or particularization, they are taken to be external objects. That is why all sentient beings, since before the beginning of time, have conceived them as real Atman and real dharmas.

THE DREAM ANALOGY

> An analogy is that of a man in a dream, who, under the influence of that dream, in which his mind produces what seem to be external objects of all sorts, believes that these images are real external objects.

THE TWO TRUTHS: RELATIVE AND ABSOLUTE

> What the ignorant imagine to be a 'real' Atman and 'real' dharmas are devoid of all objective existence. They are simply fictitious constructions based on erroneous opinions and conceptions. Hence we say that they are 'fictitious constructions' (i.e., relative truths).

Thus, the seeming Atman and the seeming dharmas which evolve out of internal consciousness, although they exist as a product of various causes, are not really of the nature of a real Atman and real dharmas, despite their semblance. This, then, is the reason for calling them 'fictitious constructions'.

In other words, what we take to be external objects are the result of our erroneous opinions, and do not 'exist' in the same way as consciousness does; (that is to say, external objects are illusory (parikalpita)).

On the other hand, internal consciousness, born by reason of causes and conditions, and responsible for the appearance of external objects, is not, in its essential nature, non-existent in the same way as are external objects; (it is paratantra). Thus, we exclude the two heterodox doctrines, namely, that which affirms the additional reality of objects apart from the mind and that which, because it wrongly believes in 'voidness' , sets aside consciousness itself as non-existent, thus reducing everything to voidness or emptiness.

External objects, since they are mere fictitious constructions arising from internal consciousness, exist purely from a worldly point of view. On the other hand, inasmuch as consciousness is the essential basis from which false appearances of an external world spring, it really exists.

OBJECTION ANSWERED

How do we know that in reality there is no external sphere of objects, but only internal consciousness which brings forth what seem to be real external spheres of objects?

We know this because the existence of a real Atman or real dharmas cannot be affirmed beyond doubt.

Let us now examine, in proper sequence, the different ways of conceiving Atman and dharmas.[106]

This subtle philosophy, abstruse in its terminology and detailed in its analysis of mind and the senses, was perhaps too foreign to the Chinese culture of its day, and with the passing of the two masters the Faxiang School rapidly declined. When Xuanzang died, in 664, the emperor cancelled his audiences for three days out of veneration and respect. As Tripitaka, the adventurous pilgrim monk in *The Journey to the West*, Xuanzang lives on in the popular Chinese imagination – an archetype of wise heroism.

Hakuin, on the left, grasps his kyōsaku, or 'wake-up' stick. Kūkai holds a vajra and rosary, Dōgen teaches the Dharma, and Shinran holds up his rosary.

Japan

Hakuin

Zen Buddhism in Japan has long been divided into two principal schools: the Sōtō School, founded by Dōgen, and the Rinzai, which had preceded it. Rinzai originated with Linji, a great Chinese master of the ninth century, and had been brought to Japan by Eisai Zenji in the twelfth century.

Whereas Sōtō Zen placed a primary emphasis on *zazen*, Rinzai tended to focus on the contemplation of *kōans* as the primary means of training. Essential to a *kōan* is paradox – it is a proposition or question that can be resolved only by going beyond logic and leaping to another level of comprehension.

Born into a family of commoners in eastern Japan in 1689, Hakuin, a frail and sensitive teenager, persuaded his parents to allow him to become a monk at fifteen. He had, from an early age, an overwhelming fear of the hells, which pushed him ever deeper into spiritual practice. At first his spiritual quest was filled with doubts, disappointments, and even breakdowns but, by studying Zen texts, searching out teachers, and applying himself remorselessly to the *kōans* they set him, he achieved a number of major breakthroughs. After achieving a number of great and small *satoris*, or 'spiritual insights', he came to be famed as a great teacher and used his influence to revitalize the Rinzai tradition to which he belonged, and which by the seventeenth century had degenerated considerably. He condemned, in no uncertain terms, what he saw as laxity, wrong understanding, and wrong practice:

On the day I first committed myself to a life of Zen practice, I pledged to summon all the faith and courage at my command and dedicate myself with steadfast resolve to the pursuit of the Buddha Way. I embarked on a regimen of rigorous austerities, which I continued for several years, pushing myself relentlessly.[107]

Properly undertaken, *kōan* practice propels one into a state of 'Great Doubt'. One's *kōan* then feels 'like a red-hot iron ball stuck in the throat'; you can't swallow it down and you can't vomit it up. One day, while absorbed in just such a state, Hakuin heard the ringing of a temple bell. Suddenly his fears and doubts evaporated and he cried out, 'Wonderful, wonderful! There's no cycle of birth and death! There's no Enlightenment to strive for! The kōans transmitted by the ancients are worthless!'

This experience was so overwhelming that he believed it was unique. 'My pride rose up like a mighty mountain; my arrogance swelled like an ocean wave.' But his master, Dōkyō Etan, seeing the incomplete nature of this breakthrough, would not confirm it as a genuine insight, and subjected Hakuin to further severe training, driving him deeper and deeper to ever more profound realizations. In time, Hakuin became Dōkyō's Dharma successor. He singlehandedly remoulded and revitalized Rinzai in Japan, systematizing the practice of *kōan* contemplation and creating his own famous *kōan*:

If someone claps his hands one hears a sound at once. Listen now to the sound of a single hand![108]

Hakuin travelled the country, lecturing on the sūtras and meeting people individually. He wrote and published many books:

I decided I would be far better off if I followed the parting advice Shōju had given me: to devote my energy to liberating the countless suffering beings of the world by imparting the great gift of the Dharma; to assemble a few select monks capable of passing through the barrier into genuine kenshō; to strive diligently toward creating conditions for the realization of a Buddha-land on earth and, in the process, carry into practice Bodhisattva vows.

When I resolved to embark on this grand and far-reaching program and send a handful of genuine monks out into the world, it was because I wanted to repay the immense debt I owed to the Buddhas and patriarchs.

Little by little, I worked out methods for imparting the Dharma gift. At first, I had only two or three monks here with me. Later, they were joined by others, like attracting like, until eventually their number swelled to more than a hundred and fifty. In recent years, we usually have three hundred monks in residence in and around the temple.

Through all those years, in response to circumstances, in answer to requests, I have travelled extensively, visiting many different provinces, carrying out my mission of imparting the Dharma wherever I went. I don't remember all the temples, monasteries, and laymen's homes I have been to....

At meetings during those visits, I have given Zen lectures (teishō) on a great many texts: four or five times each on the Lotus, Shurangama, and Vimalakīrti Sūtras; six or seven times on the Blue Cliff Record and the Record of Hsü-t'ang; two or three times each on Praise of the True School and the Three Teachings of the Buddha Patriarchs. More times than I can remember on the Kannon Sūtra. In addition, I have lectured on the Record of Lin-chi; Ta-hui's Letters; the Records of Daitō, Fa-yen, Sung-yuan, and Bukkō; the Tsung-ying Verse Collection; the Poems of Cold Mountain; Spurring Students through the Zen Barrier; the Four-Part Collection; Ta-hui's Arsenal; Manjushri's Held-in-Hand Sūtra; The Precious Mirror Samādhi; Dream Words from the Land of Dreams; Poison Stamens in a Thicket of Thorns; the Record of Daiō; The Song of the Mind-King; and others so numerous I can't recall them all.

There is an old saying: 'When a superior man speaks a thousand words, he may make a single mistake. When an inferior man speaks a thousand words, he may achieve a single benefit.' If within this rambling nonsense of mine a single benefit is indeed to be found, it might perhaps serve as a small Dharma gift.

My writing is gross-grained, the strokes of my brush a thick, vulgar chicken-scratch. Both of them are riddled with blunders of various kinds. Characters miswritten. One word mistaken for another. I just scribble it down on the paper, make them a 'fair copy.' They take it and carve it on to wooden blocks and print it off. Altogether I must have written twenty books that way. No matter. Any wise man who claps eyes on them is sure to fling them on the ground in disgust and spew them contemptuously with spit.[109]

Besides being an outstanding Zen master, Hakuin was also an important painter, master of calligraphy, and sculptor, and his ink paintings are among the most renowned works of Zen painting. He stressed three things above all: overriding faith, Great Doubt when contemplating *kōans*, and strong aspiration and perseverance. He also stressed practice in the midst of activity, and daily physical work was an important element in the regime at his monasteries where 'a day without work is a day without food'. In his *Orategama* he wrote:

I am not trying to tell you to discard completely quietistic meditation and to seek specifically for a place of activity in which to carry out your practice. What is most worthy of respect is a pure kōan meditation that neither knows nor is conscious of the two aspects, the quiet and the active. This is why it has been said that the true practicing monk walks but does not know he is walking, sits but does not know he is sitting.

For penetrating to the depths of one's own true self nature, and for attaining a vitality valid on all occasions, nothing can surpass meditation in the midst of activity.[110]

Hakuin was scathing in condemnation of those he called 'the bands of the Unborn Zennists' – 'unborn', because they stressed the teaching that Enlightenment, being immanent in all things, is unborn, unconditioned, and unmade. It cannot be pursued, for there is nothing to pursue. In reality we are all Buddhas already. Hakuin poured contempt on this attitude:

I have a verse that pours scorn on this odious race of pseudopriests:

Earth's vilest thing? From which all men recoil?
Crumbly charcoal? Firewood that's wet? Watered lamp oil?
A cartman? A boatman? A stepmother?
Skunks? Mosquitoes? Lice? Blue flies? Rats? Thieving monks.

Ahh! Monks! Priests! You can't all be thieves, every last one of you. And when I talk about thieving priests, I refer to those 'silent illumination' Zennists who now infest the land.

Where our Zen school is concerned, anyone who achieves kenshō and leaves the house of birth and death is a house-leaver. Not just someone who forsakes the family home and goes off to get his skull shaved. Still, you find people going around making unfounded claims: 'I've left home, I'm a priest. I'm a priest.' If that weren't bad enough, they then proceed to pocket the charity and donations they hoodwink lay-people, the householders, into giving them.[111]

In contrast to this attitude, Hakuin stressed the need for continuous spiritual practice, even after one's first Awakening:

These people ... do not do a single thing. They engage in no act of religious practice; they don't develop a shred of wisdom. They just waste their lives dozing idly away like comatose badgers, useless to their contemporaries while they live, completely forgotten after they die. They aren't capable of leaving behind even a syllable of their own to repay the profound debt they owe to the Buddha patriarchs.

Maintaining come hell or high water, 'We are Buddhas just as we are – plain unvarnished bowls,' they proceed to consume heaping piles of rice day after day. They then disburden themselves of steaming loads of horse flop – great copious pillows of the stuff! That is the sum total of their achievements. They can't help a single person to the other shore of emancipation so as to repay the obligation they owe to their own parents. To them, the Buddhist saying 'If one child leaves home for the priesthood, his kinsmen will be born in the heavenly realms for nine generations' is just so much hogwash.

To them, I say: 'Surely you must know there are fifty-two stages of practice a Bodhisattva passes through in becoming a Buddha, beginning with the arising of the religious mind and ending with the final stages of supreme enlightenment. For some Bodhisattvas, enlightenment comes suddenly; and for some, it is gradual. For some, attainment is complete, and for others, it is partial. If you are right about "being as you are" in this "plain bowl" suchness of yours, then the stages of Bodhisattva practice that were set forth long ago are mistaken. If the stages passed down from the past are correct, then being as you are, like a "plain bowl," is wrong. The Buddha once told his disciples he would rather they be reborn as cankered old foxes than to see them becoming followers of the Two Vehicles [Hinayāna]. But followers of the Two Vehicles are nothing compared to you, you ignorant, shameless, unconscionable, self-indulgent pack of scoundrels!'[112]

Hakuin was the abbot of several Zen monasteries, among them Ryūtaku-ji, which continues to be one of the most important monasteries in Japan. He died in 1769. His *Chant in Praise of Zazen* emphasizes the importance he placed on dedicated sitting practice. It is still regularly intoned in Zen temples in Japan, and is often used in translation in the West:

> All beings are from the very beginning Buddhas.
> It is like water and ice:
> Apart from water, no ice,
> Outside living beings, no Buddhas.
> Not knowing it is near, they seek it afar. What a pity!
> It is like one in the water who cries out for thirst;
> It is like the child of a rich house who has strayed away among
>   the poor.
> The cause of our circling through the six worlds
> Is that we are on the dark paths of ignorance.
> Dark path upon dark path treading,

When shall we escape from birth-and-death?
The Zen meditation of the Mahāyāna
Is beyond all our praise.
Giving and morality and the other perfections,
Taking of the Name, repentance, discipline,
And the many other right actions,
All come back to the practice of meditation.
By the merit of a single sitting
He destroys innumerable accumulated sins.
How should there be wrong paths for him?
The Pure Land paradise is not far.
When in reverence this truth is heard even once,
He who praises it and gladly embraces it has merit without end.
How much more he who turns within
And confirms directly his own nature,
That his own nature is no-nature –
Such has transcended vain words.
The gate opens, and cause and effect are one;
Straight runs the way – not two, not three.
Taking as form the form of no-form,
Going or returning, he is ever at home.
Taking as thought the thought of no-thought,
Singing and dancing, all is the voice of truth.
Wide is the heaven of boundless Samādhi,
Radiant the full moon of the fourfold wisdom.
What remains to be sought? Nirvāṇa is clear before him,
This very place the lotus paradise, this very body the Buddha.[113]

Kūkai

Kūkai, who is also known as Kōbō Daishi, founded the Shingon
School of Japanese Buddhism. Shingon, which literally means
'School of the True Word', i.e. the Mantra School, is an esoteric
tradition centred on truths communicated by the Buddha Vairocana
that only the initiated can fully understand. Kūkai brought the
Shingon teachings from China to Japan and dedicated his life to
popularizing them. Despite its esotericism, Shingon has around
ten thousand temples in Japan today and claims about ten million

adherents. From that point of view alone, Kūkai was outstandingly successful, but he is remembered also for his calligraphy and poetry, the creativity he brought to the design of his temples, the interpretation of Dharma texts, and also for his attention to the education of the poor. His motto, 'Attaining Enlightenment in this very existence', reflects his affirmative attitude to the phenomenal world. It is *this* world in which we live, *this* world in which we practise.

Kūkai was born in 774 into an aristocratic family. At the age of 15 he took up the study of Chinese classics with an uncle, a distinguished Confucian scholar, who, recognizing his genius, took him to the capital to further his education. There he read widely, taking a special interest in the Buddhist scriptures, but he felt that what he was learning was only 'the dregs derived from men of old'. He saw that it was essential to learn the ultimate Truth, and at the age of 20 he took the lay precepts and withdrew to the mountains where he took up ascetic practices and began to have powerful mystical experiences.

In Japan at this time Buddhism was divided into two major strands. There were the state-supported functionary priests and the so-called 'private priests' who devoted themselves to asceticism, divination, and preaching. Dissatisfied with the vain, pompous affairs of urban Buddhist establishments, many private priests retired to the mountains for meditation. In his memoirs, Kūkai described the life of the wandering ascetic:

> The blue sky was the ceiling of his hut and the clouds hanging over the mountains were his curtains; he did not need to worry about where he lived or where he slept. In summer he opened his neck band in a relaxed mood and delighted in the gentle breezes as though he were a great king, but in winter he watched the fire with his neck drawn into his shoulders. If he had enough horse chestnuts and bitter vegetables to last ten days, he was lucky. His bare shoulders showed through his paper robe and clothes padded with grass cloth.... Though his appearance was laughable, his deep-rooted will could not be taken away from him.[114]

At the age of 24 Kūkai decided to dedicate himself to Buddhist monasticism and devoted himself to seeking out the highest teachings:

> I, disciple Kūkai, being driven by an inner urge, had all the while thought of returning to the Source. Not knowing the way to it, I cried many a time standing at the crossroad. My sincere wish was rewarded, however; I found this, the Esoteric Buddhist approach. I started reading (the *Mahāvairocana Sūtra*) only to find that I was unable to understand it; I wished to visit China.[115]

Eventually, at the age of 32, he sailed for China – an extremely hazardous voyage in those days – and after many difficulties he finally met his master, Huiguo, at Ximing temple in Chang'an. Huiguo was a master of two lineages of Vajrayāna Buddhism, one based on the *Mahāvairocana Sūtra* and the other on the *Vajraśekhara Sūtra*, or 'Diamond Peak *Sūtra*'. Both of these lineages had arrived in China directly from India in the early eighth century and the sūtras upon which they are founded continue to be the basic canonical texts of Shingon:

> I called on the abbot in the company of five or six monks from the Ximing Temple. As soon as he saw me he smiled with pleasure and joyfully said, 'I knew that you would come! I have waited for such a long time. What pleasure it gives me to look upon you today at last! My life is drawing to an end, and until you came there was no one to whom I could transmit the teachings. Go without delay to the altar of *abhiṣeka* with incense and a flower.' I returned to the temple where I had been staying and got the things which were necessary for the ceremony. It was early in the sixth month then that I entered the altar of *abhiṣeka* for primary initiation.[116]

A mere three months later, Kūkai was permitted the final initiation and was ordained by Master Huiguo into the esoteric Mantra School (Japanese, 'Shingon') of Buddhism, becoming its eighth patriarch.

Shingon practice consists of elaborate rituals, recitation of *dhāraṇīs* and mantras, and meditation on mandalas. Through the practice of mudrā and meditation, practitioners unite their minds with particular Buddhas and Bodhisattvas. Dainichi (Sanskrit, Mahāvairocana) is the central Buddha of the Shingon School.

One day, approaching death, Huiguo gave Kūkai his final instructions:

Now my existence on earth approaches its term, and I cannot long remain. I urge you, therefore, to take the mandalas of both realms and the hundred volumes of the teachings of the Diamond Vehicle, together with the ritual implements and these objects which were left to me by my master. Return to your country and propagate the teachings there.[117]

Kūkai gradually rose to prominence, eventually finding favour at the Imperial Court. In 816 he petitioned the emperor to grant him Mount Kōya, where he wished to establish a monastery:

According to the meditation sūtras, meditation should be practised preferably on a flat area deep in the mountains. When young, I, Kūkai, often walked through mountainous areas.... There is a quiet, open place called Kōya.... High peaks surround [it] in all four directions; no human tracks, still less trails, are to be seen there. I should like to ... build a monastery there for the practice of meditation, for the benefit of the nation and of those who desire to discipline themselves.[118]

The emperor granted his request, and although Kūkai had received an imperial order to act as adviser to the secretary of state, he often climbed to Mount Kōya to supervise the work there, sending his personal supporters letters such as this: 'We are out of nails; the carpenters cannot finish their work. I sincerely wish that you would send me some nails as soon as possible.' He received invitations from friends in the capital and responded with poems in which he tried to explain his feelings for the Dharma and the mountains:

Teachers of Enlightenment

You ask me why I entered the mountain deep and cold,
Awesome, surrounded by steep peaks and grotesque rocks,
A place that is painful to climb and difficult to descend,
Wherein reside the gods of the mountain and the spirits of
trees.

Have you not seen, O have you not seen,
The peach and plum blossoms in the royal garden?
They must be in full bloom, pink and fragrant,
Now opening in the April showers, now falling in the spring
    gales;
Flying high and low, all over the garden the petals scatter.
Some sprigs may be plucked by the strolling spring maidens,
And the flying petals picked by the flittering spring orioles.

Have you not seen, O have you not seen,
The water gushing up in the divine spring of the garden?
No sooner does it arise than it flows away forever:
Thousands of shining lines flow as they come forth,
Flowing, flowing, flowing into an unfathomable abyss;
Turning, whirling again, they flow on forever,
And no one knows where they will stop.

Have you not seen, O have you not seen,
That billions have lived in China, in Japan?
None have been immortal, from time immemorial:
Ancient sage kings or tyrants, good subjects or bad,
Fair ladies and homely – who could enjoy eternal youth?
Noble men and lowly alike, without exception, die away;
They have all died, reduced to dust and ashes;
The singing halls and dancing stages have become the abodes of
    foxes.
Transient as dreams, bubbles or lightning, all are perpetual
    travellers.

Have you not seen, O have you not seen,
This has been man's fate, how can you alone live forever?
Thinking of this, my heart always feels torn;
You, too, are like the sun going down in the western mountains,
Or a living corpse whose span of life is nearly over.

Futile would be my stay in the capital;
Away, away, I must go, I must not stay there.
Release me, for I shall be master of the great void;
A child of Shingon must not stay there.

I have never tired of watching the pine trees and the rocks at
    Mt Kōya;
The limpid stream of the mountain is the source of my
    inexhaustible joy.
Discard pride in earthly gains;
Do not be scorched in the burning house, the triple world!
Discipline in the woods alone lets us soon enter the eternal
    Realm.[119]

In 823 the emperor granted Kūkai possession of Tō-ji, the second state temple of the new capital at Kyoto, entrusting him with the completion of the temple and granting him exclusive use of it for the new Shingon sect. Shingon had now finally become fully established. At the age of 50, Kūkai was the pre-eminent religious personality in Japan, unequalled in breadth of learning, religious authority, and popularity among all classes of society.

While still working to complete Kongōbu-ji Monastery on Mount Kōya, he founded a School of Arts and Sciences in Kyoto. As the first school open to everyone, regardless of social status or economic means, it was the first in Japan to provide universal education, and behind it lay Kūkai's conviction of the oneness of humanity, his ideal of equal opportunity in education, and his belief in the intrinsic value of each individual.

After finally completing his chief work on thought and religion – *The Ten Stages of the Development of Mind* – which was the first attempt in the history of Japanese Buddhism to expound the teachings of a school while taking into account the doctrines of other schools, both Buddhist and non-Buddhist, Kūkai died in 835, on his beloved Mount Kōya.

Dōgen

Dōgen Zenji, who lived between 1200 and 1253, is regarded as the pre-eminent Sōtō Zen master of Japan and as one of that country's foremost religious personalities.

Dōgen lost his father when he was two, and his mother when he was only seven. In grief and solitude he realized the frailty of all earthly things. After his mother's death he was adopted by an uncle, a powerful aristocrat, who wanted him to become his heir. At the age of twelve, informed of the fate in store for him, he fled his uncle's house just before the date set for the rites of puberty and his entrance upon a secular career and joined a younger uncle who lived as a hermit at the foot of Mount Hiei. There he entered a monastery and fully devoted himself to the religious life and the study of sacred writings.

But the young monk was plagued by a question which none of the Tendai scholar-monks of his monastery could answer to his satisfaction: 'If all beings already possess Buddha-nature, why does one need to arouse the Will to Enlightenment and engage in practices to realize it?'

His quest for an answer eventually led him to China, and the monastery of Rujing, a master of the Caodong (in Japanese, Sōtō) School, where meditation was practised with great intensity. One night, during a late session of meditation, Ju-Ching yelled at the monk sitting next to Dōgen, 'When you study under a master you must drop the body and mind! What use is single-minded intense sleeping?' At these words Dōgen suddenly experienced the dropping of body and mind. His dilemma was resolved. From Ju-Ching he received the seal and mantle of succession to the patriarchate of the Sōtō sect and returned to Japan to teach. Contrary to the practice of other Buddhist pilgrims to China, Dōgen returned to Japan without new sūtras, rites, or sacred images. In his own words, he came 'empty handed', knowing nothing more than 'the eyes are horizontal and the nose is vertical', but, nonetheless, 'with a heavy burden on my shoulders'.[120]

The key element in Dōgen's teaching is the ultimate non-duality of all phenomena. Such non-duality is not merely conceptual, however. To truly know it is to experience it at all times. His original dilemma had come about from assuming that Buddha-nature and the practices one undertook to realize it were separate. Now he saw that they were in fact one and the same thing. Practice *is* Enlightenment.

Above all he emphasized *zazen* – formal sitting meditation practice. But *zazen* was not a practice one engaged with in order to attain Enlightenment in the future, for *zazen*, properly practised, transcends the dichotomy between 'practice' and 'Enlightenment':

> To practise the Way single-heartedly is, in itself,
> Enlightenment. There is no gap between practice and
> Enlightenment or *zazen* and daily life.[121]

Practice, in Dōgen's terms, is itself the manifestation of an intrinsic realization. The Dharma is amply present in all beings, but unless one practises it is not manifested and, without realization, it is not attained. Attainment, however, is no-attainment: it is not the result of aiming at anything. All things are always the Buddha-nature. Seeing this, perfectly, as it is in the present moment, with complete at-oneness with the events around one, in total openness to its wonder and perfection – as, in fact, absolute reality itself – is both the nature of practice and the nature of Enlightenment.

The identity between Buddhist practice and daily life is brought out in his treatise *Instructions to the Tenzo* (the head cook, who occupied a very important position in the monastery):

> Maintain an attitude that tries to build great temples from
> ordinary greens, that expounds the buddhadharma through
> the most trivial activity. When making soup with ordinary
> greens, do not be carried away by feelings of dislike towards
> them nor regard them lightly; neither jump for joy simply
> because you have been given ingredients of superior
> quality.[122]

As an aristocrat, Dōgen was expected to associate with the court and political authorities of the Shōgunate, but he shunned such involvements until 1247 when he received an official invitation to the capital, where he taught for a time, eventually receiving the purple robe – the highest state honour for a monk. Eihei-ji, the monastery that Dōgen founded in north central Japan, is still the headquarters of the Sōtō Order. Today there are about 15,000 Sōtō temples in Japan, and the Sōtō claim to have around 7,000,000 adherents.

In 1253, his health failing, Dōgen left Eihei-ji and returned to Kyoto for medical treatment. He died there the same year – seated in *zazen*.

The *Shōbōgenzō Zuimonki* consists largely of brief talks, exhortations, and instructions given by Dōgen, recorded by his disciple Ejō and edited by Ejō's disciples after his death. It does not contain the philosophical subtleties of Dōgen's *Shōbōgenzō*, nor does it give the full scope of Dōgen's thought, but it directly communicates the flavour of Dōgen's approach to monastic life and Zen practice:

One day Dōgen instructed: You should understand that a man who is born into a certain household and wants to enter the family occupation must first train himself in the family speciality. It is a mistake to strive for knowledge and training in an area outside your own speciality and competence.

Now, as men who have left your homes, if you are to enter the Buddha's house and become priests, you must learn thoroughly what you are supposed to do. To learn these things and to maintain the regulations mean to cast aside attachments to the Self and to conform to the teachings of the Zen Masters. The essential requisite is to abandon avarice. To do this, you must first free yourselves from egoism. To be free from egoism is to have a deep understanding of transiency. This is the primary consideration.

Most people in the world like to regard themselves as good and to have others think the same of them, but such a thing seldom happens. If, however, you gradually forsake attachment to the Self and follow the advice of your teacher, you will progress. You may say that you understand but still cannot give up certain things; and practise zazen while holding on to various attachments. If you take this attitude, you sink into delusion.

For a Zen monk the primary prerequisite for improvement
is the practice of concentrated *zazen*. Without arguing about
who is clever and who inept, who is wise and who foolish, just
do *zazen*. You will then naturally improve.[123]

Shinran

Shinran Shōnin, 'Shinran the Saint', was born in 1173 and died in
1263. He founded the Jōdo Shin School of Pure Land Buddhism,
which has thrived in Japan ever since. Because of Shinran's
efforts, the faith teachings of the Jōdo Shinshū spread far and
wide throughout Japan, particularly amongst the common people.

He became a monk while still relatively young, and spent a
number of years on Mount Hiei, where the principal monasteries
of the Tendai School are located. Practising diligently, he
mastered the texts and teachings of the various Buddhist schools
that had been introduced into Japan from China, but to his
increasing dismay, neither his study nor his practice brought
him any nearer to Enlightenment. The mountain monastery,
moreover, was permeated with an atmosphere of worldliness.
So Shinran began his search for a teacher, and eventually met
Hōnen Shōnin. Hōnen, then the greatest exponent and exemplar
of the Pure Land doctrine in Japan, initiated him into the Path
of Faith and the practice of the *nembutsu*, which centres on the
recitation of the mantra '*namo amida butsu*'. Profoundly moved
by this practice, Shinran abandoned his former life, left Mount
Hiei, and joined Hōnen's following.

The Pure Land schools derive their teachings from the three
sūtras connected with the Buddha Amitābha. In one of these, the
Larger Sukhāvatīvyūha Sūtra, known within Pure Land Buddhism
simply as the *Larger Sūtra*, it is said that prior to his Enlightenment,
when he was still a Bodhisattva called Dharmākara, the Buddha
Amitābha made a series of forty-eight great vows, each embodying
a different aspect of Sukhāvatī, the pure land or Buddha-field
that he resolved to build once he had become a Buddha. These
forty-eight vows are central to Pure Land doctrine, and of them
the eighteenth and the nineteenth were particularly important to
Shinran:

Teachers of Enlightenment

If, when I attain Buddhahood, among the sentient beings in
the ten directions those who, with sincere mind, rejoice in
faith, aspire to be born in my land, think thus even ten times,
are not born there, may I not realize perfect enlightenment.
Excluded are those who commit the five grave offences and
those who slander the right Dharma.[124]

According to Shinran, one could never gain Enlightenment by
way of 'self-power' (*jiriki*). Such endeavours only strengthened
one's attachment to self, for, after all, how can the self let go of
the self? The more the self tries to let go of the self, the more it is
bound up in the effort of the self and the more the sense of self is
strengthened. Only by relying on 'other-power' (*tariki*), the salvific
effort of the Buddha Amitābha, is salvation possible.

What was needed was great faith in, and gratitude to, the
Buddha for his great salvific effort. When such faith arises, the
ego dies and all our tormented cravings and delusions are turned
into Enlightenment. But by 'faith' Shinran does not mean to imply
the generation of any intentional volition on our part. That belongs
to self-power. The faith (Japanese, *shinjin*) which Shinran talks
about involves a *complete* letting go. This cannot come from the
egoistic, defiled individual. In that sense the faith of Jōdo Shin is
very difficult. The ego is always egoistic and it is therefore very
difficult to let it go completely. It is 'most difficult among the
difficult'. In another sense, however, it is not difficult at all, for one
does not actually have to *do* anything. Faith can save because it is
other-power. Faith in this sense is the action of Amitābha himself,
shining from within.

To translate this into Sangharakshita's terms, the faith that
Shinran speaks of is *Real* Faith – the affective counterpart of Real
Going for Refuge or the Real arising of the bodhicitta.

In his *Kyōgyōshinshō* Shinran wrote:

As I contemplate matters, I see that the acquirement of
Serene Faith arises out of the Tathāgata's Selected Vow, and
that the awakening of True Mind is made possible by the
compassionate, skilful means of the Great Sage.

However, priests and laymen of the Declining Age and masters of these days, sunken in the idea 'that one's true nature is Buddha' and 'that the Buddha's Pure Land exists in one's mind', degrade (the belief in) the True Enlightenment in the Pure Land; or, being deluded by the mind of self-power to practise meditative and non-meditative good deeds, they are blind to the Adamantine True Faith.[125]

All the ocean-like multitudinous beings, since the beginningless past, have been transmigrating in the sea of ignorance, drowning in the cycle of existences, bound to the cycle of sufferings, and having no pure, serene faith. They have, as a natural consequence, no true serene faith. Therefore, it is difficult to meet the highest virtue and difficult to receive the supreme, pure Faith. All the common and petty persons at all times constantly defile their good minds with greed and lust, and their anger and hatred constantly burn the treasure of Dharma. Even though they work and practise as busily as though they were sweeping fire off their heads, their practices are called poisoned and mixed good deeds and also called deluded and deceitful practices; hence, they are not called true acts. If one desires to be born in the Land of Infinite Light with these deluded and poisoned good [deeds], he cannot possibly attain it.

Why is it so? Because when the Tathāgata performed the Bodhisattva practices, His three kinds of actions were not mingled with doubt even for a thought or a moment.

Since this mind (Serene Faith) is the Tathāgata's Great Compassionate Mind, it necessarily becomes the rightly determinant cause for (Birth in) the Recompensed Land. The Tathāgata, pitying the sea of suffering multitudes, endowed the unhindered, great Pure Faith to the ocean of all beings. This is called the True Faith of the Other-Power.[126]

The Buddhist establishment of the time was deeply opposed to Pure Land Buddhism. It was rapidly gaining popularity, and was clearly a threat. Moreover, they asserted, it encouraged lawlessness and immoral conduct. This criticism is not without foundation. According to Hōnen, Amida's vow is universal and thus saves all who say his name. Some people had understood this to mean that if only one says the name there is no need to fear the consequences of immoral acts, and there had been cases of lawlessness and immorality.

In 1207 the establishment attacked. Hōnen and seven disciples, including Shinran, were exiled to distant provinces, and four disciples were executed. Shinran and Hōnen were stripped of their Tendai ordinations and given laymen's names. However, Shinran could not and would not assume the worldly attitudes and attributes of a layman. Certainly, he was no longer a monk – he married and started a family – but neither did he think of himself simply as a layman, for he continued to devote himself fully and wholeheartedly to Dharma activities. In exile he came into close contact with the common peasantry – with their everyday problems and fears – and he began to see that it was his mission to save people such as these.

After five years in exile, Shinran and Hōnen were pardoned. Nonetheless, Shinran did not return to monasticism and remained married, true to the vision he developed during his exile that the right path is to be 'neither monk nor lay' – a tradition that ordained members of the Jōdo Shinshū follow to this day.

Shinran spent the remaining sixty years of his long life travelling about the country preaching to the common people, many of whom became his friends and followers. In 1225 he founded the independent school called the Jōdo Shinshū ('True Pure Land School'), as opposed to Hōnen's Jōdo Shū ('Pure Land School'). Today, the Jōdo Shinshū is the largest of the Japanese branches of the Mahāyāna, possessing more temples (about 20,000), more full-time teachers, and more adherents than any other.

The Jōdo Shin approach was based partly on the teaching of the last age of the Dharma. The seventh-century Chinese Pure Land teacher Daochuo had taught that according to the *Great Collection Sūtra* the last age of the Dharma begins with the beginning of the fourth 500-year period after Buddha Śākyamuni. According to the information then available in Japan, the last age of the Dharma had begun in 1052. Contemporary experience strengthened people's belief in the dawning of the last age: moral corruption had appeared among the monks, and civil wars and plagues were breaking out.

In such an age, according to Daochuo, Buddhists can neither practise meditation successfully nor cultivate wisdom. External circumstances no longer allowed for that, and the individual capacity for spiritual practice was no longer what it was in the time of the ancients. Instead, people needed to develop faith by reciting the Buddha's name. Shinran believed that the new age required just such an approach:

> As I contemplate the ocean-like Great Faith, I see that it does not choose between the noble and the mean, the priest and the layman, nor does it discriminate between man and woman, old and young. The amount of sin committed is not questioned, and the length of practice is not discussed. It is neither 'practice' nor 'good', neither 'abrupt' nor 'gradual', neither 'meditative' nor 'non-meditative', neither 'right meditation' nor 'wrong meditation', neither 'contemplative' nor 'non-contemplative', neither 'while living' nor 'at the end of life', neither 'many utterances ' nor 'one thought'. Faith is the inconceivable, indescribable, and ineffable Serene Faith. It is like the *agada* which destroys all poisons. The medicine of the Tathāgata's Vow destroys the poisons of wisdom and ignorance.[127]

Sangharakshita, in the centre of the bottom row, sits in his Order robes wearing a golden kesa: a piece of cloth that members of the Triratna Buddhist Order wear round their necks. He is holding another kesa is readiness to perform an ordination. He is flanked by Yogi Chen on our left and Bhikkhu Jagdish Kashyap, who has a begging bowl, on our right. Kachu Rimpoche sits above Sangharakshita, flanked by Chetul Sangye Dorje to the left and Dhardo Rimpoche to the right. On the top row, Jamyang Khyentse Chökyi Lodrö is flanked by Dudjom Rimpoche on our left and Dilgo Khyentse Rimpoche on our right.

Chapter Twelve

The Teachers of the Present

The teachers of the present, sitting on the lotus in front of the Buddhas of the Three Times, are iconographically closest to us as we gaze upon the Refuge Tree. This reflects their historical position in relation to the Tree, but there is more to it than that. They are, between them, our gateway into the mandala of Going for Refuge. Through our contact with them, directly or indirectly, we enter the vast mandala of spiritual influence represented by the Tree itself.

Between them, the teachers of the present represent an assortment of approaches to Dharma practice. There is a Chan/Vajrayāna yogi hermit, a Theravādin scholar-monk, a Gelug monk, and four Nyingma lamas. Four of these teachers lived as celibate renunciants and four with their wives and families. Some of them had their Dharma education in the context of a formal monastic structure from an early age, others seem almost to have found it out for themselves. Some were born into Buddhist families, others decided they were Buddhists later in life. Some of them related to Sangharakshita as a personal friend, others had a more formal relationship with him. All of them, however, exhibit certain similar characteristics. That they all had a profound knowledge of and commitment to the Dharma goes without saying, but, among their contemporaries, they all stand out as unusually broad-minded people, strongly ecumenical in their approach to spiritual practice.

Sangharakshita had a profound insight experience at the age of 16. Ever since then, he once said, there were few occasions when he did not reflect on the Dharma and – in all his later learning about Buddhism and in all his subsequent experience – he found nothing that caused him to question that first instance of insight; everything that came after only served to broaden and deepen it.

What, then, did he get from his eight main teachers? After all, he had all but completed his *Survey of Buddhism* before meeting seven of them, and the Theravādin bhikkhu Jagdish Kashyap, whom he had met before writing it, can hardly have influenced very much of it, based as it partly is on Mahāyāna Buddhist doctrine.

This question was once put to Sangharakshita, and he replied that he had certainly gained a great deal of Dharma knowledge from many of his teachers, and had received initiations and information about meditation practices from many of them. But he got most from them by observing how, in the context of their daily lives, the Dharma life was truly to be lived.

This process of exemplification continues down to us today. We too can reflect on the lives and teachings of the teachers of the present, if not in the flesh then through their teachings and the stories of their lives. It is to be hoped that this process will continue in the lives of Sangharakshita's senior disciples, their disciples, and their disciples' disciples, for, in the end, it is only through living contact and the practice of spiritual friendship that we can follow these great teachers and ourselves enter the mandala of Going for Refuge.

In their own way, each of the teachers of the present dedicated their lives to Dharma practice and to handing on the great treasure they had found to the next generation. We too, each in our own way, can follow in their footsteps.

Urgyen Sangharakshita

Poet, scholar, commentator, critic, mystic, organizer, teacher, and friend – Sangharakshita was a man of many talents and great genius. It is too soon to say how history will regard his contribution to the development of Buddhism, both in the West and in the East, but if the spiritual movement he founded lives up to his vision, it will be judged to have been very great indeed.

Born in 1925 to working-class parents in South London, Sangharakshita was confined to bed at an early age, and there he began a life-long programme of self-education, immersing himself in the classics of Western and Eastern literature and philosophy. At the age of 17 he read the *Diamond Sūtra* and the *Sūtra of Wei Lang* (Huineng) and began to have psychical and mystical experiences:

> When I read the *Diamond Sūtra* I knew that I was a Buddhist. Though this book epitomizes a teaching of such rarefied sublimity that even Arahants ... are said to become confused and afraid when they hear it for the first time, I at once joyfully embraced it with an unqualified acceptance and assent. To me the *Diamond Sūtra* was not new. I had known it and believed it and realized it ages before and the reading of the *Sūtra* as it were awoke me to the existence of something I had forgotten. Once I realized that I was a Buddhist it seemed that I had always been one, that it was the most natural thing in the world to be, and that I had never been anything else. My experience of the *Sūtra* of Wei Lang, ... though taking place at a slightly lower level, was repeated with much greater frequency.
>   Whenever I read the text I would be thrown into a kind of ecstasy.[128]

In May 1944, during the Buddhist Society's Wesak celebrations in London, Sangharakshita formally became a Buddhist, reciting the Refuges and Precepts for the first time. That same year he was conscripted and sent by the Army to South Asia, where he sought out religiously minded men in Sri Lanka and learned meditation for the first time.

At the end of the war, while stationed in Singapore, Sangharakshita learned that his unit was to return to England before demobilization. Checking-in his equipment, he left camp and made for India where, at the age of 22, he burned his identification papers, gave away his possessions, and, dressed in a simple ochre-stained robe, went forth as a wandering ascetic, following the example of the Buddha:

> As we left Kasauli it was raining, but, as in the course of our descent we emerged from the clouds into the bright sunshine

below, we saw arching the road, at intervals of a few dozen yards, not only single but double and triple rainbows. Every time we turned a bend we found more rainbows waiting for us. We passed through them as though through the multicoloured arcades of some celestial palace. Against the background of bright sunshine, jewel-like glittering raindrops, and hills of the freshest and most vivid green, this plethora of delicate seven-hued bows seemed like the epiphany of another world.[129]

For the next two years he and a friend wandered, mainly in South India, seeking out ashrams and teachers. While meditating in a cave above Ramana Maharshi's ashram, Sangharakshita had an overwhelming vision of the Buddha Amitābha and took this as confirmation that he should seek ordination as a Buddhist monk. He and his companion set out first for Sarnath and then Kuśinagara where, in May 1949, the Burmese monk U Chandramani granted them the novice ordination. Full ordination followed the next year, and – after a brief period of wandering in Nepal – Sangharakshita settled down for seven months with his first teacher, Ven. Jagdish Kashyap. After a pilgrimage together, Kashyapji and Sangharakshita parted in the small Himalayan hill-station of Kalimpong:[130]

After weeks of indecision, Kashyap-ji had finally made up his mind not to return to the Benares Hindu University. Instead, he would spend some time meditating in the jungles of Bihar, where a yogi whom he knew had a hermitage. Perhaps, as he meditated, it would become clear to him what he ought to do next. Meanwhile, I was to remain in Kalimpong. 'Stay here and work for the good of Buddhism,' he told me, squeezing himself into the front seat of the jeep that was taking him to Siliguri. 'The Newars will look after you.' There was little that I could say. Though I did not really feel experienced enough to work for Buddhism on my own, and though I doubted whether the Newars were quite so ready to look after me as Kashyap-ji supposed, the word of the guru was not to be disobeyed. Bowing my head in acquiescence, I paid my respects in the traditional manner, Kashyap-ji gave me his blessing, and the jeep was off.

I was left facing Mount Kanchenjunga.[131]

Finding the existing Buddhist organizations in the Himalayan border region too factious and sectarian, he founded a new one, the Young Men's Buddhist Association, which offered Buddhist teaching and practice as well as social and cultural activities and tutorial classes to help the young men pass their exams.

Eventually acquiring his own property – the Triyāna Vardhana Vihāra – Sangharakshita worked energetically to revitalize and promote the Dharma throughout the region, giving talks and hosting meetings in a wide variety of places, as well as producing a new publication, Stepping-Stones, which soon attracted an impressive list of contributors (Lama Govinda, Herbert Guenther, Edward Conze, and Prince Peter of Greece among others) and brought Sangharakshita to the attention of the English-speaking Buddhist world. He also became the principal editor of the *Maha Bodhi Journal*.

In 1956, Dr Bhimrao Ambedkar, the great leader of those who were known as India's Untouchables, or Dalits, asked Sangharakshita to preside at his conversion ceremony. Sangharakshita suggested that the ceremony would carry more weight if it were undertaken by U Chandramani, then the seniormost bhikkhu in India, and, in October that year, Ambedkar and nearly 400,000 of his followers duly took the Refuges and Precepts. Six weeks later Ambedkar died, and Sangharakshita, who was visiting the plains at that time, threw himself into the task of rallying the grief-stricken multitudes, addressing nearly thirty mass meetings in four days and initiating 30,000 people into Buddhism:

The condolence meeting was held in the Kasturchand Park, which was little more than a large open space part of which was occupied by a small pavilion. Roads apparently debouched into it from a number of directions, for on my arrival there at seven o'clock, by which time night had fallen, it was the dark centre of a gigantic wheel the golden spokes of which were formed by the lighted candles carried by the long columns of mourners who were converging on the place from all over the city. As the columns entered the park I saw that the men, women, and children carrying the candles were all clad in white – the same white that only seven weeks ago they had worn for the conversion ceremony. Whether on account of their demoralized state, or because there was not enough time, the organizers of the meeting had done little more than rig up a microphone and loudspeakers. There was no stage and, apart from a petromax or two, no illumination other than that provided by the thousands of candles. By the time I rose to speak – standing on the seat of a rickshaw and with someone holding the microphone up in front of me – about 100,000 people had assembled. Under normal circumstances I would have been the last speaker, but on this occasion I was the first. In fact as things turned out I was the only speaker. Though some five or six of Ambedkar's most prominent local supporters one by one attempted to pay tribute to their departed leader, they were so overcome by emotion that, after uttering only a few words, they burst into tears and had to sit down. Their example was contagious. When I started to speak the whole vast gathering was weeping, and sobs and groans filled the air. In the cold blue light of the petromax I could see grey-haired men rolling in agonies of grief at my feet.

Though deeply moved by the sight of so much anguish and despair, I realized that for me, at least, this was no time to indulge in emotion. Ambedkar's followers had received a terrible shock. They had been Buddhists for only seven weeks, and now their leader, in whom their trust was total, and on whose guidance in the difficult days ahead they had been relying, had been snatched away. Poor and illiterate as the vast majority of them were, and faced by the unrelenting hostility of the Caste Hindus, they did not know which way to turn and there was a possibility that the whole movement of conversion to Buddhism would come to a halt or even collapse. I therefore delivered a vigorous and stirring speech in which, after extolling the greatness of Ambedkar's achievement, I exhorted my audience to continue the work he had so gloriously begun and bring it to a successful conclusion. 'Baba Saheb' was not dead but alive. To the extent that they were faithful to the ideals for which he stood and for which he had, quite literally, sacrificed himself, he lived on in them. This speech, which lasted for an hour or more, was not without effect. Ambedkar's stricken followers began to realize that it was not the end of the world, that there was a future for them even after their beloved Baba Saheb's death, and that the future was not altogether devoid of hope.

While I was speaking I had an extraordinary experience. Above the crowd there hung an enormous Presence. Whether the Presence was Ambedkar's departed consciousness hovering over the heads of his followers, or whether it was the collective product of their thoughts at that time of trial and crisis, I do not know, but it was as real to me as the people I was addressing.[132]

From then until he left India he spent several months nearly every year teaching and lecturing among the new Buddhists of western India. He personally conducted the conversion ceremonies of more than 200,000 people. Despite all this activity, Sangharakshita continued with his writing, meditation, reflection, and Dharma studies, maintaining a 'rains retreat' at his vihara for three months each year. He continued to write poetry, published *A Survey of Buddhism*, his magnum opus, and wrote both *The Three Jewels* and *The Eternal Legacy*.

While living in Kalimpong, Sangharakshita met the rest of his principal teachers. Yogi Chen lived there as a hermit. Chetul Sangye Dorje often passed through there and, in 1956, Sangharakshita received his first initiation from him. He later received initiations and teachings from Jamyang Khyentse Rimpoche, Dilgo Khyentse Rimpoche, Dudjom Rimpoche, and Kachu Rimpoche. In 1962 he received the Bodhisattva ordination from Dhardo Rimpoche.

In 1964 Sangharakshita was invited to London to help bring harmony to the small but fractious British Buddhist community. Seeing great potential for the spread of the Dharma in Britain, Sangharakshita decided to remain at London's Hampstead Buddhist Vihara, where he was the incumbent. But his non-sectarian approach and his refusal to fit in with narrow expectations of what a Buddhist monk ought to be turned some of the Vihara's trustees against him, and while he was on a farewell tour in India he received notice that he would not be allowed to return to his former post.

This left him free to start a new Buddhist movement and, with the blessings of his teachers, he returned to England. There, in April 1967, he founded the Friends of the Western Buddhist Order with a small group of his disciples from the Vihara. One year later he ordained the first thirteen men and women into the new Western Buddhist Order.

By 1973 he judged the FWBO and the Order to be sufficiently firmly established to allow him to withdraw from day-to-day involvement in its activities, and he moved away to the countryside where he focused on his writing as well as keeping up a growing correspondence and seeing many visitors. From then on, Sangharakshita tended to follow the same daily regime. He kept his mornings free for meditation and for writing, seeing visitors and conducting his correspondence in the afternoons.

In 1989 he handed on responsibility for ordinations to some of his leading disciples, and in 1993 he created the Preceptors' College Council, a body of thirteen men and women to whom he largely handed over his remaining organizational responsibilities. Sangharakshita died in 2018 at the age of 93.

The Movement that he founded has grown enormously from its small beginnings. At the time of writing there are, what we now call Triratna Buddhist Community, activities on all but one continent, and well over a hundred centres and groups. Throughout his life, Sangharakshita took a vivid interest in the movement he founded and stayed in spiritual contact with those he personally ordained as well as with his many personal friends.

Sangharakshita's approach to the Dharma is marked by its emphasis on the fact of the centrality in the Buddhist spiritual life of the act of Going for Refuge to the Three Jewels:

A Buddhist is one who goes for Refuge in response to the Buddha and his teaching. A Buddhist is one who commits himself. He gives himself to the Three Jewels. This was the criterion in the Buddha's day and remains the criterion today.[133]

His recognition of the centrality of the act of Going for Refuge also allowed Sangharakshita to distinguish between commitment and lifestyle. What is important is that one goes for Refuge, one commits oneself to spiritual practice, and the lifestyle that one then follows – be it as a celibate renunciant, a married householder, or any other – is then a secondary (although by no means unimportant) matter. The order that he founded therefore contains people who follow a wide variety of lifestyles.

By discerning in this way what is essential in Buddhism from what is peripheral, and determined more by the historical and cultural conditions under which the Dharma is practised than by any essential spiritual reality, Sangharakshita was able to create a path of practice suited to contemporary conditions. He emphasized the need for people to remain rooted in their own culture, using what is best in it to further their Dharma practice. Thus he encouraged his students to develop and pursue interests in art, literature, and music, and to relate their experiences in these areas to their practice and understanding of the Dharma.

Perhaps more than any other teacher, Sangharakshita emphasized the importance for spiritual life of the practice of spiritual friendship – not only with those more developed than oneself, which is common throughout the tradition, but also with one's peers. In the modern world, where so many people suffer from isolation and alienation from the fragmented society around them, this has enabled the movement he founded to develop as a healthy, thriving sangha.

This valuation of the idea of spiritual friendship carried over into Sangharakshita's relationship to the Order and Movement. Although clearly occupying a special position as founder and as preceptor to hundreds of Order members, he preferred not to think of himself as a 'guru', with all that that connotes in the West today:

> I would ... preferably not apply the word 'guru' to myself
> nor have it applied to me by others. We have in Buddhism
> the wonderful term 'spiritual friend' and this I am more
> than content to apply to myself and to have applied to me
> by others. Indeed, there are times when I think that 'spiritual
> friend' is almost too much and that just 'friend' would be

enough. The English word 'spiritual' is in any case not the exact equivalent of the Indian word 'kalyāṇa'. According to the PTS Pāli-English Dictionary, 'kalyāṇa' means 'beautiful, charming, auspicious, helpful, morally good'. Obviously I cannot claim to be beautiful, at least not in the literal sense, and I can hardly be described as charming, though I may be auspicious and helpful on occasion and morally good to some extent. Let me, therefore, be content with the appellation 'friend' and stand to the Order simply in the relation of friend.[134]

Yogi Chen

 Sangharakshita first came into contact with Yogi Chen in the late 1950s, while he was living in Kalimpong. At that time, Yogi Chen was living in a small bungalow on the outskirts of the bazaar area. He lived there as a hermit and, during the whole time Sangharakshita was in Kalimpong, Yogi Chen never went outdoors – not even once. Nor did he generally receive visitors. Instead, he spent the greater part of his day engaged in different forms of meditation. At the same time, he devoted half an hour each day to writing, producing a number of books and booklets, in Chinese and in English.

After getting to know him, Sangharakshita was permitted to spend an evening with him every week. This went on for several years, and Sangharakshita found his teacher to be very communicative:

I learned quite a lot from him, mainly about the Vajrayāna and about Chan and Mahāyāna and Chinese Buddhism in general. I must add that he absolutely refused to consider himself a teacher, and did not allow anyone to refer to him as their teacher or their guru. He absolutely would not accept this. He wouldn't accept disciples in the formal sense, and would certainly not give initiations. If anyone approached him for initiation he would send them along to the appropriate incarnate lama. This did not, however, prevent him from criticizing some incarnate lamas very vigorously – and he was very critical of them indeed.[135]

Yogi Chen knew English quite well, and could read almost any English book, but, according to Sangharakshita, his spoken English was dreadful:

> He had a very, very strong Chinese accent and very strange ideas about English grammar. If you hadn't known him for quite a while you couldn't make out what he was saying. Even when he spoke English he needed an interpreter into English.[136]

He was also somewhat eccentric, especially with regard to dress. Sometimes Sangharakshita would find him wearing a kind of cowboy outfit, at other times a very formal Chinese scholar's dress with a black cap and long grey-blue robe. He was also very excitable:

> He was so excitable, so explosive, so emotional. In the end I came to the conclusion that perhaps lots of energy was generated in his meditation and it spilled over. That was the only explanation I could think of.[137]

On one occasion, Sangharakshita gave him a book on Zen that had been written by a British writer, and after reading it Yogi Chen shed tears. 'To think,' he said, 'that people in the West are being given this sort of stuff rather than the real thing.' For all this, what most impressed Sangharakshita about Yogi Chen was his extraordinary intellect:

> I used to ask him all sorts of questions, and he gave me the clearest replies that I got from any of my teachers. In the midst of all his eccentricity there was an absolute clarity of understanding. He clarified things that no one else had been able to clarify.[138]

He was also very learned, and once told Sangharakshita that when he was in China he had read the entire Chinese *Tripiṭaka* twice. Some catalogues put that at over 2,000 separate works! His *Buddhist Meditation: Systematic and Practical*[139] is the record of a number of conversations between Yogi Chen, Sangharakshita, and his friend Khantipalo, which took place in Yogi Chen's hermitage in Kalimpong. 'On this first occasion,' Khantipalo wrote, 'it was decided that an outline of his biography would be a good introduction to his explanation of practice and realization.' So the two monks asked him to tell his story. Yogi Chen replied:

> Autobiography is based on the 'I', but in practice no 'I' is found, so why should we deal with it? All that we can talk about is a certain mass passing through a period of time and being constantly identified as the same person. Though I have practised meditation for more than twenty years, still no 'I' has been discovered; while on the other hand voidness does not mean nothing....
>
> But one lives from day to day and traces remain; life is just a continuous mass of traces with nothing that can be held to either by you or by me. But just as the Bodhisattva went to Vimalakīrti and there was nothing to talk on but you have come so far and all this is at command. Under such a glorified condition of you. How could I keep in silence?[140]

He then related some of his biography. The young Chen was born covered by an unbroken placenta and so 'undefiled' by the mother's blood. Nor did he cry at birth as most children do. His mother noticed in his forehead a depression between or a little above the eyes – an evil omen according to normal Chinese standards, but a favourable sign for a Bodhisattva.

There were eight in the family, four girls and four boys. He was the fourth child, but while he was still young most of his brothers and sisters died. One day, a fortune-teller told his mother that the young Chen too would have a short life. Hearing this, he became greatly afraid of death. At the same time his father took a second wife and was always running after women, spending the family's money on them and on drink.

Fearing death and poverty, the young Chen saw that the world was a painful place. He had no need, he said, to read books to be convinced of the first Noble Truth of *duḥkha*: it was his own early experience. But, much as he wanted to, he could not Go Forth as he still had to care for his parents – there was no one else to look after them.

A sickly child, he nonetheless studied hard and was always first in school. Eventually, despite many difficulties, he graduated and obtained a post as a teacher in a high school. There he read the works of Ven. Taixu, a vigorous reformer of Chinese Buddhism who blended the modern scientific approach with ancient wisdom. So impressed was he with Ven. Taixu that he moved to Sichuan to work under him in the new Buddhist college the venerable master had founded. He took up the study of the *Avataṃsaka Sūtra*, and was particularly interested by the chapter on Good Conduct:

> This chapter sets forth how daily life should be well-accompanied by the Bodhicitta.... When we walk we should think of the sentient beings all walking on the great path of Buddhism; when we sit we should wish that all sentient beings are sitting on the Vajrāsana;.... [and so on]. In this way almost every action of our daily life is well-accompanied by the bodhicitta....
>
> I wrote out the whole of this chapter in good and vigorous style so that many copies might be made for presentation to others. Since then, I myself have always used and followed these same gāthās in my own life, well preserving the precepts of the Bodhicitta and constantly accompanied by the Bodhicitta itself.[141]

At this point, Yogi Chen took up with a Taoist teacher, and studied with him for a time before meeting his first Vajrayāna teacher, a Gelug lama called Gelu Rimpoche, under whose instruction he practised the Four Mūla Yogas. To find the time to do this, he had to rise at 3 a.m. and practise until it was time to leave for work at 9 o'clock.

At some point Yogi Chen married and started a family, but he does not tell us when. Instead, we learn that he always longed to Go Forth and that he left his wife for a time to practise with the Nyingma hermit Lola Hutuku, who passed on to him the Ati Yoga doctrines of Mahāmudrā and Dzogchen and told him that he ought to study Chan, 'because its realizations went very deep'.

Returning from the hermitage, doubts about the Dharma arose in Yogi Chen's mind, so he shut himself away for three days to fast and meditate. On the third day he had a vision of the Iron Pagoda, the abode of Vajrasattva where Nāgārjuna received the texts and instructions of the *Mahāvairocana* and *Vajraśekhara Sūtras*. At the same time, he realized that the Truth could never be contained in words, and all his doubts vanished – never to return.

Yogi Chen said that he had four kinds of guru: outward ones, such as his Taoist and Confucian teachers; inward ones, such as Ven. Taixu, who taught him exoteric teachings and with whom he read the *Tripiṭaka*, and who also appeared to him in dreams and meditations; secret teachers, such as Mahākāla, who gave him many instructions in dreams and meditations; and finally the guru of the *dharmakāya* – 'the wisdom of non-guru'.

During school vacations Yogi Chen practised as a solitary hermit for two months in the summer and one month in the winter, and although he still yearned to Go Forth, he was prevented by family obligations. Nonetheless, he managed to find the money necessary to maintain his family while he travelled in Tibet seeking teachings. He had a dream in which the young Karmapa instructed him to come to him, and so he did:

It is a traditional Buddhist practice that when a pilgrim newly arrives at a holy place, he should first pay his respects by circumambulating it clockwise (thus keeping it on his right side). I was doing this around the temple where the Karmapa was staying, all the time keeping my mind completely concentrated on his *mantra*. So closely did I attend to this, that I did not know some pilgrims had already arrived to see the Karmapa, and while they were in the temple worshipping him, they left their dogs outside to roam about. By 'dogs' I do not mean the tame ones in Europe, but great hulking mastiffs with bloody mouths like tigers and long sharp teeth. Then they saw me coming and went for me, one lunging at my

Teachers of Enlightenment

throat. With my mind totally focused upon the Karmapa, I pointed at the dog with one finger. The dog became quiet, sat down, and stared at me. I stood still and continually repeated the *mantra* with my hand remaining in this pointing gesture. Then many people came running and shouting. 'They will kill you,' they said. I just said I was sorry to trouble their dogs and went along the path with my practice unbroken.[142]

While travelling in Tibet Yogi Chen encountered Jamyang Khyentse Rimpoche, from whom he received many teachings. Remaining in Tibet for a time, he wandered about, receiving initiations and teachings from teachers in all the principal Tibetan traditions.

After practising in seclusion for a time, he realized that he had to return to China to rescue his family from the privations of the Second World War and, having settled them safely, he lived alone, practising in a cave for two years. In 1947 he made a pilgrimage to the holy places in India and then settled in Kalimpong where he lived as a hermit for the next twenty-five years, devoting himself to meditation. During this period he devoted half an hour each day to correspondence and writing, keeping in touch with people all over the world and producing 148 'Chenian booklets' that included sūtras, commentaries, teachings, and meditation instruction and which he distributed widely without charge. In 1972 he moved to America, where he died in 1987:

> The first mistake is not having a foundation of renunciation
> as a firm base for their practice of meditation. Quite often
> I receive correspondence from America, and my friends
> ... there say that to renounce is very easy for people in the
> East but very hard for Westerners. They complain that in
> the West there are so many things to give up so that it is
> made more difficult. To them I reply that the right thing to
> do is to lay even more stress on renunciation. If a boy finds
> mathematics difficult to study, the only way in which he can
> learn and progress is to make even greater efforts. So it is with
> renunciation. If we find it difficult, we should struggle and
> put forth great effort in order to overcome our attachments
> and enable us to give them up completely.[143]

Ven. Jagdish Kashyap

In his day, Ven. Jagdish Kashyap was one of the greatest Indian scholars of Buddhism. Sangharakshita remembers him as being of medium height, very dark in complexion and very, very, fat:

He told me very shortly after I met him that had I come a year earlier, he would have been unable to go out with me for a walk because he was so fat. He used to go everywhere by cycle-rickshaw, and paid the cycle-rickshaw wallah double fare. He was very humble, very unassuming. Despite his vast learning he never arrogated anything to himself. He was in some ways quite a childlike sort of person, very simple in his way of life with regard to dress, food, and accommodation. He was a terrific worker; he could work day and night without food or sleep, but if he had no work he'd simply lie on his string bed and sleep, hour after hour. He would reason, 'Well, if there's no work to do then why not just sleep?'[144]

Sangharakshita spent some of the happiest months of his life studying Pāli and Buddhist logic with Kashyapji at Benares Hindu University in 1949:

However conventional Kashyap-ji's teaching methods might have been, his manner of teaching was unconventional enough. When I entered his room (the communicating door was always left open) it was generally to find him stretched out on his string bed like a stranded whale, sound asleep, for though he could work day and night when necessary he could sleep day and night too with equal ease. As Professor of Pāli and Buddhist Philosophy his duties were minimal, and much of his time was therefore spent on the string bed, which creaked protestingly from time to time, and where he slept without benefit of either mattress or pillow. On my coughing, or murmuring 'Bhante!' a single eyelid would twitch, whereupon I would put my question, which was generally on some knotty point of Pāli grammar, or Abhidhamma, or Logic, which I had not been able to unravel by myself. Without opening his eyes, and without moving, Kashyap-ji would proceed to clear up the difficulty, heaving the words up from the depths of his enormous frame and rolling them around on his tongue before releasing them in slow, deliberate utterance. Sometimes he rumbled on for only a few minutes, sometimes for half an hour. Whatever he said was clear, precise, and to the point. If I asked about a particular passage of text, he always knew whereabouts it came, what had come before, and what followed. Yet all the time he had hardly bothered to wake up. As I returned to my room I would hear behind me a sigh and a snore and before I had settled down at my table Kashyap-ji would be sound asleep again.[145]

Bhikkhu Jagdish Kashyap was born Jagdish Narain in 1908 in the state of Bihar in northern India. During his early schooldays Jagdish acquired a reputation for being somewhat radical and unconventional. Instead of the 'respectable' Western dress of the local middle classes he adopted the rustic homespun *dhoti* and *kurta*, and often went to school barefoot.

He did well at school, and after graduating with a BA from Patna College went on to Varanasi, where he enrolled at the Benares Hindu University. There he completed two MAs, one in Philosophy and the other in Sanskrit. He lived simply at the university, actively enjoying austerity, and growing increasingly involved in the Indian nationalist movement as well as campaigns for social reform. He joined the Arya Samaj, a Hindu nationalist reform movement whose purpose was to return Hinduism to the basic teachings of the Vedas.

In order to be free to dedicate himself to the service of his country, Jagdish refused all attempts to involve him in marriage and instead adopted a celibate life. He threw his considerable energies into the work of the Arya Samaj, but he eventually grew disillusioned with it. He was increasingly concerned about the gap between its precepts and its practices, particularly with regard to the caste system. His fellow members of the Samaj seemed to him to be unable to free themselves from caste prejudice. Not only that; he also found the teachings of the Vedas extremely dispiriting. They seemed to him to comprise mainly hymns of worship and a variety of rituals, as well as spells for destroying enemies and attracting love. Where was all the sublime philosophy that the Samaj promised? Later on he would tell Sangharakshita that 'the best way to wean a Hindu away from Hinduism is to get them to study the Vedas'. In exasperation he considered converting to Islam.

While studying Sanskrit at university, however, Jagdish was attracted to Buddhism, and decided he would like to take up a doctorate in Buddhist philosophy. In order to do so, his teachers advised him first to become acquainted with the Pāli *Tipiṭaka* in the original language. In 1933, therefore, he left for Sri Lanka, where he joined the Vidyalankara Parivena monastic college. One year later he was ordained into the bhikkhu sangha, taking the name Jagdish Kashyap.

Kashyapji was astonished by the religious formalism he found in Sri Lanka, and he treated it with great irony. Sinhalese monks seemed to him to be as inquisitive about which monastic sect one belonged to as Hindus were about caste. When asked which *nikāya*, or sect, he belonged to, his usual reply was that he belonged to the 'Buddha Nikāya'. Once, a group of monks, not satisfied with that answer, persisted by asking him which shoulder he covered on leaving his monastery (the various nikāyas followed different practices in this respect). 'When it's cold,' Kashyapji replied, 'I cover both shoulders, when it's hot I keep one shoulder uncovered, and when it's very hot I don't wear any robe at all!'

While still in Sri Lanka, Kashyapji began to translate the *Dīgha-Nikāya* into Hindi together with his Indian bhikkhu friend Ven. Rahula Sankrityayan. Rahula had long planned a journey to Japan and invited Kashyapji to join him on his travels. They set out by boat from Calcutta, taking the *Dīgha* manuscript with them. Despite seasickness, they continued to work on the translation throughout the journey until the ship docked in Penang, where the local British Imperial police detained Kashyapji. They had received word from India asking them not to permit him to travel any further on account of his involvement in Gandhi's non-cooperation movement. Rahula and Kashyapji accordingly parted company and Kashyapji remained for one year in Penang where he continued the work of translation, eventually sending the completed manuscript to printers in India.

Kashyapji got on very well in Penang. He was the first Indian Buddhist monk to be seen there and was much in demand as a lecturer. He learned meditation from some Chinese monks and developed an interest in, and respect for, the Mahāyāna approach. Upon returning to Sri Lanka he retired to a forest hermitage for one year in order to meditate. One day he found himself standing face to face with a deadly cobra that was blocking the exit from his cave. This, he said, severely tested his practice of *mettā*.

In 1936, Kashyapji returned to India, settling eventually in Sarnath where he became involved in the work of the Maha Bodhi Society. Along with translation and literary work, he now became increasingly involved in social work, and became the headmaster of a new high school in Sarnath. He undertook a wide range of humanitarian work in the local villages, helping the poor and oppressed wherever he was able. Such actions were not without personal risk, and at one point, because of his support for the oppressed classes, he became the target of an arson attack. Rather than formally lodge a complaint, he simply went on a short pilgrimage until things calmed down.

Throughout this time his scholarly work continued and he developed an international reputation. In 1940 he was awarded the degree of Tripiṭakācārya by the Vidyalankara Parivena of Sri Lanka and began to teach Pāli at his Alma Mater, Benares Hindu University, where the philanthropist Jugal Kishore Birla built him a cottage called Buddha Kuti. It was here that Sangharakshita stayed with him.

Sangharakshita was puzzled at this time by the problem of the ego, and was much impressed by something he read in Thomas Merton's *Seeds of Contemplation*. There, the Trappist monk recommended that one could begin to overcome egoism by entirely surrendering oneself to one's spiritual superior. Sangharakshita decided to apply this in his relations with Kashyapji, a mild and unassuming man who always consulted Sangharakshita's wishes before deciding on anything.

By 1950 Kashyapji finally tired of the caste-ridden atmosphere of the University, with its Brahminical prejudice against Buddhist studies, and he and Sangharakshita embarked on a short holiday, visiting the Buddhist holy places in Bihar and ending up in the small hill-station of Kalimpong, in the foothills of the Himalayas, where Kashyapji finally decided to relinquish his post at the university. He determined to spend some time meditating in the jungles of Bihar, where a yogi he knew had a hermitage. There he hoped to become clear about what to do next. In the meantime Sangharakshita was to stay in Kalimpong and work for Buddhism. Having resolved always to obey his teacher, there was little Sangharakshita could say, and the two parted company.

Kashyapji now spent some time wandering in the districts that made up the ancient kingdom of Magadha. This was his native area and he deeply wished to re-establish the Dharma there. Eventually he conceived the idea of restoring the Buddhist University at Nālandā where, after much struggle, he established the Nava Nalanda Mahavihara which came to house a celebrated Pāli Institute.

All this time he never relinquished his ambition to see the *Tripiṭaka* made available in the contemporary language and scripts of India, and he kept up his own translation work accordingly. Eventually he persuaded the Government of India and the State of Bihar jointly to fund a five-year project to publish the whole of the *Tripiṭaka* in Devanagari script for the first time. The project was divided into three centres, where three teams of his students lived in or near the printing presses. Working sixteen or eighteen hours a day, cutting through red tape, and brooking no delay from the printers – even selling his house to release funds for salaries – Kashyapji managed to get the first volume of the series brought out in 1956 in time for the Buddha Jayanti celebrations.

Throughout the last part of his life Kashyapji continued to promote the cause of Buddhist studies in and around the Buddhist holy places. He developed his own friendly contacts with Buddhists from different traditions, actively helping the new Tibetan refugee community while taking his responsibilities within the Indian monastic sangha very seriously. He became involved in Dr Ambedkar's mass conversion movement and was particularly concerned with the training of monks from the new Indian Buddhist community.

He died at the Japanese Buddhist Temple at Rajgir in January 1976. News of his death spread rapidly and thousands of people from the villages around Nālandā and Rajgir came to pay their final respects at the state funeral organized by the Government of Bihar.

Dhardo Rimpoche

Sangharakshita and Dhardo Rimpoche became close friends when they were members of a delegation of 'eminent Buddhists from the border areas' that the Government of India had invited to Delhi, via the Buddhist holy places, as part of the celebrations held in 1956–7 to mark 2,500 years of Buddhism – the 'Buddha Jayanti':

What used to happen was this – our government-sponsored train would take us from one holy place to another, and we usually saw a holy place in the morning and a dam or factory in the afternoon. Our official guide would say 'this morning we are going to the holy place and this afternoon we are going to the factory', and if we were going to the holy place we would always take incense and candles and so on, to perform a little pūjā. One day, perhaps it was at Kusinara, the guide said 'We are not going to the holy place this morning, we will go this afternoon. This morning it's something else.' So we didn't bother about candles and incense or anything of that sort, and off we trooped. But it so happened that actually we found ourselves in a Buddhist temple in one of the holy places and we hadn't got any candles or any incense. And for traditionally-minded Buddhists it's a big thing to turn up at a holy place with nothing to offer. So all fifty-seven people were really quite upset – except Dhardo Rimpoche.

Tibetan monks have got very voluminous red robes, and while everybody else was expressing their regret and being a bit annoyed with the guide, Rimpoche unfolded his capacious robe and, with a big smile, he pulled out bundles of incense and candles, and distributed them to everybody. And there was really quite enough for all fifty-seven of us. So he wasn't only mindful – you never seemed to catch him napping. He always seemed prepared: he always seemed to anticipate what was going to happen and to be ready to meet it.[146]

Dhardo Rimpoche placed little value on the matter of reincarnation. *Maybe* he was a reincarnation, he said: when he was very young he had had memories of his previous life, but they had faded like dreams. He never *felt* like a great lama, although everyone treated him as one. Nonetheless, it occurred to him, he ought to *act* like one by developing wisdom and compassion. In this way, he said, he *became* a Rimpoche. 'You too can become Rimpoches,' he once told visiting Order members. 'All you have to do is to start acting with wisdom and compassion.'

He was born in 1918 in Dhartsendo, in the east of Tibet towards the Chinese border, the son of a prosperous merchant and his aristocratic wife, and was soon recognized as the thirteenth Dhardo Tulku. The name 'Dhardo' is a contraction of Dhartsendo, and Dhardo Rimpoche's previous incarnations had been the Nyingma abbots of the Dorje Drak Gompa there. The twelfth incarnation, however, took up residence at the great Drepung monastery near Lhasa, where he became allied with the Gelugpa, rising in due course to become the Khenpo Tripa, or chief abbot – a position of considerable spiritual and political consequence.

At his parents' request, the young tulku spent the first years after his discovery living not far from them at Nam Chod Gompa – a local Gelug monastery. From an early age his life was devoted to spiritual learning and discipline. While still only four years old he was expected to rise at 4 a.m. to memorize eight or ten lines of verse. Then, before he was allowed his morning tea or breakfast, he had to recite everything he had learned. After that there was reading or writing until noon and then he was allowed to play until 4 p.m. That was followed by more recitation and chanting. He had to learn all the rituals that a tulku was expected to perform.

In 1927 Rimpoche's family moved to Lhasa, where he was enthroned in magnificent state and ceremony at Drepung, the largest Tibetan Buddhist monastery, where the young lama Yeshe Lhondup was assigned to him as tutor. Rimpoche was deeply devoted to Lhondup, despite his strictness and the occasional beatings he received. For seventeen years they studied closely together, concentrating on the course of *geshe* studies. Candidates for the *geshe* degree are expected to acquire a detailed knowledge of the sūtras, commentaries, and classical texts of Indo-Tibetan Buddhism, as well as an understanding of their underlying philosophy. Accordingly, Rimpoche studied the texts along with logic, epistemology, phenomenology, and ethics, sharpening his understanding at the highly stylized debates in which students contested points of doctrine and interpretation. In the last years of the course, Geshe Lhondup also arranged for Rimpoche to attend gatherings at which distinguished lamas gave initiations or teachings.

In 1944 Rimpoche passed his examination as a *Lharampa* geshe, that is, with distinction, and he was accordingly enrolled in a Tantric college whose severely ascetic regime caused Rimpoche's health to give way. Much to his regret he was forced to withdraw from the college and, in 1947, Rimpoche journeyed to India to seek medical help.

On his arrival in Kalimpong he was given a rapturous welcome by the local Tibetan merchant community – so few high-ranking lamas ever made the journey to India – and after finding a doctor in nearby Darjeeling, Rimpoche's health gradually improved. He made a pilgrimage to Bodh Gaya and, before returning to Lhasa, spent some time teaching in Kalimpong, much to the delight of the local Tibetan Buddhist community.

When he had been back in Lhasa for only eighteen months, the regent of the young Dalai Lama, having heard of Rimpoche's success in Kalimpong, ordered him to return to India to take on the incumbency of the newly founded Tibetan gompa at Bodh Gaya.

Rimpoche remained in Bodh Gaya for twelve years, revitalizing the gompa, raising funds for new buildings and extensions, and sometimes even working alongside the labourers on the site. After insisting that all who lived there follow a strict monastic regime, Rimpoche began to meet a great deal of opposition from some of the residents. Nonetheless, he was deeply impressed with the responsibility he had to carry at the Bodh Gaya Gompa, especially after the Chinese invasion of Tibet when he realized that henceforth the light of the Dharma might well be extinguished in Tibet and would therefore have to be well preserved in exile.

Every year Rimpoche left the scorching plains of India for a small house which he rented for his mother and her attendants in the hills of Kalimpong, where he came to play an important part in the religious life of the local Buddhist community. In 1951 he was invited to become the abbot of Yi-Gah Chö-Ling Monastery in nearby Ghoom, which was famous for the beautiful statue of Maitreya which Tomo Geshe Rimpoche installed there.

By 1953 Rimpoche and his friends saw quite clearly the weight of the disaster that was about to befall Tibet. They knew that the refugees already in Kalimpong would soon be joined by many others and that they would find conditions in exile very hard indeed. Already the children of poor Tibetan families wandered the streets and orphans struggled to make a living. Realizing that children who grew up in India would have little sense of the culture their parents had left behind, Rimpoche decided that a school to provide a traditional Tibetan education was badly needed, and together with others he founded a society to raise funds for it. In 1954 the Indo-Tibet Buddhist Cultural Institute (ITBCI) School opened its doors.

Rimpoche had occasionally considered going to the West to teach the Dharma, but he recognized there were two obstacles. In the first place, although he had managed to pick up some Hindi while working with the labourers in Bodh Gaya, he was not a natural linguist and language would always be a barrier. He also recognized that his Buddhism was deeply embedded in Tibetan culture, which was very different to that of the West. In 1953, however, he met Sangharakshita in Kalimpong (having previously seen him in passing in Bodh Gaya). At first he privately doubted whether the young English monk would be able to understand the Dharma in its depths or be able to follow the difficult life of a Buddhist monk. But when they started to discuss the Dharma,

Rimpoche realized there was no need for him to travel to the West. He now had a student who would be able to effect a translation of the Dharma into the terms of Western culture in his stead. In an interview many years later he said:

> If you are asking whether Bhikṣu Sangharakshita is the reincarnation of a Rimpoche or not, that I cannot say straight out. But I am a hundred percent sure that he is a truly remarkable and outstanding, deep-minded person. I say this because when we used to talk about the profoundest aspects of Buddhism, Bhikṣu Sangharakshita had no difficulty at all in understanding them with ease. That in itself is proof that he has a natural inborn ability to understand the higher things which ordinary people cannot understand easily.... I did not have any other disciples like Sangharakshita. He was unique in the sense that he used to learn [something] from me, and at the same time practise it, and then he used to teach it to other people. Only a few people can do this – learn and teach at the same time – because most students do not understand what they have learned and so can't teach it to others.[147]

In 1959, following the Lhasa uprising, a flood of refugees began to pour into Kalimpong. The refugee community was desperately poor. Monks disrobed in order to be able to scrape a living on the road gangs, and children stole in order to eat. All were hungry and destitute, and disease spread rapidly amongst them. Seeing the need, Rimpoche opened the ITBCI orphanage which soon housed fifty children.

He was also deeply concerned about the future of the Tantric colleges. Monks from these had been resettled in different areas and their studies had effectively come to an end. So long as the colleges remained closed the great cycles of Tantric texts and rituals which they had passed on were in danger of being lost. The Tibetan Government-in-exile had been unable to resolve the difficulties. Few were fluent in English or Hindi and they did not understand the complex workings of Indian bureaucracy. Rimpoche was begged to intervene and, within a month, the colleges were reopened in Dalhousie.

Rimpoche had already fallen out with a Tibetan government officer in Bodh Gaya who was now actively maligning him. He now saw that his success with the Tantric colleges would be interpreted as undue interference in government business. He considered the directness and outspokenness of his character and concluded that dealing with those who held political power would always bring him trouble. Fearing the possible repercussions for his school, his orphanage, and his monasteries he therefore took a solemn oath never again to do anything which would involve him in government work.

In 1962 Rimpoche's opponents in Bodh Gaya finally succeeded in having him removed as abbot, and he subsequently concentrated his energies on his projects in Kalimpong, where there was still much to do. In particular, the ITBCI School and orphanage were desperately short of money and Rimpoche was very aware that although they were able to provide some places for orphans, there were still many in Kalimpong whom he was unable to accommodate.

During this period Rimpoche and Sangharakshita deepened their friendship. Sangharakshita was able to help Rimpoche with fundraising, translation, and correspondence. Rimpoche, for his part, opened for Sangharakshita the treasure-house of the Tibetan Buddhist canon. But the teacher found that he could also learn from his pupil:

Before meeting Sangharakshita, Dhardo Rimpoche had been accustomed to teaching in the 'classical' style, seated on a throne while his disciples sat below. Traditionally, the lama is regarded, at such times, as the very Buddha himself and it must be difficult to feel anything for him other than profound awe. While teacher–disciple bonds were usually very strong, Rimpoche commented that it was rare for a lama to develop a close *friendship* with a pupil. Thus it came as a revelation when he realized that something remarkable had developed between himself and Sangharakshita. They had become intimate friends.[148]

By 1962 Sangharakshita realized that in Dhardo Rimpoche he had met someone whom he could revere as being himself a living Bodhisattva. Accordingly, he asked Rimpoche for the Bodhisattva ordination, which Rimpoche happily bestowed along with a detailed explanation of all the sixty-four Bodhisattva precepts.

For many years Rimpoche struggled to keep his school open in the face of constant financial hardship. In 1985, however, the charity Aid For India (later the Karuna Trust), run by some of Sangharakshita's disciples in England, undertook the financial support of the school, and Rimpoche's long financial struggles were finally over.

Around this time too, some of Sangharakshita's disciples began making their own pilgrimages to Kalimpong to meet the great lama who had had such an influence on their own teacher. Rimpoche always received them gladly, making his time freely available. 'I do not make any distinction between my own disciples and those of Sangharakshita,' he said.

In January 1990 Rimpoche realized that the portents for his own health were highly unfavourable. He therefore undertook a pilgrimage to the Buddhist sites in Nepal, making gifts to temples, monks, and beggars wherever he found them. Returning to Kalimpong in March, he suffered a stroke and, after a brief remission, finally passed away. Asked about how his own reincarnation might be recognized, Rimpoche said, 'The boy must have the same qualities as I have. I don't have ordinary feelings – I have continual compassion for people. Only a boy with those qualities will do.'

Chetul Sangye Dorje

Chetul Sangye Dorje, also known as Chetul (or Chatral) Rimpoche, is one of the most outstanding Nyingma lamas of his generation. Sangharakshita met him in 1956. After hearing that Rimpoche was staying in Kalimpong, and being told something of his great reputation, Sangharakshita was determined to take his first Tantric initiation from him:

What I had expected the famous Nyingma lama to look like I cannot say, but on meeting him I received a shock. He was of indeterminate age, perhaps somewhere between thirty and forty, his coarse black hair was cut short, like a monk's, and he was clad in a nondescript maroon garment lined with what appeared to be grubby sheepskin. What I was most struck by, however, was his face, which was coarse and unrefined almost to the point of brutality, and could easily have passed for that of a horny-handed peasant with no thought beyond his pigs and poultry. At the same time, his whole being communicated such an impression of strength and reliability that one could not but feel reassured, and it was not long before the two of us were deep in conversation.[149]

Sangharakshita asked Rimpoche to tell him who his *yidam* was and, after a moment of reflection, Rimpoche told him it was Green Tārā and then gave him the appropriate initiation. 'Many great pandits of India and Tibet have done this practice,' he said. Sangharakshita performed it faithfully every day for the next seven years.

Rimpoche came to some prominence in the West after the Trappist monk and poet Thomas Merton described a meeting with him in his *Asian Journal*. The meeting took place in 1968 after the Dalai Lama had recommended that Merton, who wanted to know about DzogChen, seek Rimpoche out:

> And there was Chatral, the greatest rimpoche I have met so far and a very impressive person.
>
> Chatral looked like a vigorous old peasant in a Bhutanese jacket tied at the neck with thongs and a red woollen cap on his head. He had a week's growth of beard, bright eyes, and a strong voice, and was very articulate,... We started talking about dzogchen and Nyingmapa meditation and 'direct realization' and soon saw that we agreed very well....
>
> The unspoken or half-spoken message of the talk was our complete understanding of each other as people who were somehow on the edge of great realization and knew it and were trying, somehow or other, to go out and get lost in it – and that it was a grace for us to meet one another. I wish I could see more of Chatral.... I was profoundly moved, because he is so obviously a great man, the true practitioner

of dzogchen, the best of the Nyingmapa lamas, marked by complete simplicity and freedom.... If I were going to settle down with a Tibetan guru, I think Chatral would be the one I'd choose.[150]

Although they met up a number of times, Sangharakshita found it was not always easy to meet Chatral Rimpoche, because he was always wandering about and would not tell anyone what his movements were going to be. 'He'd just up and off, he'd never take anything with him, and was altogether quite a strange, mysterious character.'[151]

Chatral Sangye Dorje was born in the Abse tribal group in Kham in eastern Tibet, and at an early age he migrated with the members of his tribe to Amdo, where he began to take an intense interest in spiritual matters.

At the age of 15 he abandoned his ties with his family and went about seeking spiritual teachers with whom to study and practice. He gave up riding, travelling instead on foot, and refused to enter houses or the tents of household people, staying only in hermitages, caves, or his own small tent. In the course of his wanderings at this time Rimpoche received many teachings and transmissions in the Nyingma tradition. Kathok Khenpo Ngawang Palzang was his most important root teacher, but he received many transmissions from Jamyang Khyentse Chökyi Lodrö and was one of the principal disciples of Dudjom Rimpoche.

When Chatrul Rimpoche was about 35 years old, the regent of Tibet, Reting Rimpoche, invited him to Lhasa to teach, and there he developed a great reputation. Large numbers of nobles and others flocked to him to make offerings and to receive teachings. Eventually, at the conclusion of a lengthy Tantric initiation, which had lasted for several days, the Regent made the customary offerings which, in his case, were very valuable. Rimpoche swept them all on to a cloth, tied the cloth up into a bundle, handed the bundle to the Regent, saying, 'Look after it for me,' and resumed his wanderings. In the mountains, he meditated in the caves blessed by Padmasambhava and other great teachers of the past. For several decades he lived as a hermit and became known as Chetul, 'One Without Concerns'. Coming and going as he pleased, he traversed the borders of India, Tibet, and Nepal.

At the end of the 1950s he moved to Bhutan and then to India, where he restored a simple temple in a village above Darjeeling and created a facility there for people to enter the three-year retreat, the only such facility to be established by a refugee lama at that time.

The day after he gave Sangharakshita the Green Tārā initiation, Rimpoche visited Sangharakshita at his rented vihara and, after explaining the Green Tārā sādhana to him at greater length, predicted that he would soon come to own a vihara himself. 'At that stage I didn't know I was going to get a vihara,' said Sangharakshita, 'I certainly didn't have the money for one.' Rimpoche then bestowed a name on the vihara-to-be: it was to be called the Triyana Vardhana Vihara, 'The Place Where the Three Yanas Flourish', and he spontaneously composed the following stanzas:

> In a sky devoid of limits, the teaching of the Buddha is
> The sun, spreading the thousand rays of spiritual discipline;
> Continually shining in the radiance of the impartial disciples,
> May this realm of the Triyana be fair!
> In accordance with this request, made in the Fire-Monkey Year
> On the ninth day of the first month by the Maha Sthavira
>   Sangharakshita,
> This was written by the Shakya-upasaka, the Vidyadhara
>   Sangye Dorje:
> May there be happiness and blessings![152]

Rimpoche built many temples, stupas, and retreat facilities in India and Nepal. He has many disciples from Tibet, Bhutan, Nepal, India, and the West. With his consort, Kamala, he had two daughters, but he continued to lead a peripatetic, unpredictable life and to resist all involvement in monastic or bureaucratic structures. At the end of his life he was based in Pharping, a Nepalese pilgrimage spot associated with Padmasambhava. He died there on 30 December 2015.

Kachu Rimpoche

Dudjom Dorje Khacheod Rimpoche, or Kachu Rimpoche, born in 1920, was the eighth tulku of Lhatsun Rimpoche, who had introduced Buddhism into Sikkim. He was a man of great learning, a gifted sculptor, and a very deep meditator and visionary.

Sangharakshita was introduced to Rimpoche by one of his Western acquaintances in Kalimpong. She was a nun who had been ordained by Dhardo Rimpoche but had become rather frustrated with him because (according to her) he was not teaching her fast enough. One day she was wandering in the jungle in Sikkim, in quite a distraught state, when she came upon a clearing, and there, sitting in the clearing, was a Tibetan lama. Since she was dissatisfied with Dhardo Rimpoche, this really cheered her up. 'Oh, a new guru, how wonderful!' she thought. She approached him and they fell into conversation. The lama, who was Kachu Rimpoche, explained that he was the new abbot of Pema Yangtse Gompa, the Royal Monastery of Sikkim, and that he had just come to take charge of the monastery. According to custom, however, he had to enter the monastery on a certain auspicious day and, since that day had not yet come, he was waiting in the clearing, in his little tent, for the day on which he would make his official entrance. 'Oh, this is wonderful, this is providential!' the nun exclaimed. Then Kachu Rimpoche, as was customary, began to make enquiries of her – 'Who are you? Who ordained you?' and so on. 'I'm a Frenchwoman, ordained by Dhardo Rimpoche,' she replied. 'And what meditation practice are you doing?' he asked. 'I'm doing such-and-such practice,' she answered. 'No you're not!' Rimpoche responded, 'You haven't done that practice for six months,' and it was true.

From the time of their first meeting Rimpoche went out of his way to befriend Sangharakshita, who would visit him in his monastery in Gangtok. Rimpoche also visited Sangharakshita at his vihara, often turning up unannounced.

Sometimes Sangharakshita used to function as Rimpoche's translator from Nepali when he was visited by religious seekers. Once an American couple wanted to meet him, so Sangharakshita invited Rimpoche and them to lunch. They asked all sorts of questions and Rimpoche replied. Some of the questions concerned quite technical and abstruse points, such as the nature of nirvāna and so on, and as the conversation flowed on Sangharakshita suddenly realized that Rimpoche was answering their questions without waiting for him to translate. Since Rimpoche knew not a word of English, Sangharakshita concluded that he must have been telepathic.

Apart from Yogi Chen, Sangharakshita believes that of all his teachers, Kachu Rimpoche was the one most committed to meditation. He relied very much on the inspiration it gave him and would act upon any vision that arose in the course of his practice. Once, when he was staying at the Triyana Vardhana Vihara, he told Sangharakshita at breakfast, 'In my meditation this morning, I saw a banner of victory on the roof of your vihara. We've got to put one there.' So he went straight to the bazaar, saw the carpenter, and had a frame made; went to the cloth merchant and got all the different coloured silks; went to the tailor and had it all stitched up; and then returned and erected it himself on the roof of the vihara with all the necessary ceremonies and offerings. That, Sangharakshita said, was typical of him.

Kachu Rimpoche urged Sangharakshita to ask Jamyang Khyentse Chökyi Lodrö for initiations. After these had been given Jamyang Khyentse Rimpoche handed Sangharakshita over – as it were – to Kachu Rimpoche for further teaching, insisting especially that he be given the Padmasambhava initiation.

In 1962 Rimpoche came to stay for a time at Sangharakshita's vihara and gave him the Padmasambhava initiation. He also gave him the name 'Urgyen' – the Tibetan version of the Sanskrit 'Uḍḍiyāna', Padmasambhava's mythical homeland. The day after the initiation, as we saw earlier, Sangharakshita came upon a Tibetan monk selling a few woodblock prints of Tibetan script in the local bazaar. Wanting to help the man, who was clearly destitute, Sangharakshita gave him what money he had in exchange for texts. Returning to the vihara he showed them to Rimpoche, who was delighted to find that they were Nyingma texts, mainly concerned with Padmasambhava. One of the texts was the *Tharpe Delam*, or 'Easy Path to Emancipation', which, among other things, gives an account of the four foundation yogas. In particular it described the Going for Refuge and Prostration practice, based on a Refuge Tree which centred upon Padmasambhava. After obtaining Kachu Rimpoche's permission, Sangharakshita translated the text with the help of Dhardo Rimpoche and took up the prostration practice for the remainder of his stay in Kalimpong.

Despite giving him several initiations, and therefore standing in a formal guru–disciple relationship to him, Rimpoche continued to be very much a friend to Sangharakshita:

> He was by nature a very cheerful, very lively, very unassuming person, very warm-hearted; but unlike my other teachers he was a bit rough, not very polished or elegant, a bit rough-and-ready. But very good-hearted, very warm-hearted, very generous, very communicative, and with an earthy sense of humour. He was deeply, very deeply, devoted to Khyentse Rimpoche and to the Nyingma tradition.[153]

Kachu Rimpoche died on 4 July 1981 in Kathmandu, while he was there for medical treatment.

Dudjom Rimpoche

Dudjom Rimpoche was a great scholar and a gifted meditator. After so many leading lamas from the Tibetan community had gone into exile, the Dalai Lama decided to appoint heads for the different schools in order to help preserve harmony among them, and he asked Dudjom Rimpoche to assume the post of head of the Nyingma School. Sangharakshita met Rimpoche in Kalimpong, where he was staying in rather regal style with his wife and family. Sangharakshita received a number of initiations from him:

Dudjom Rimpoche was very much the Tantric guru, unafraid of worldly powers. He would sometimes dress in Western clothes, such as Hawaiian shirts, with a huge wad of notes in his top pocket! He gave me the Vajrasattva initiation wearing a cowboy hat! He had been married a number of times, and was rather fond of whisky – although I never heard of him being intoxicated.[154]

Dudjom Rimpoche was born in 1904, in the Pemako region on the frontier of Tibet, into an aristocratic family. His predecessor, the great Rime master Dudjom Lingpa, was still alive when he was born, but gave very precise instructions to his followers on how to discover his next reincarnation. 'Go to the secret region of Pema Ko,' he told them, 'Before you young ones get there, I, the old one, will already be there.' And so it was. When they arrived in Pema Ko they found his reincarnation.

The young Dudjom Rimpoche was a spiritually gifted child. From the age of five, it is claimed, he began discovering *termas*. He quickly mastered many complex teachings, and was able to give empowerments and oral transmissions on the collected treasure texts of the Nyingma lineage by the age of fourteen. From then on he gave major empowerments relating to the different treasure cycles, and composed many sādhanas. He wrote commentaries both on his predecessor's teachings and on his own *termas* and, aged seventeen, composed a celebrated treatise on Dzogchen. He became widely renowned as a scholar and meditation master and developed a huge following of students in Tibet and throughout the Himalayan region. In his teaching, he stressed the Dzogchen view:

Since pure awareness of nowness is the real buddha,
In openness and contentment I found the Lama in my heart.
When we realize this unending natural mind is the very nature
    of the Lama,
Then there is no need for attached, grasping, or weeping
    prayers or artificial complaints.
By simply relaxing in this uncontrived, open, and natural state,
We obtain the blessing of aimless self-liberation of whatever
    arises.[155]

Teachers of Enlightenment

Foreseeing the coming Chinese invasion, he and his family left Tibet for India in 1958. It was here, in Kalimpong, that Sogyal Rimpoche first met him:

> He was small, with a beautiful and gentle face, exquisite hands, and a delicate, almost feminine presence. He wore his hair long and tied up like a yogin in a knot; his eyes always glittered with secret amusement. His voice seemed like the voice of compassion itself, soft and a little hoarse.[156]

After his arrival in India, Rimpoche established many temples and monasteries, including impressive foundations in Kalimpong, Orissa, Rewalsar, and at Bodhnath in Nepal. He had a huge following in India, where he strongly encouraged the exiled Tibetan community to study the Nyingma tradition. His literary output was prodigious and includes the compendious two volumes on *The Nyingma School of Tibetan Buddhism* which has been published in the West.

In the final phase of his teaching Rimpoche travelled extensively in the West, giving formal Dharma teachings and initiations, and personally supervising students in their meditation practice and on retreat. He established meditation and retreat centres in France, Hong Kong, and the United States. Rimpoche was, however, not uncritical of Western values:

> One day he was driving through France with his wife, admiring the countryside as they went along. They passed a long cemetery, which had been freshly painted and decorated with flowers. Dudjom Rimpoche's wife said, 'Rimpoche, look how everything in the West is so neat and clean. Even the places where they keep corpses are spotless. In the East not even the houses that people live in are anything like as clean as this.'
>
> 'Ah yes,' he replied, 'that's true; this is such a civilized country. They have such marvelous houses for dead corpses. But haven't you noticed? They have such wonderful houses for the living corpses too.'[157]

Rimpoche died in the Dordogne region of France in 1987, and his embalmed body was placed in a specially constructed stupa in Bodhnath, Nepal in 1989.

Dilgo Khyentse Rimpoche

 Sangharakshita met Dilgo Khyentse Rimpoche in Kalimpong in 1959. Having just come into exile in India, and having fled Tibet rather suddenly and without preparation, the previously wealthy, aristocratic lama was living in great poverty. But this seemed not to disturb him at all, nor did it curb his innate generosity:

He was a very gentle, very kindly person, and a very great scholar – he was always reading. Whenever I went to see him, he always had a book in his hand, which he put aside as I entered. I used to study with him and our relationship was always of a teacher-pupil kind. I received many initiations from him, including the Amitābha initiation.

He was a very humble, very unassuming person, who never made much of a splash, who never looked for disciples. I must mention that both he and his wife – in fact the whole family – were very very tall, at least six and a half feet, they were absolute giants! After he came out of Tibet he was very, very poor. When I left Kalimpong for the West I went to visit Dilgo Khyentse and his wife and they gave me a knife as a leaving present.... This was all they had in their house to give at that time.[158]

Dilgo Khyentse Rimpoche was born in 1910, the fourth son of the Dilgo family, which traces its descent from King Trisong Detsen. Even before his birth, the great lama Mipham Rimpoche took an active interest in the fourth child of this noble family, and shortly after his birth the lama blessed the boy by performing a Mañjuśrī empowerment ceremony and undertaking to take care of him throughout all his future lives. 'I feel that this blessing of his was the single most important event in my life,' Dilgo Khyentse Rimpoche later wrote in his autobiography.[159]

One of the principal lamas of the Dilgo family was the great Jamyang Khyentse Wangpo, who died in 1892, and when the boy was one year old, Loter Wangpo, the foremost Sakya disciple of Jamyang Khyentse Wangpo, came to pay them a visit. He immediately recognized their fourth child as an emanation of his teacher. Mipham Rimpoche, however, counselled that the recognition should not be made public 'as it might provoke obstacles'. On several occasions after that, various lamas recognized the boy's outstanding qualities, but his father objected strongly. 'The lamas won't let me keep this son. But I'm not going to let him become a lama. We have a large family estate and much land to look after. I want him to remain a layman so that he can take care of it all.'

When he was ten years old the young boy was badly scalded in an accident and became seriously ill. 'What ceremonies will help you get better?' his father asked. 'If there's anything that can save your life we must do it!' The lad very much wanted to become a monk, so he replied, 'It would help if I could wear monk's robes.' His father complied and the child recovered. For the next two years he trained as a monk with various accomplished teachers in the Nyingma tradition and, when he was twelve, Shechen Gyaltsap Rimpoche formally recognized him as the mind emanation of Jamyang Khyentse Wangpo.[160]

Dilgo Khyentse spent the next five years living under the guidance of Gyaltsap Rimpoche at Shechen, one of the six principal Nyingma monasteries, studying with him and with Jamyang Khyentse Chökyi Lodrö who, although seventeen years older than Dilgo Khyentse, was also an emanation of Jamyang Khyentse Wangpo. Gyaltsap Rimpoche made a profound impression on the youth:

> While he was giving empowerments, I was often
> overwhelmed by the splendor and magnificence of his
> expression and his eyes as, with a gesture pointing in my
> direction, he introduced the nature of mind. I felt that, apart
> from my own feeble devotion that made me see the teacher
> as an ordinary man, this was in fact exactly the same as the

great Guru Padmasambhava himself giving empowerments to the twenty-five disciples. My confidence grew stronger and stronger, and when again he would gaze and point at me asking, 'What is the nature of mind?,' I would think with great devotion, 'This is truly a great yogi who can see the absolute nature of reality!' and began to understand, myself, how to meditate.[161]

Returning home, he practised alone in a cave for a time and received teachings from other lamas. He then received a letter from his father telling him that Gyaltsap Rimpoche had died:

> For a moment my mind went blank. Then suddenly the memory of my teacher arose so strongly that I was overwhelmed and wept. That day I felt as though my heart had been torn from my chest. I went back to Denkhok and started a period of retreat in the mountains that would last thirteen years.[162]

Shechen Gyaltsap had given the young Khyentse Rimpoche many teachings and had shown him the true nature of his own mind. He, in turn, had promised his teacher that he would show the same unstinting generosity to all who asked him for instruction. In order to prepare himself he spent the next thirteen years in silent retreat:

> I practised from the early hours before dawn until noon, and from afternoon until late into the night. At midday I read from my books, reciting the texts aloud to learn them by heart....
>
> I lived in the cave at Cliff Hermitage without coming out of retreat for seven years.... I was sixteen when I started that retreat. I sat all the time in a four-sided wooden box, occasionally stretching my legs out. Shedrup, my elder brother, was my retreat teacher and he told me that unless I sometimes took a walk outside I might end up deranged; but I felt not the slightest wish to go out.[163]

During this period Khyentse Rimpoche became seriously ill. Jamyang Khyentse Chökyi Lodrö and several other lamas unanimously agreed that the time had come for him to take a consort, as was necessary for him as a *tertön* (a finder of the spiritual treasures concealed by Padmasambhava). Accordingly, he married Lhamo, a simple girl from an ordinary farming family. From then on his health improved; he had many deep visions and revealed many of the mind treasures of Padmasambhava.

After completing his retreat, at the age of 28, Khyentse Rimpoche spent many years with Jamyang Khyentse Chökyi Lodrö, whom he thought of as his second main teacher. After receiving a cycle of empowerments from him, Khyentse Rimpoche expressed the desire to spend the rest of his life in solitary retreat. But his teacher was adamant, 'Your mind and mine are one,' he said, 'The time has come for you to teach and transmit to others the countless precious teachings you have received.' From then on Khyentse Rimpoche worked constantly for the benefit of living beings.

In 1959 the Dilgo estates in Kham were confiscated by the Chinese, and Rimpoche and his family barely escaped to Bhutan. He arrived in Sikkim, penniless, just in time to perform the cremation of Jamyang Khyentse Chökyi Lodrö, who had recently died, and he went on to stay in the Kalimpong and Darjeeling region, where he met and exchanged teachings with other great lamas such as Dudjom Rimpoche and Kangyur Rimpoche.

At the request of the royal family, Rimpoche went to live in Bhutan where he became a schoolteacher near the capital. Disciples gradually became drawn to him and he became the foremost Buddhist teacher in the kingdom, revered by all, from the king to the humblest peasant.

Around this time he also became one of the main teachers of the Dalai Lama, offering him most of the major teachings from the Nyingma tradition. He re-founded Shechen Monastery, building a magnificent complex near the great stupa at Bodhnath in Nepal, and he travelled extensively – visiting Tibet twice and the West several times. Wherever he was he would rise before dawn to pray and meditate for several hours before embarking on a continuous flow of activity until late at night. He accomplished a huge workload with effortless serenity. He taught in every free moment of the day, tirelessly responding to all requests for instruction and spiritual guidance. He died in Bhutan in 1991.

Pure perception, the extraordinary outlook of the Adamantine Vehicle, is to recognize the Buddha-nature in all sentient beings and to see primordial purity and perfection in all phenomena. Every sentient being is endowed with the essence of Buddhahood, just as oil pervades every sesame seed. Ignorance is simply to be unaware of this Buddha-nature, like a poor man who does not know that there is a pot of gold buried beneath his hovel. The journey to enlightenment is thus a rediscovery of this forgotten nature, like seeing the ever-brilliant sun again as the clouds that have been hiding it are blown away.[164]

Jamyang Khyentse Rimpoche

Jamyang Khyentse Chökyi Lodrö is widely thought to have been the greatest master of many Tibetan Buddhist lineages of the twentieth century. Although himself the abbot of a Sakya monastery, his chief affiliation was Nyingma and he was a leading exponent of the Rime approach to Tibetan Buddhism. The Rime (pronounced *ree-may*, and meaning 'no boundaries') movement began in the nineteenth century in eastern Tibet, where a number of lamas belonging to different traditions met together and exchanged initiations so as to create a more unified tradition. Rimpoche's predecessor, Jamyang Khyentse Wangpo, also known as Jamyang Khyentse the Great, played a significant part in the founding of the movement. Sangharakshita has always thought it significant that he had a strong personal connection with Jamyang Khyentse Rimpoche, a representative of 'ecumenical' Tibetan Buddhism, because the Triratna Buddhist Order tries to follow that same approach with regard to the whole Buddhist tradition.

Rimpoche himself was very learned and very widely read, as Sangharakshita explains on one of his first meetings with him:

He looked up from his book,... a very grey and dignified figure, very regal, but very kindly, and said to me, 'Do you know anything about dancing?' And I had to say 'No.' Because I didn't. So he said, 'Pity. I've been reading about dancing ... in the Kanjur there are several works on dance, and I've been studying them recently.'

Of course those Indian works on dance are the choreographic basis of the Tibetan so-called 'lama dances'. That's why he was interested and why he was studying them. But this just illustrated the extent of his studies and his researches. He was reading all these texts on dance and wanted to gather further information on the subject if he could, even from Western sources. He was a little bit disappointed that I couldn't tell him anything about dance.[165]

Jamyang Khyentse Chökyi Lodrö was born in 1893. His father was a Tantric master and himself the son of a *tertön*. When he was seven, the nephew of Jamyang Khyentse Wangpo recognized Rimpoche as the action-emanation of his uncle, and took him to Kathok Monastery.

When Rimpoche was ten years old, his tutor, Khenpo Thupten Rigdzin, became ill and Rimpoche nursed him personally – cooking, washing him, fetching water, and so on – until he died three years later. Rimpoche later said that this service of his not only pleased his tutor, it also purified his own qualities.

When he was 15, the young Khyentse Tulku at Dzongsar Monastery – the seat of Khyentse Wangpo – died, and Rimpoche was installed in his place. There was a great deal of opposition to his taking over the seat there, but the young Rimpoche faced the challenge and slowly calmed everything down with his skill, fearlessness, tolerance, and compassion.

Over the subsequent years he travelled throughout Tibet, receiving teachings and initiations in all the main schools. He spent many years in retreat and was widely acclaimed as a master of all the many Tibetan Buddhist traditions. He was a renowned visionary and many miraculous incidents were attributed to him.

At the age of 56 he married Khandro Tsering Chodron, who is now regarded as the foremost female master in Tibetan Buddhism.

In 1955, aged 63, he arrived in India, and after making an extensive pilgrimage based himself at the Palace Chapel of the king of Sikkim. Sangharakshita met him in 1957 and asked him for the Mañjughoṣa initiation. Rimpoche, however, decided to give him the initiations of Avalokiteśvara, Vajrapāṇi, and Green Tārā as well. He then commissioned a thangka for Sangharakshita that depicted the four Bodhisattvas and nineteen great Buddhist teachers. Sangharakshita himself was shown twice, once teaching the Dharma and once meditating in a cave. Rimpoche explained that through this initiation he had transmitted to Sangharakshita the essence of all the teachings of all the gurus in the thangka. Sangharakshita was now, he said, their spiritual heir and successor.

Sangharakshita has described how Rimpoche looked while conducting this ordination. He seemed to be gazing upwards, at the actual rainbow-bodied forms of the Bodhisattvas themselves, just as if he were actually seeing them there, like old friends, and effecting an introduction between them and Sangharakshita. By virtue of Rimpoche's spiritual eminence and the nature of this particular initiation, Sangharakshita thinks of Rimpoche as his 'root guru'.

Jamyang Khentse Rimpoche, Dudjom Rimpoche, and Chetul Sangye Dorje maintained a particularly close connection with one another. They had a number of disciples in common. One day, a discussion arose among some of those disciples as to which of the three was the greatest and most enlightened. So one of the disciples was deputed to ask Rimpoche which lama was the greatest of the three. Was there one of them who was more enlightened, or spiritually developed, than the other two? Rimpoche heard the questioner out and then nodded and replied, 'Yes, yes, very interesting. As a matter of fact, out of the three of us, one is definitely more enlightened than the other two. But you people will never know which one!' In *The Tibetan Book of Living and Dying* Sogyal Rimpoche paints a vivid picture of this great teacher:

> My master, Jamyang Khyentse, was tall for a Tibetan, and he always seemed to stand a good head above others in a crowd. He had silver hair, cut very short, and kind eyes that glowed with humour. His ears were long, like those of the Buddha. But what you noticed most about him was his presence. His

glance and bearing told you that he was a wise and holy man. He had a rich, deep, enchanting voice, and when he taught his head would tilt slightly backward and the teaching would flow from him in a stream of eloquence and poetry. And for all the respect and even awe which he commanded, there was humility in everything he did.[166]

Rimpoche had a profound respect for all the Buddhist traditions, and worked tirelessly to overcome inter-Buddhist sectarianism. As he wrote in *The Opening of the Dharma*:

The Buddha's many vehicles, his paths of wisdom and insight (such as Mahayana and Hinayana), are without any limit, and the various traditions of the different practices of Dharma are profound beyond all imagination....

The Lion of the Shakya Clan, the All-Knowing Master, has turned the wheel of Dharma on three different occasions. With the first turning, the Buddha eliminated the incorrect view of not believing in cause and effect. With the next turning, the Buddha eliminated the incorrect view of the inherent existence of an independent ego-identity, the basis for deluded ego-grasping. With the last turning, the Buddha eliminated the basis of wrong views altogether, that is, the belief in the independent inherent existence of any phenomenon whatsoever, permanent or impermanent....

Taking refuge is the stable and secure foundation of all the paths to Enlightenment and of all other vows. It is what differentiates Buddhists from non-Buddhists and what protects us from harm from either humans or the spirits. By taking refuge, all our wishes for happiness both in this lifetime and in future ones will be fulfilled. Therefore we must completely entrust ourselves to the Three Jewels of Refuge: to the Buddha, the true teacher; to the Dharma, the true protection; and to the Sangha, the true guides. We must not take refuge just with our words, but from our hearts, having developed the complete confidence that the Three Refuges will never disappoint us. Then we must be very careful to honour always our commitments....

The Sangha Community of Buddhists should all be friendly to each other, and we must abandon all divisive talk of sectarianism. Do not take sides and say that this is my Sect and that is his Sect. Do not fabricate contradictions among the teachings of the many Traditions of the Buddha (for there are none). Do not abandon being respectful to the Dharma (by saying there are contradictions in its various Traditions). The teachings of the Buddha are as vast and deep as the ocean. We must understand that all the teachings are intended as methods for taming our minds, and we must put them into sincere practice accordingly. Externally we should be peaceful and relaxed, with our body, speech and mind always under control; inwardly we must have self-awareness at all times, mustering the forces of alertness and memory....

As for myself, I am close now to my death and am experiencing the sufferings of old age. All I can do now is have good and pure wishes for the preservation of the Dharma. Although I have no powers or abilities to benefit directly the teachings of the Buddha, I am always making efforts in praying for propagation of the Dharma.[167]

Rimpoche died in 1959. Most of his remains are enshrined in a small golden stupa in the Royal Chapel in Sikkim.

On the left is Dr Ambedkar, wearing a garland. On the right,
Anagarika Dharmapala in his renunciates robes.

Reviving Buddhism in Modern India

On either side of the teachers of the present sit Dr Babasaheb
Ambedkar on the left, and Anagarika Dharmapala on the right. Both
sit on white lotus thrones on branches that stem from the Refuge
Tree. These figures were responsible for the revival of Buddhism
in modern India. They influenced both how Sangharakshita
understood Buddhism and how it might be practised in the modern
world. They also informed the way he founded his new Buddhist
Movement, the Triratna Buddhist Community. Sangharakshita
said that, along with the Buddha and Milarepa, Dharmapala and
Ambedkar are the figures that inspired him most in his life.[168]

Sangharakshita started to correspond with Dr Ambedkar in 1950
after Ambedkar wrote an article called 'Buddha and the Future of
His Religion' for the *Maha Bodhi* journal.[169] They met three times after
that, meetings that were important for Sangharakshita both personally
and for the future of the Dharma in India. Inspired by Dr Ambedkar,
Sangharakshita taught the Dharma to those Indians newly converted
to Buddhism.[170] After he left India and in the 1970s, Sangharakshita
encouraged his disciples to do likewise. Through his meetings with

Dr Ambedkar, Sangharakshita realized that Buddhism itself could have a transformative effect on society. In fact it could not *but* have an effect on society, just as society has an effect on individuals practising Buddhism. 'After my contact with Dr Ambedkar, I became much more aware of the social dimension of Buddhism, in fact the social dimension of existence itself.[171]

In contrast, Sangharakshita never met Dharmapala. But in 1952 he started a biographical sketch of Dharmapala, having known very little about his life in advance. Such was his enthusiasm on finding out more about him that he finished his work in only three weeks. He said he wrote it *'con amore'* as he became aware of 'the towering moral spiritual and grandeur of the man... the picture of utter devotion to the work of spreading the Dharma which his whole life presented'.[172]

Dharmapala and Ambedkar were originally part of the Refuge Tree of the Triratna Buddhist Order in India. Buddhism had largely ended in the land of its birth by the thirteenth century and both men had central roles in its revival. It is through the example of Dr Ambedkar in particular that many Indians continue to be inspired to become Buddhists.

In 2018, Sangharakshita requested that Dharmapala and Ambedkar be included on the Refuge Tree throughout the Triratna Buddhist Community. He said that they belong to our lineage of inspiration and deserve a place on the Tree we all use. We too can be inspired by the lives of these two men who devoted their lives to the spread of the Dharma in the demanding conditions of the modern world. Sangharakshita added that 'now the Refuge Tree is complete'.[173]

Anagarika Dharmapala

Dharmapala, or 'Protector of the Dharma', was also known as 'The Lion of Lanka' because of his courageous determination to re-establish the Dhamma once more in India and Sri Lanka, and to spread Buddhism in countries newly taking an interest in 'Eastern Religion'. He was born in 1864 into a middle-class Buddhist family in Colombo and, like most Sri Lankans, had to take a Christian name.

Buddhism, while not openly outlawed, was repressed by the British colonial administration. Children had to be taken for registration at a church and educated in church-run schools. Dharmapala, or David Hewavitarne as he was known at the time, was no exception. Rather than making him turn against the religion of his ancestors, however, studying Christianity convinced him of his Buddhist faith.

There were two turning points for this. The first was when, as a boy, his school fellow died. The body was laid out and the teachers asked the students to offer prayers. Looking around at their grave faces, Dharmapala realised that the prayers were born of a fear of death. He decided at that moment that he did not want to pray out of fear or live a life of fear. The other incident was in 1883 when a peaceful Buddhist procession was attacked by an angry Christian mob. Dharmapala's father refused to have his son continue to study at a Christian school and withdrew him, despite him not having finished his schooling. Interestingly, his school warden gave him an excellent certificate. Evidently Dharmapala earned the respect of his elders. Every Wesak festival day, when the Buddhists in Sri Lanka celebrated the Buddha's Enlightenment, Dharmapala would go to the office of the Warden and ask for a day's holiday to join in the festival, and every Wesak Warden Millar would refuse. Dharmapala would gather his belongings and walk out of the school anyway. The following day, he would be beaten for his insolence.

Sangharakshita said of Dharmapala that 'with him, religion was not an intellectual conviction, but an instinct'. Dharmapala was searching to deepen his understanding and practice of Buddhism and spiritual experience. He went to the library and read philosophy, psychology, history and poetry, particularly the English Romantic poetry of Shelley and Keats. He also pursued his interest in Theosophy. In 1880, the famous Theosophists Col. Olcott and Mme. Blavatsky came to Sri Lanka, making history by being the first Westerners in Sri Lanka to repeat the Buddhist Refuges and Precepts after a Buddhist monk. The people of Sri Lanka had long been used to Westerners attacking the Dhamma, and it was a cause of much celebration when they embraced it. David started a lifelong connection with the Theosophical Society, joining the Society while still under age. He went to Adyar, their headquarters in India, where he was encouraged to learn about Buddhism rather than studying the occult, with which Theosophy was more commonly associated.

Returning to Colombo, he took up the vows of homelessness and celibacy, and decided to devote his life to working for Buddhism. He became Anagarika Dharmapala; Anagarika meaning 'homeless one', and Dharmapala meaning 'Protector of the Dharma'. He lived a full time, semi-monastic, Buddhist life while not a full monk. He wore robes, though not the traditional ones of a monk, and his hair was short rather than shaved. Tirelessly touring around Sri Lanka and later Japan, the U.S., South East Asia, India and Europe, he encouraged people to follow and practise the Buddha-Dhamma. He also set up schools and hospitals in Sri Lanka, and temples and viharas in India and Sri Lanka.

In 1893 he was invited to Chicago to address the World Parliament of Religions. He proved a very popular speaker, impressing people with his sincerity and energy and filling the halls in which he spoke to beyond capacity. On that visit, the first person to formally go for refuge to the Three Jewels in America took the refuges and precepts from Dharmapala as his preceptor. Dharmapala offered a simple and direct message: practise ethics, meditation, love, and wisdom. This message had a huge effect on those who heard it and sowed the seeds for Buddhism in the West:

> In the religion of Buddha is found a comprehensive system of
> ethics, and a transcendental metaphysic embracing a sublime
> psychology. To the simple-minded it offers a code of morality,
> to the earnest student a system of pure thought. But the basic
> doctrine is the self-purification of man. Spiritual progress
> is impossible for him who does not lead a life of purity and
> compassion. The rays of the sunlight of truth enter the mind
> of him who is fearless to examine truth, who is free from
> prejudice, who is not tied by the sensual passions and who has
> reasoning faculties to think.

Dharmapala also had a more personal vision. In 1891 he visited the Mahabodhi temple at Bodh Gaya, the sacred place where the

Buddha is reported to have gained Enlightenment. At that time, the temple was owned by the Hindu Mahant, who not only neglected the temple, but also sold off some of its sculptures. Dharmapala vowed that he would re-establish the Sangha there and enable the Buddhists to take custody of the temple and care for it. The vow emerged from a feeling of deep inspiration that he found at that site. He said it was there that he experienced, for the first time in his life, 'that peace which passeth all understanding. How peaceful it was.' He set up 'The Mahabodhi Society' shortly afterwards to help him achieve his aims, though it was fraught with difficulties: financial, legal and from the impact of religious intolerance. There were even threats of violence. At the time of his death in 1933 at the age of 68, the Temple at Bodh Gaya was still under the control of the Hindu Mahant, and the only visible fruits of Dharmapala's labour was the Maha Bodhi Guest House located nearby. However, others carried on his mission. In 1949 the management of the Temple was passed over to the Bodhgaya Temple Management Committee, composed of Buddhists and Hindus. There are still calls for exclusively Buddhist management.

Anagarika Dharmapala received the lower and higher ordination of a monk shortly before his death. It was his last wish, having had an aspiration to a simple life of brahmacarya, or celibacy and purity, since he was eight years old. He was finally able to shed his enormous responsibilities and hand over all worldly affairs, no longer handling money, which is not allowed in monastic rules. As Sangharakshita points out:

> It behoves us to remember, in this connection, that in spite
> of his devastatingly energetic career of practical activities
> and achievements, Dharmapala's temperament had a
> pronouncedly ascetic side which was no less characteristic of
> the man as a whole. He loved solitude, meditation and study,
> and if these do not occupy a more prominent position in his
> biography the fact is due not to his own lack of inclination
> for them, but to the circumstances in which he lived, when
> the task of rousing the Buddhist world from its centuries
> long slumber was the one which made the most imperative
> demand upon the resources of his genius.

In recent years, Dharmapala's life has been identified primarily with his work to revitalise Buddhism and restore a sense of national pride in Sri Lanka. However, Dharmapala's impact on the world was much more than that. His life is an example of the *vīrya*, or energy, of a Bodhisattva, who works for the good of others. To do that work, he drew on a life of simplicity, meditation, particularly meditation on *maitrī*, or loving kindness, and wisdom. Dharmapala kept a diary throughout most of his life. At the top of each page he wrote: 'The only Refuge for him who aspires to true perfection is the Buddha alone.'

Dr Bhimrao Ramji Ambedkar

Dr Ambedkar's first name translates as 'fearsome', and that is what he had to be as 'the most educated man in India' having been born into the community with the lowest social status. Indian society is divided into four main 'castes' with the Brahmins, the priestly caste, at the top, followed by the warriors, the merchants, and the servants. Below these four castes are the community of what was formally known as 'the untouchables'. They were deemed 'untouchable' by those of higher caste. They are now known as the 'Dalits' or oppressed, or what Dr Ambedkar called 'the scheduled castes'. Each caste is divided into many subcastes. Dr Ambedkar called this a system of 'graded inequality'. Caste norms dictated who you could marry or be friends with and where you could eat, drink, walk, or sit. Those in the scheduled castes were denied access to education, owning land, and religious knowledge, and the system was kept in place by violence and oppression.

Dr Ambedkar was born into one of the scheduled castes in 1891. His father was in the Indian army, and this enabled Ambedkar to get an education, and he was the first member of his caste to matriculate from high school. Sponsored by the forward-thinking Maharaja of Baroda who recognised his talent, he became a master of arts and doctorate in economics at Columbia University in New York; master of science and doctor of science in economics at the London School of Economics, and a barrister-at-law at Grey's Inn, London. With that kind of education, Dr Ambedkar could have become a wealthy man, perhaps living abroad where caste discrimination would no longer touch him. Instead he dedicated his life to the eradication not only of caste discrimination, but of all kinds of inequality in society.

His followers often tell the story of the moment when he made this commitment. After finishing his education in New York and starting his studies in London, Dr Ambedkar's funds from the Maharaja ran out. Dr Ambedkar was required to work for the Baroda State government in return for his scholarship, and he was forced by poverty to return to India and fulfil his commitment. Even though he was highly educated with a good government job, he was unable to find accommodation due to his caste. In desperation he assumed a Parsi name and lived in a Parsi boarding house. His working life was no easier. His colleagues never accepted his position there. They criticised him openly and threw his papers onto his desk to avoid any physical contact. The situation became untenable when the Parsi community learned of his deception and demanded his expulsion from the guest house, threatening to beat him up. Ambedkar had nowhere to go. He visited the Maharaja to explain his situation, but the Maharaja was unable to help. Defeated, Ambedkar sat in tears on a bench near the palace. He reflected that if he was to be treated this way despite his learning and experience, how much worse it must be for other members of his caste. He decided that he would not rest until he had removed caste discrimination in India and challenged inequality in the world.

Dr Ambedkar tried many methods to fulfil his aim. He tried social action, most famously in 1927 at the Chavadar Tank (reservoir) in Mahad. A resolution had been passed to enable all castes use public water sources, but in practice, the scheduled castes were intimidated and threatened so that they couldn't use it. In March of that year, Ambedkar led 3,000 people to drink from the tank. When they got there they found it ritually 'purified' with 108 pots of cow dung, urine, milk, yoghurt and ghee by members of the higher castes. Later that year Ambedkar organised another social action in which 10,000 people gathered to burn a copy of the *Manusmṛti*, the text outlining the most discriminative caste laws.

Dr Ambedkar realised he needed more than social action. He advocated for political, economic, and social reform, becoming the first Law Minister of independent India and drafting the constitution. In 1936 he was invited to a conference on how to annihilate caste distinctions, but the paper he was to deliver was deemed too inflammatory and his invitation rescinded. He published it nonetheless, arguing that caste is not a real entity, but a state of mind. For that reason, it can only be overcome by the mind itself:

> Caste is not a physical object like a wall of bricks or a line of
> barbed wire... which has, therefore, to be pulled down. Caste
> is a notion, it is a state of the mind. The destruction of Caste
> does not therefore mean the destruction of a physical barrier.
> It means a *notional* change.[174]

How can one change the mind itself to overcome inequality? For Ambedkar, the answer lay in Buddhism, which has a clear method of transforming mental states into love and wisdom. 'If the new world – which be it realised is very different from the old – must have a religion – and the new world needs religion far more than the old world did – then it can only be the religion of the Buddha.'[175] Buddhism teaches a path of ethics and the fundamental virtues of liberty, equality and fraternity, or maitrī. These qualities could help India, and the world, throw off the shackles of all inequality in society. For Ambedkar, Buddhism was more than a social force. All his life he had felt a strong connection to the Buddha and studied the Buddha's teachings. The last book he wrote is called *The Buddha and His Dhamma*.[176]

Sangharakshita first met Ambedkar in Mumbai in 1952 after he publicly decided to convert to Buddhism. His immediate impression of Ambedkar was of someone who evoked in his followers both devotion and respect. Sangharakshita told of how, on his first meeting, he saw how Ambedkar responded to a deputation who had come to see him:

> As Ambedkar advanced towards them, a frown on his face,
> the three or four men in Western-style reach-me-downs who
> appeared to be the leaders of the deputation produced an
> enormous marigold-and-tinsel garland which they attempted
> to place round his neck. This token of homage Ambedkar
> thrust roughly aside with every mark of impatience, not to say

irritation. Far from resenting this display of apparent rudeness the leaders of the deputation stood clutching the garland and gazing at their leader with an expression of utter devotion as, still frowning, he addressed to them (in Marathi) a few short, sharp sentences of what seemed to be rebuke. Evidently they had done something wrong, and he was scolding them. But they no more resented this than they had resented his refusal of the garland, the expression on their faces plainly saying that if instead of scolding them he was to beat them with a stick they would count it the greatest of blessings. This was my first experience of the devotion with which Ambedkar was regarded by his followers, and I never forgot that scene in the surgery. Indeed four years later it helped me to understand the readiness with which those same followers responded to his call to embrace Buddhism.[177]

Not only did Ambedkar evoke devotion, he also evoked some trepidation, and he was not always a comfortable person to be around. Ambedkar had experienced a lot of hardships in his life, and he worked impressively hard. He was serious, and he took other people seriously:

Ambedkar was of above-average height, brown- complexioned, and heavily built, with a distinct inclination to corpulence. His Western-style suit was well cut, but hung on him rather loosely, like the wrinkled hide on an elephant. As for his head, this matched his body, being large and well formed, while the pear-shaped face revealed an exceptionally lofty brow, very full jowls, a slightly aquiline nose, and a mouth the corners of which were turned down to a remarkable degree. More noticeable still was Ambedkar's expression, which was grim and lowering, as of a man who rarely smiled. So grim and so lowering was it, indeed, that watching him I had the impression of a great black storm-cloud – a storm-cloud that might discharge thunder and lightning at any minute.[178]

Fortunately, their second meeting was more cordial. Ambedkar, having decided to embrace Buddhism, asked Sangharakshita how this should be done. Sangharakshita told him how one becomes a Buddhist by reciting the Refuges and Precepts, and undertaking the practice of the Five Precepts. 'By this time Ambedkar and I had been talking a good while, and a feeling of warmth and confidence had sprung up between us, as though we were members of the same family.'[179]

Between their second and third meeting, Dr Ambedkar had embraced Buddhism with 400,000 of his followers. It was a joyous occasion, with Ambedkar's followers pouring into Nagpur dressed in the cleanest white and shouting slogans of victory. But Ambedkar was not well, suffering from diabetes and arthritis. When Sangharakshita last saw him he was very tired, and though Sangharakshita made every attempt to shorten the meeting, Ambedkar urged him to stay:

> There was evidently much that was weighing on his mind,
> much that he wanted to speak to me about, and he had
> no intention of allowing bodily weakness and suffering to
> prevent him from continuing the conversation. The longer
> he spoke, though, the more concerned about him I became,
> for his head gradually sank until it almost touched his
> outstretched arms, which were resting on the surface of
> the table. Sitting there in that way, like an Atlas for whom
> the globe had at last become almost too heavy for him to
> bear, he spoke of his hopes and fears – mostly fears – for
> the movement of conversion to Buddhism that he had
> inaugurated.[180]

Ambedkar had a deep conviction that Buddhism could be a force for goodness in the world, but he died before he could fulfil his vision to establish Buddhism in India and further afield. Who could carry on the work that he had started? Sangharakshita said:

> I had the distinct impression that he somehow knew we
> would not be meeting again and that he wanted to transfer to
> my shoulders some of the weight that he was no longer able to
> bear himself. There was still so much to be done, the sad, tired
> voice was saying ... so much to be done...[181]

Sangharakshita was in Nagpur when he received the news of Ambedkar's death only two months after the conversion ceremony. Being in the heartland of Ambedkar's followers, over the next four days he was able to console hundreds of thousands of people who had embraced Buddhism with such hope and inspiration, only to have their great leader pass from them. They needed guidance and encouragement. Not only did Sangharakshita help the new Buddhists of Nagpur, he was also very affected by his communication with those he met and the events he took part in:

> My own spiritual experience during this period was most peculiar. I felt that I was not a person but an impersonal force. At one stage I was working quite literally without any thought, just as one is in *samādhi*. Also I felt hardly any tiredness – certainly not at all what one would have expected from such a tremendous strain. When I left Nagpur I felt quite refreshed and rested.[182]

Sangharakshita went on to visit the Indian Buddhists on the plains regularly. When he left to set up a new Buddhist movement in the West, he asked some of his British disciples to carry on his work back in India. Today around a third of the Triratna Buddhist Order is in India. Sangharakshita described how he felt as if the Triratna Buddhist Order was founded by a 'supra-personal force'[183] working through him. He describes it in similar terms as the force he felt when addressing the crowds of new Buddhists after Ambedkar's death. Looking at Dr Ambedkar's life, we can imagine that the same force worked through Dr Ambedkar's thoughts and actions, leading him to devote his whole life to the welfare of others.

Conclusion

We have now briefly visited all forty-six figures on the Refuge Tree. Each of them has, in their own right, an inspiring and fascinating story to tell. Taken together, they are a great blaze of spiritual inspiration, holding out to all of us the constant prospect of self-transformation. But the Refuge Tree, in its widest sense, is much more even than that.

The true Refuge Tree is not the image we see in pictures, nor the symbol we visualize in meditation. Nor is it confined to the myths and stories of the forty-six great figures upon it. All sentient beings experience an unavoidable urge to reach outside themselves to find security. The most creative possible manifestation of this great common urge is the act of Going for Refuge to the Three Jewels. The Refuge Tree, from its most cosmic and most general perspective, is a symbol of this act. The true Refuge Tree is a symbol of the great will to growth that manifests wherever there is life.

This expanded vision of the Refuge Tree encompasses all possible levels of Going for Refuge. With us, at the foot of the Tree, stand all unenlightened living beings. Between us we make up the levels of cultural, provisional, and effective Going for Refuge. Upon the Refuge Tree are not just the forty-six figures we have been looking at, but rather all those who are further along the path than we are, in particular those beings whose Going for Refuge is Real and those for whom it is Absolute. And this image, in its totality, is an image of Cosmic Going for Refuge – a term that Sangharakshita has used poetically to stand for the urge to growth and self-transcendence that is inherent in life itself.[184]

When we see this fact in its fullness, then the previously grey, two-dimensional world of materialist thought breaks into colour and takes on the added dimension of spiritual depth. The will to growth is there in all living beings. Some forms of life show only the smallest spark of it. In others it manifests as a blaze of spiritual glory.

Looked at in this way, the Refuge Tree exhibits the hierarchical nature of Buddhist thought, which follows from the hierarchical nature of life itself. If growth is possible at all, it necessarily follows that some will have grown more than others. The figures on the Tree are further along the path than we are and even on the Tree itself there are some who are more and some who are less developed. The Refuge Tree is perhaps the only symbol in Buddhism of the spiral tendency within conditionality that Dhammadinnā referred to in her teaching.

We, of course, are in no position to rank the outstanding figures on the Refuge Tree. As we saw in the story of Jamyang Khyentse Rimpoche, we will never know which figures are higher than others, and this is not important. It is far more important that we allow the image of the Tree to act upon us, that we open ourselves up to it and to the image of the vast potential for growth and development that it represents. As we are now, we experience only the tiniest portion of our own potential and that of others. Looking up to the figures on the Tree, coming into relationship with them, feeling a sense of gratitude, love, and devotion to them, we begin to open ourselves up to the awesome extent of their spiritual development. Then, seeing our current place in the scheme of things, we may also awaken, to some extent at least, to our own true potential.

When we engage with the Refuge Tree, placing our heart upon that which is highest, we begin to find out 'where we are at'. All kinds of resistance to the practice emerge, and we soon find out where we really place our hearts. When we see this, if we are honest in our endeavours, we get a clearer sense of our place in the cosmic scheme of things.

We are deluded, as yet unenlightened, beings. Yet, somehow, by our great good fortune, we have come into contact with the Refuge Tree and the endless vistas of change for the better that it represents. If only we can align ourselves with it, keep it steady before us, and go to it for Refuge, again and again, what can we not achieve?

Teachers of Enlightenment

Notes and References

Preface to the 2000 edition

1 Lord Alfred Tennyson, *Idylls of the King*, ed. J. M. Gray, Penguin, London 1996.
2 Sangharakshita (trans.), *Dhammapada* 188–92, Windhorse, Cambridge 2010, pp.168–9.
3 Kenneth Clark, *Monuments of Vision*, John Murray 1981, p.68.

Part One
Chapter One

4 Sangharakshita, *Facing Mount Kanchenjunga*, Windhorse, Glasgow 1991, p.100.

Chapter Two

5 Trans. H. Saddhatissa, *Sutta-Nipāta*, Curzon Press, London 1985, pp.131–3.
6 Sangharakshita, *The Priceless Jewel*, Windhorse, Glasgow 1993, p.57.
7 Wordsworth, 'The world is too much with us'.

Chapter Three

8 Sangharakshita (trans.), *Dhammapada* 188–92, Windhorse, Cambridge 2010, pp.168–9.
9 For a fuller treatment of this, see Subhuti, *Sangharakshita: a New Voice in the Buddhist Tradition*, Windhorse, Birmingham 1994, p.92.

Chapter Four

10 *Ratnaguṇa-saṃcayagāthā*, from Edward Conze, *The Perfection of Wisdom in Eight Thousand Lines and its Verse Summary*, Four Seasons Foundation, San Francisco 1983, p.9.

Part Two
Chapter Five

11 *Samyutta-Nikāya* ii.178ff.
12 *Sutta-Nipāta*, op. cit., p.46.
13 Ibid., p.47.
14 Ibid., p.47.
15 *Majjhima-Nikāya* i.245–8 in Bhikkhu Ñāṇamoli and Bhikkhu Bodhi (trans.), *The Middle Length Discourses of the Buddha*, Wisdom Publications, Boston 1995, p.339.
16 From Canto 11 of the *Buddhacarita*, or 'The Acts of the Buddha', by Aśvaghoṣa. Edward Conze, *Buddhist Scriptures*, Penguin, London 1959, pp.48–9.
17 Ibid., p.49.
18 *Sutta-Nipāta*, op. cit., p.75.
19 *The Mahāvastu*, in *Buddhist Scriptures*, op. cit., pp.21–3.
20 'Metteyya' is the Pāli form of the Sanskrit 'Maitreya'.
21 Maurice Walshe (trans.), *The Long Discourses of the Buddha*, Wisdom Publications, London 1995, pp.403–4.

22 Edward Conze (ed. and trans.),
    Buddhist Scriptures, op. cit.,
    pp.238–42.
23 Lama Anagarika Govinda, *The
    Way of the White Clouds*, Rider,
    London 1966, p.17.
24 Ibid., p.9.

Chapter Six

25 Quoted in H.W. Schumann,
    Buddhism, Wheaton, Ill. 1974,
    p.168.
26 Sangharakshita, *The Rainbow
    Road*, Windhorse, Birmingham
    1997, p.338.
27 Fremantle and Trungpa, *The
    Tibetan Book of the Dead*, trans.
    with commentary by Francesca
    Fremantle and Chögyam
    Trungpa, Shambhala, Boston and
    London 1987, pp.48–9.
28 Thomas Cleary (trans.), *Entry
    into the Realm of Reality: The
    Text*, Shambhala, Boston and
    Shaftesbury 1986, p.365.

Chapter Seven

29 See Reginald Ray, *Buddhist Saints
    in India*, Oxford University Press,
    New York and Oxford 1994, for a
    full account of this phenomenon.
30 Quoted in Nyanaponika Thera
    and Hellmuth Hecker, *Great
    Disciples of the Buddha*, Wisdom
    Publications, Boston 1997, p.7.
    The complete story is found at
    Vinaya i.39ff.
31 Vinaya ii.12; iii.182–3.
32 *Samyutta-Nikāya* iv.251.
33 Udāna iii.iv, quoted in *Great
    Disciples of the Buddha*, op. cit.,
    p.37.
34 *Samyutta-Nikāya* xii.32, quoted in
    ibid., p.46.
35 *Theragāthā* 1146–9, from K.R.
    Norman (trans.), *The Elders Verses
    I*, Pali Text Society, Oxford 1990,
    p.106.
36 *Majjhima-Nikāya* iii.248, in *The
    Middle Length Discourses of the
    Buddha*, op. cit., p.1097.

37 *Dhammapada* commentary,
    vv.137–40, quoted in *Great
    Disciples of the Buddha*, op. cit.,
    p.103.
38 *Samyutta-Nikāya* v.2.
39 Jataka 296, quoted in *Great
    Disciples of the Buddha*, op. cit.,
    p.142.
40 *Aṅguttara-Nikāya*, iii.78.
41 *Theragāthā* 1030–31, quoted in
    Great Disciples of the Buddha, op.
    cit., p.153.
42 Quoted in ibid., p.154.
43 Adapted from Vinaya ii.253f.
44 *Theragāthā* 1041–3, quoted in
    Great Disciples of the Buddha, op.
    cit, p.148.
45 Mahāparinibbāna Sutta, *Dīgha-
    Nikāya* 16, in *The Long Discourses
    of the Buddha*, op. cit., p.265.
46 Ibid.
47 Ibid.
48 *Samyutta-Nikāya* ix.5, quoted in
    Great Disciples of the Buddha, op.
    cit., p.179.
49 From *Jātaka* 469, quoted in ibid.,
    p.118.
50 Adapted from *Theragāthā* 1057.
51 *Theragāthā* 1062–71, quoted in
    Great Disciples of the Buddha, op.
    cit., pp.134–6.
52 *Majjhima-Nikāya* i.299, in *The
    Middle Length Discourses of the
    Buddha*, op. cit., p.396.
53 Ibid., v.29, p.403.
54 Susan Murcott, *The First Buddhist
    Women*, Parallax, Berkeley 1991,
    p.64.

Chapter Eight

55 *Devotion to Avalokiteśvara*, from
    ed. Edward Conze, *Buddhist Texts
    Through the Ages*, Oneworld,
    Oxford 1995, pp.195–6. © Muriel
    Conze, 1995.
56 From the *Śūraṃgama Sūtra*, in
    Dwight Goddard (ed.), *A Buddhist
    Bible*, Beacon Press, Boston 1994,
    p.257.
57 Je Tsong Khapa, 'The Ocean
    of Clouds of Praises of the

Guru Manjughosha', in *Life and Teachings of Tsong Khapa*, ed. and trans. Robert A.F. Thurman, Library of Tibetan Works and Archives, Dharamsala 1982, p.192.

58 Robert A.F. Thurman, *The Holy Teaching of Vimalakīrti: A Mahāyāna Scripture*, Penn State, University Park and London 1976, p.77.

59 Ibid.

60 Sangharakshita, *The Inconceivable Emancipation: Themes from the Vimalakīrti Nirdeśa*, Windhorse, Birmingham 1995, p.113.

61 *The Long Discourses of the Buddha*, op. cit., p.116.

62 Available in English as *Sūtra of the Past Vows of Earth Store Bodhisattva: collected lectures of Tripitika Master Hsüan Hua*, trans. Bhikshu Heng Ching, Chinese Text Translation Society, New York 1974.

63 Pitt Chin Hui (trans.), Kṣitigarbha Bodhisattva *Sūtra*, published for free download at www.tbsn. org/english/library/sutras/ksitigarbha/opnpge.htm

64 Martin Willson, *In Praise of Tārā: Songs of the Saviouress*, Wisdom Publications, London 1986, p.179.

65 Ibid., pp.99–100.

Chapter Ten

66 *Tiratana Vandanā*, translated by Sangharakshita, in *Puja: The FWBO Book of Buddhist Devotional Texts*, Windhorse, Birmingham 1999, p.41.

67 F.L. Woodward (trans.), *The Minor Anthologies of the Pali Canon, part ii, Udāna: Verses of Uplift and Itivuttaka: As it Was Said*, Oxford University Press, London 1948, p.65.

68 Ibid., p.67.

69 Anguttara Nikāya, 65. (Ven Soma Thera, trans). https://www.buddhanet.net/e-learning/kalama1.htm. Accessed 28 December 2022.

70 Published in Sangharakshita, *The Priceless Jewel*, Windhorse, Glasgow 1993.

71 Cyril Birch (ed.), *Anthology of Chinese Literature*, Penguin, London 1967, p.225.

72 Ibid., p.222.

73 Burton Watson (trans.), *The Lotus Sūtra*, Columbia University Press, New York 1993, pp.l00–l.

Chapter Eleven

74 Adapted from *Mūla-madhyamaka-kārikā* 24.18, in Kenneth K. Inada (trans.), *Nāgārjuna: a Translation of his Mūlamadhyamakakārikā*, Hokuseido, Japan 1970, p.148.

75 Adapted from ibid., p.39.

76 Ibid., 24-9–11, p.146.

77 *Trisvabhāvanirdeśa*, trans. Sujitkumar Mukhopadhyaya, Visvabharati, 1939, vv.27–30, p.55.

78 *Bodhicaryāvatāra*, ch.9 v.34.

79 Trans. Stephen Batchelor, *A Guide to the Bodhisattva's Way of Life*, Library of Tibetan Works and Archives, Dharamsala 1979, ch.3, vv.18–19, p.32.

80 Ibid., ch.8, vv.129–30, p.120.

81 Trans. Kate Crosby and Andrew Skilton, *The Bodhicaryāvatāra*, Oxford University Press, Oxford 1996, ch.2, vv.10–11, p.15.

82 Ibid., ch.6, vv.14–15, p.51.

83 Ibid., ch.9, v.26, p.117.

84 *Visuddhimagga* xix.20, quoted in Sangharakshita, *A Survey of Buddhism*, Windhorse, Glasgow 1993, p.125.

85 Buddhaghosa, *Visuddhimagga*, in Bhikkhu Ñāṇamoli (trans.), *The Path of Purification*, Buddhist

Publication Society, Kandy 1991, chapter 9, vv.1–13, pp.288–90.

86 Ibid., v.44, p.300.

87 From 'The Song of a Yogi's Joy', in Garma C.C. Chang (trans.), *The Hundred Thousand Songs of Milarepa*, Shambhala, Boston and London 1999, pp.74–5. Published by arrangement with Carol Publishing Group, Inc., Secaucus, NJ 01962. Oriental Studies Foundation. All rights reserved. Reprinted by permission of Citadel Press.

88 Geshe Wangyal, *Door of Liberation*, Wisdom Publications, Boston 1995, p.84.

89 Ibid., p.86.

90 Ibid., pp.84–5.

91 Yeshe Tsogyal, *The Life and Liberation of Padmasambhava*, trans. Tarthang Tulku et al, Dharma Publishing, Berkeley 1978.

92 Ibid., canto 22, p.141.

93 Ibid., canto 22, p.142.

94 Ibid., canto 61, pp.377–83.

95 Ibid., canto 62, p.388.

96 'Praise of Buddha Śākyamuni for His Teaching of Relativity', in *Life and Teachings of Tsong Khapa*, op. cit., pp.99–100.

97 *Door of Liberation*, op. cit., pp.135–7.

98 A.F. Price and Wong Mou-lam (trans.), *The Diamond Sūtra and the Sūtra of Huineng*, Shambhala, Boston 1990, p.70.

99 Ibid., p.72.

100 Ibid., p.129.

101 Ibid., pp.151–3.

102 Wai-tao (trans.), 'Dhyana for Beginners', in Dwight Goddard (ed.), *A Buddhist Bible*, op. cit., pp.438–40.

103 Anthony C. Yu (trans.), *The Journey to the West (Xi You Ji)*, University of Chicago Press, 1980.

104 Samuel Beal (trans.), *Si-yu-ki: Buddhist Records of the Western World*, Motilal Banarsidass, Delhi 1981, pp.170–1.

105 Ibid., pp.172–3.

106 Tripiṭaka-Master Hsüan Tsang, *Ch'eng Wei-Shih Lun: Doctine of Mere-Consciousness*, trans. Wei Tat, Ch'eng Wei-Shih Lun Publication Committee, Hong Kong 1973, pp.11 and 13.

107 Norman Waddell (trans.), *Wild Ivy: the Spiritual Autobiography of Zen Master Hakuin*, Shambhala, Boston and London 1999, p.87.

108 Heinrich Dumoulin, *Zen Buddhism: a History*, vol. 2: Japan, New York and London 1990.

109 *Wild Ivy*, op.cit., pp.84–6.

110 Trans. Philip B. Yampolsky, *The Zen Master Hakuin: Selected Writings*, Columbia University Press, New York 1971, pp.33–4.

111 *Wild Ivy*, op. cit., pp.3–4.

112 Ibid., pp.65–6.

113 Trevor Leggett (trans.), *A First Zen Reader*, Charles E. Tuttle, Rutland 1960, pp.67–8.

114 *Kōbō daishi zenshū* III.305, quoted in Yoshito S. Hakeda, *Kūkai: Major Works*, Columbia University Press, New York 1972, p.22.

115 III.476, ibid., p.27.

116 I.19, ibid., pp.31–2.

117 I.100, ibid., p.32.

118 III.524, ibid., p.47.

119 III.406–7, ibid., pp.51–2.

120 Stephen Batchelor, *The Awakening of the West: The Encounter of Buddhism and Western Culture*, Aquarian, London 1994, p.127.

121 Yuho Yokoi, *Zen Master Dōgen: an introduction with selected writings*, Weatherhill, New York and Tokyo 1976.

122 Dōgen, *From the Zen Kitchen to Enlightenment*, Weatherhill, New York 1983, p.7.

123 Reihö Masunaga (trans.), *A Primer of Sōtō Zen: a translation of Dōgen's Shōbōgenzō Zuimonki,*

University of Hawaii, Honolulu 1971, pp.7–8.

124 Unpublished translation by the Ryukoku Translation Center, Ryukoku University, Kyoto 1999.

125 Hisao Inagaki, Kosho Yukawa, and Thomas R. Okano (trans.), *Kyō Gyō Shin Shō: The Teaching, Practice, Faith, and Enlightenment, a collection of passages revealing the true teaching, practice, and enlightenment of Pure Land Buddhism*, vol.5, Ryukoku Translation Center, Ryukoku University, Kyoto 1983, p.84.

126 Ibid., pp.107–8.

127 Ibid., pp.113–14.

Chapter Twelve

128 Sangharakshita, *The Rainbow Road*, Windhorse, Birmingham 1997, p.80.

129 Ibid., p.219.

130 The suffix 'ji' is an Indian honorific.

131 Ibid., p.456.

132 Sangharakshita, *In the Sign of the Golden Wheel*, Windhorse, Birmingham 1996, pp.340–1.

133 Sangharakshita, *A Guide to the Buddhist Path*, Windhorse, Birmingham 1996, p.103.

134 Sangharakshita, *My Relation to the Order*, Windhorse, Birmingham 1998, p.26.

135 Sangharakshita, 'My Eight Main Teachers', unpublished talk given in the USA and slightly edited.

136 Ibid.

137 Ibid.

138 Ibid.

139 Yogi C.M. Chen, *Buddhist Meditation: Systematic and Practical*, published by Dharma Friends of Dr Lin, 1980, free copies available from Dr Yutang Lin, 705 Midcrest Way, El Cerrito, CA94530, USA.

140 Ibid., pp.xiv–xv.

141 Ibid., p.xviii.

142 Ibid., pp.66–7.

143 Ibid., p.17.

144 Sangharakshita, 'My Eight Main Teachers', op. cit.

145 Sangharakshita, *The Rainbow Road* op. cit.

146 'My Eight Main Teachers', op. cit.

147 Interview with Suvajra, January 1988, WBO Tape Archive.

148 Suvajra, *The Wheel and the Diamond: the Life of Dhardo Tulku* op. cit.

149 Sangharakshita, *In the Sign of the Golden Wheel* op. cit.

150 Naomi Burton, Patrick Hart, and James Laughlin (eds), *The Asian Journal of Thomas Merton*, New Directions, New York 1973, pp.143–4.

151 'My Eight Main Teachers', op. cit.

152 Subhuti, *Bringing Buddhism to the West*, Windhorse, Birmingham 1995, p.70.

153 'My Eight Main Teachers', op. cit.

154 'My Eight Main Teachers', op. cit.

155 Dudjom Rimpoche, *Calling the Lama from Afar*, Rigpa, London 1980, as quoted in Sogyal Rimpoche, *The Tibetan Book of Living and Dying*, Rider, London 1998, p.44.

156 *The Tibetan Book of Living and Dying*, op.cit., p.45.

157 Ibid., p.17.

158 'My Eight Main Teachers', op. cit.

159 Matthieu Ricard, *Journey to Enlightenment: The Life and World of Khyentse Rimpoche, Spiritual Teacher from Tibet*, Aperture, New York 1996, p.13.

160 Jamyang Khyentse Wangpo had five emanations: those of his body, speech, mind, qualities, and activity.

161 *Journey to Enlightenment*, op. cit., pp.33–4.

162 Ibid., p.34.

163 Ibid., p.40.

164 Ibid., p.82.

165 'My Eight Main Teachers', op. cit.

166 *The Tibetan Book of Living and Dying*, op.cit., p.xi.

167 *The Opening of the Dharma (a brief exposition of the Essence of the Buddha's Many Vehicles)*, Library of Tibetan Works and Archives, Dharamsala 1982, pp.9, 21, 25–7.

168 'Sangharakshita and his Legacy' https://vimeo.com/3693791. Accessed 28 December 2022.

169 Magazine '*Maha Bodhi*': Maha Bodhi Society Journal, Calcutta; Vaishak Number, Vol. 58, May 1950. Also published in *Dr Babasaheb Ambedkar Writings and Speeches Vol.17*. Part 2, Section-I, Article 17. Government of Maharashtra, Mumbai, 2003.

170 Dr Ambedkar converted to Buddhism in 1956 with around 400,000 followers. For more information, please refer to *The Complete Works: Volume 9, Dr Ambedkar and the Revival of Buddhism 1*, published by Windhorse Publications.

171 Sangharakshita, interview with Saddhanandi, 2015 See thebuddhistcentre.com 'Nine Decades: A Life in Objects 1955–65 https://thebuddhistcentre. com/stories/decades/1955–1965/. Accessed 28 December 2022.

172 Sangharakshita, *Flame in Darkness: The Life and Sayings of Dharmapala*, Preface to the 1980 edition.

173 https://thebuddhistcentre. com/preceptors/chairs-letter-%E2%80%93-april-2020

174 Dr Ambedkar, *Annihilation of Caste*, Navayana Publishing.

175 Dr Ambedkar, *Buddhism and the Future of His Religion*, Mahabodhi Journal, May 1950.

176 Bhimrao Ramji Ambedkar, Aakash Singh Rathore, Ajay Verma (eds) (2011), *The Buddha and His Dhamma: a critical edition*. Oxford University Press.

177 Sangharakshita, *The Complete Works: Volume 9, Dr Ambedkar and the Revival of Buddhism 1*, Windhorse Publications 2016, p.15.

178 Ibid., p.16.

179 Ibid., p.17.

180 Ibid., p.20.

181 Ibid., p.21.

182 Sangharakshita, *Dear Dinoo: Letters to a Friend*, Ibis Publications, 2012.

183 Subhuti, *A Supra Personal Force*, 2011.

Conclusion

184 For a fuller treatment of this theme see Aloka, 'The Cosmic Refuge Tree', *Articles Shabda*, November 1998, published privately.

Selected Reading

General

Andrew Skilton, *A Concise History of Buddhism*, Windhorse, Birmingham 1997

H. Kohn (trans.), *The Shambhala Dictionary of Buddhism and Zen*, Shambhala, Boston 1991

Paul Williams, *Mahāyāna Buddhism*, Routledge, London 1989

Sangharakshita, *A Guide to the Buddhist Path*, Windhorse, Birmingham 1996

Sangharakshita, *The Three Jewels*, Windhorse, Birmingham 1998

Lokabandhu (ed.), *Readings from the Refuge Tree of the Western Buddhist Order*, published privately.

Stephen Batchelor, *The Awakening of the West*, Aquarian, London 1994

Subhuti, *The Mythic Context*, published privately by Padmaloka Books, 1990

Aloka, *The Refuge Tree as Mythic Context*, published privately by Padmaloka Books, 1994

Dhammadinnā, *The New Refuge Tree*, a talk delivered at the WBO Convention 1991, published by Tiratanaloka Books.

The Buddhas of the Three Times

Bhikkhu Ñāṇamoli, *The Life of the Buddha*, Buddhist Publication Society, Kandy 1992

Aśvaghoṣa, *The Buddhacarita, or 'Acts of the Buddha'*, trans. E.H. Johnston, Motilal Banarsidass, Delhi 1984

J.J. Jones (trans.), *The Mahāvastu* (3 vols), Pali Text Society, London 1976–87

G.P. Malalasekera, *Dictionary of Pāli Proper Names* (3 vols), Pali Text Society, Oxford 1997

Maurice Walshe (trans.), *Cakkavatti-Sīhanāda Sutta, Dīgha-Nikāya* in *The Long Discourses of the Buddha*, Wisdom Publications, Boston 1995

Sangharakshita, *Who is the Buddha?* Windhorse, Birmingham 1994

Gwendolyn Bays (trans.), *The Voice of the Buddha (Lalitavistara Sūtra)* (2 vols), Dharma Publishing, Berkeley 1983

The Five Jinas

Vessantara, *Meeting the Buddhas: a Guide to Buddhas, Bodhisattvas, and Tantric Deities*, Windhorse, Birmingham 1998

The Larger Sukhāvatī-vyūha Sūtra, The Smaller Sukhāvatī-vyūha Sūtra, The Amitāyur Dhyāna Sūtra, all in F. Max Müller (ed.), *Buddhist Mahāyāna Texts*, Motilal Banarsidass, Delhi 1997

Franscesca Fremantle and Chögyam Trungpa, *The Tibetan Book of the Dead*, Shambhala, Boulder and London 1975

Thomas Cleary (trans.), *Entry in the Realm of Reality: the Text*, Shambhala, Boston and Dorset 1987

The Arhants

Nyanaponika Thera and Hellmuth Hecker, *Great Disciples of the Buddha: Their Lives, Their Works, Their Legacy*, Wisdom Publications, Boston 1997
Zenno Ishigami, *Disciples of the Buddha*, Kosei Publishing Co., Tokyo 1989
G.P Malalasekera, *Dictionary of Pāli Proper Names* (3 vols), Pali Text Society, Oxford 1997
K.R. Norman (trans.), *Theragāthā I*, Pali Text Society, Oxford 1990
Susan Murcott, *The First Buddhist Women*, Parallax, Berkeley 1991

The Bodhisattvas (including Vajrasattva)

Vessantara, *Meeting the Buddhas: a Guide to Buddhas, Bodhisattvas, and Tantric Deities*, Windhorse, Birmingham 1998
David Snellgrove, *Indo-Tibetan Buddhism: Indian Buddhists and Their Tibetan Successors*, Serindia, London 1987
Martin Willson, *In Praise of Tārā: Songs of the Saviouress*, Wisdom Publications, London 1986
Paul Williams, *Mahāyāna Buddhism*, Routledge, London 1989
John Blofeld, *Bodhisattva of Compassion: the Mystical Tradition of Kuan Yin*, Shambhala, Boston 1988

The Dharma Texts

Sangharakshita, *The Eternal Legacy*, Tharpa, London 1985

Andrew Skilton, *A Concise History of Buddhism*, Windhorse, Birmingham 1997
Paul Williams, *Mahāyāna Buddhism*, Routledge, London 1989

The Teachers of the Past

General

H. Kohn (trans.), *The Shambhala Dictionary of Buddhism and Zen*, Shambhala, Boston 1991
Lobsang N. Tsonawa, *Indian Buddhist Pandits from 'The Jewel Garland of Buddhist History'*, Library of Tibetan Works and Archives, Dharamsala 1985

Nāgārjuna

Keith Dowman, *Masters of Mahāmudrā: Songs and Histories of the Eighty-Four Buddhist Siddhas*, SUNY, New York 1985
K. Venkata Ramanan, *Nāgārjuna's Philosophy*, Motilal Banarsidass, Delhi 1976
Chr. Lindtner, *Master of Wisdom: Writings of the Buddhist Master Nāgārjuna*, Dharma Publishing, Berkeley 1986
David J. Kalupahana, *Nāgārjuna: The Philosophy of the Middle Way*, SUNY, New York 1986
Kenneth K. Inada, *Nāgārjuna: a Translation of his Mūlamadhyamakakārikā with an Introductory Essay*, Hokuseido, 1970

Asaṅga

Geshe Wangyal, *Door of Liberation*, Wisdom Publications, Boston 1995
Janice Dean Willis (trans.), *On Knowing Reality: the Tattvārtha Chapter of Asaṅga's Bodhisattvabhūmi*, Columbia University Press, New York 1979
Yajneshwar S. Shastri, *Mahāyānasūtrālaṅkāra of Asaṅga:*

a Study in Vijñānavāda Buddhism,
Sri Satguru, Delhi 1989

Vasubandhu

Sujitkumar Mukhopadhyaya (trans.),
Trisvabhāva-nirdeśa, Visvabharati,
Calcutta 1939
Stefan Anacker, Seven Works
of Vasubandhu: The Buddhist
Psychological Doctor, Motilal
Banarsidass, Delhi 1984

Śāntideva

Marion L. Matics (trans.), Entering
the Path of Enlightenment, the
Bodhicaryāvatāra of the Buddhist
Poet Śāntideva, George Allen and
Unwin, London 1971
Stephen Batchelor (trans.), A Guide
to the Bodhisattva's Way of Life,
Library of Tibetan Works and
Archives, Dharamsala 1988
Kate Crosby and Andrew Skilton
(trans.), The Bodhicaryāvatāra,
Oxford University Press, 1996
Cecil Bendall and W.H.D. Rouse
(trans.), Śikṣā-Samuccaya, a
Compendium of Buddhist Doctrine,
Motilal Banarsidass, Delhi 1971

Buddhaghosa

Pe Maung Tin (trans.), The Path of
Purity (3 vols), Pali Text Society,
Oxford 1975
Bhikkhu Nānamoli (trans.), The Path
of Purification (Visuddhimagga),
Buddhist Publication Society,
Kandy, 1985

Milarepa

Garma C.C. Chang (trans.), The
Hundred Thousand Songs of
Milarepa, Shambhala, Boston and
London, 1995
Lobsang P Lhalungpa (trans.), The
Life of Milarepa, Shambhala,
Boston and London 1984

Atiéa

Geshe Wangyal, Door of Liberation,
Shambhala, Boston 1995
Richard Sherburne (trans.), A Lamp
for the Path and Commentary,
George Allen and Unwin, London
1983
Lama Thubten Kalsang, Atisha, a
Biography of the Renowned Buddhist
Sage, Social Science Association
Press, Bangkok 1974

Padmasambhava

Yeshe Tsogyal, The Life and Liberation
of Padmasambhava, trans. Tarthang
Tulku et al. Dharma Publishing,
Berkeley 1978
Keith Dowman, The Legend of the
Great Stupa, Dharma Publishing,
Berkeley 1973

Tsongkhapa

Robert Thurman (ed. and trans.), The
Life and Teachings of Tsongkhapa,
Library of Tibetan Works and
Archives, Dharamsala 1982

Huineng

A.F. Price and Wong Mou-Lam
(trans.), The Diamond Sūtra and
the Sūtra of Huineng, Shambhala,
Boston 1990

Zhiyi

Wai tao (trans.), 'Dhyana for
Beginners', in Dwight Goddard
(ed.), A Buddhist Bible, Beacon
Press, Boston 1994

Xuanzang

Anthony C. Yu (trans.), The Journey
to the West (Hsi-yu chi) (4 vols),
University of Chicago Press, 1980
Samuel Beal (trans.), Si-yu-ki:
Buddhist Records of the Western
World, Motilal Banarsidass, Delhi
1981

Tripiṭaka-Master Hsüan Tsang, *Ch'eng Wei-Shih Lun: Doctrine of Mere Consciousness*, trans. Wei Tat, The Ch'eng Wei-Shih Lun Publication Committee, Hong Kong 1973

Hakuin

Norman Waddell (trans.), *Wild Ivy: the Spiritual Autobiography of Zen Master Hakuin*, Shambhala, Boston and London, 1999

Heinrich Dumoulin, *Zen Buddhism: a History*, vol. 2: Japan, Macmillan, New York and London 1989

Philip B. Yampolsky (trans.), *The Zen Master Hakuin: Selected Writings*, Columbia University Press, New York, 1971

Kūkai

Yoshito S. Hakeda, *Kūkai: Major Works*, Columbia University Press, New York 1972

Dōgen

Yuho Yokoi, *Zen Master Dōgen: an introduction with selected writings*, Weatherhill, New York and Tokyo 1976

Reihö Masunaga (trans.), *A Primer of Sōtō Zen: a translation of Dōgen's Shōbōgenzō Zuimonki*, University of Hawaii, Honolulu 1971

Shinran

Y. Ueda and D. Hirota, *Shinran: an Introduction to His Thought*, Hongwanji International Center, Kyoto, 1989

H. Inagaki, *The Three Pure Land Sūtras*, Nagata Bunshodo, Kyoto, 1994

The Teachers of the Present

Urgyen Sangharakshita

Subhuti, *Bringing Buddhism to the West, a Life of Sangharakshita*, Windhorse, Birmingham 1995

Sangharakshita, *The Rainbow Road*, Windhorse, Birmingham 1997

Sangharakshita, *Facing Mount Kanchenjunga*, Windhorse, Glasgow 1991

Sangharakshita, *In the Sign of the Golden Wheel*, Windhorse, Birmingham 1996

Yogi Chen

Buddhist Meditation Systematic and Practical, published by Dharma Friends of Dr Lin (see note 139 above).

Ven. Jagdish Kashyap

Dr A.K. Narain (ed.), *Studies in Pāli and Buddhism: a Memorial Volume in Honour of Bhikkhu Jagdish Kashyap*, B.R. Publishing Corporation, Delhi 1979

Dhardo Rimpoche

Sara Hagel (ed.), *Dhardo Rimpoche: a Celebration*, Windhorse, Birmingham 2000

Suvajra, *The Wheel and the Diamond: the Life of Dhardo Tulku*, Windhorse, Glasgow 1991

Chetul Sangye Dorje

Tulku Thondup, *Masters of Meditation and Miracles: the Longchen Nyingthig Lineage of Tibetan Buddhism*, Harold Talbott (ed.), Shambhala, Boston and London 1996

Naomi Burton, Patrick Hart, and James Laughlin (eds), *The Asian Journal of Thomas Merton*, New Directions, New York 1973

Dudjom Rimpoche

Dudjom Rimpoche, *The Nyingma School of Tibetan Buddhism: Its Fundamentals and History*, Wisdom Publications, Boston 1991

Dudjom Rimpoche, *Calling the Lama from Afar*, Rigpa, London 1980

Dilgo Khyentse Rimpoche

Tulku Thondup, *Masters of Meditation and Miracles: the Longchen Nyingthig Lineage of Tibetan Buddhism*, Harold Talbott (ed.), Shambhala, Boston and London 1996

Matthieu Ricard, *Journey to Enlightenment: the Life and World of Khyentse Rimpoche, Spiritual Teacher from Tibet*, Aperture, New York 1996

Dilgo Khyentse, *Enlightened Courage: an Explanation of Atisha's Seven Point Mind Training*, trans. Padmakara Translation Group, Editions Padmakara, Peyzac-le-Moustier 1992

Jamyang Khyentse Rimpoche

Tulku Thondup, *Masters of Meditation and Miracles: the Longchen Nyingthig Lineage of Tibetan Buddhism*, Harold Talbott (ed.), Shambhala, Boston and London 1996

Jamyang Khyentse Rimpoche, *The Opening of the Dharma (a brief exposition of the Essence of the Buddha's Many Vehicles)*, Library of Tibetan Works and Archives, Dharamsala, 1974

Index

Introductory Note

References such as '178–9' indicate (not necessarily continuous) discussion of a topic across a range of pages. Wherever possible in the case of topics with many references, these have either been divided into sub-topics or only the most significant discussions of the topic are listed. Because the entire work is about 'teachers of Enlightenment', the use of this term (and certain others which occur constantly throughout the book) as an entry point has been restricted. Information will be found under the corresponding detailed topics.

abbots 5, 68, 199, 212, 215, 250, 252, 254
Abhidharma 93, 143, 156, 159, 175
Abhirati 73–4
abilities 95, 144, 166, 253, 272
absolute nature 161, 266
absolute truth 155–6
absorption 59, 167–8
ādi-buddha 2, 13, 135
aggregates, five 109
air 81, 98, 104, 234
    open 93, 106
Akṣayamati-nirdeśa-sūtra 160
Akṣobhya 12, 70, 72–5, 123
alms 55, 60, 91, 94, 106
alms-bowls 91, 96, 106
alms-food 96
altruistic dimension 42–3, 113
Ambaṭṭha 123–4
Ambedkar, Dr Bhimrao Ramji 11, 41, 233–5, 273–4, 278–83
Amitābha 13, 70, 72, 77–80, 113–14, 117–18, 222–3, 232
Amitāyur Dhyāna Sūtra 77
Amoghasiddhi 13, 70, 80–3
amṛta 124–5

Anagarika Dharmapala 11, 273–8
Ānanda 11, 61–2, 78, 88, 98–104
ancestors 124, 275
    spiritual 44, 150
anger 39, 73, 94, 131, 177, 224
Anuruddha 90, 98, 104
apprehension 23, 26, 143, 172
archetypal Buddhas 12, 71–3, 144
archetypal figures 3, 72
archetypes 24, 89–90, 205
Arhants 14, 50, 63, 89–112
aristocratic families 81, 95, 175, 214, 262, 264
Aristotle 35
armies 56, 58, 75, 96, 231
Arya Samaj, *see* Samaj
Āryatārā 129–32
Asaṅga 152, 156–61, 175, 203
asceticism 57, 59–60, 84, 107, 214
ascetics 60, 63, 65, 93, 97, 171
    wandering 55, 61, 89, 214, 231
āsuras 76, 81, 116–17, 132
Aśvajit 91, 93
Atiśa 12, 170, 174–8, 185–6
Atman 203–4

attachment 60, 94, 131, 155, 177, 221, 223, 243
    undue 43
attitudes 129, 144–5, 196, 210–11, 214, 220–1
attraction 33, 82, 177, 186
    reverse 186
austerities 57, 63, 208, 245
Avalokiteśvara 11, 16, 77–8, 112–18, 130, 132, 199, 202
Avataṃsaka Sūtra 241
Awakening 179, 182, 211, 223

Baba Saheb 235
bad karma 127, 171–2
Bamboo Grove 96, 108
bandits 174, 199
banners 85, 192, 260
bardo 81, 83, 176
Bāvari 17–18
begging 84, 89, 199
    bowls 105, 228
bhikkhus 89, 97, 107, 168
Bhutan 258, 267
Bihar 232, 245, 248–9
birds 4, 18, 78, 80–1, 108, 158, 173, 194
birth 25, 54, 179–81, 202, 208, 211, 264, 274
blessings 129, 184, 233, 236, 258, 262, 264, 281

bliss 40, 56, 78, 85, 100,
187
blood 58, 170, 179, 181,
240
blue light 73, 117, 123, 234
blue sky 136–7, 214
clear 1, 6, 14, 119, 135
Bodh Gaya 59–60, 165,
180, 199, 251–2, 254,
276–7
bodhi tree 63, 74, 191, 199
Bodhicaryāvatāra 12, 162–5
bodhicitta 33, 43–5, 75–6,
112, 114, 125, 131, 241
bodhi-mind 187
Bodhisattva Path 159, 164
Bodhisattvas 7–11, 20,
63, 68–9, 71–2, 76–7,
113–34, 212
archetypal 39, 41
great 124, 126
transcendental 160
Bodhnath 263–4, 267
body of truth 71–2
boundaries 16, 31, 37, 39,
43–4, 83
boundless love 79–80
boys 178–9, 240, 243, 255,
264–5, 275
brahmins 18, 61, 65, 90,
123, 153, 157, 165
women 126–7
brothers 98, 101, 157, 159,
161, 198, 240
Buddha patriarchs 209,
211
Buddhaghosa 12, 124,
152, 165–70
Buddhahood 23, 27, 41,
53–4, 66, 71–2, 74,
127–9
innate 20
Buddha-nature 157, 193,
219–20, 268
Buddhas, *see also individual*
names
archetypal 12, 71–3, 144
of the Three Times 1,
10, 14, 53–70, 113, 181,
229
Buddha-to-be 53, 56, 63,
65–6, 74–5, 81
Buddhavacana 111, 143–6

Cakkavatti-Sīhanāda Sutta
65
cakravartī-rāja 83
candles 1, 233–4, 249–50
captivity 131, 174
caste 60–1, 245–6, 248,
278–80
discrimination/
prejudice 123, 246,
279
scheduled 278–9
caves 158, 160, 172, 184,
243, 247, 257, 266
celibacy 122, 276–7
ceremonies 113, 215, 233,
251, 260, 265
conversion 233–5, 283
Mañjuśrī empowerment
264
Chan school 12, 106, 149,
162, 191, 229, 238
Chatral Rimpoche, *see*
Chetul Sangye Dorje
Chen, Yogi 3, 10, 228, 235,
238–43, 260
Chen dynasty 195–6
Chetul Sangye Dorje 10,
228, 235, 255–8, 270
chief disciples 5, 11, 78,
90, 93, 178
children 127, 131, 133,
211–12, 218, 240–1,
252–3, 264–5
China 9, 124, 126, 191–
206, 213, 215, 217, 219
Chinese Buddhism 7–8,
194, 196, 198, 200, 203,
238, 240–1
Chinese monks 200, 247
Chökyi Lodrö, Jamyang
Khyentse 5, 228, 257,
260, 265–9
clear blue sky 1, 6, 14,
119, 135
clinging 109
ego-based 78
cloth 100, 106, 228, 257
cotton 12, 171–2
clouds 10, 107–8, 115, 136,
146–7, 214, 231, 268
colleges 246, 251, 253
new Buddhist 241
Patna 245

Tantric 251, 253–4
colours 22–3, 76–7,
79–81, 83–4, 117, 119,
130, 134–5; *see also*
individual colours
commitment 27, 33, 84,
229, 237, 271, 279
companions 1–2, 54, 62,
84, 88, 92, 97–9, 102
compassion 60–1, 75, 77,
79, 113–14, 118, 175,
250
great 41, 114, 127, 132,
158
infinite 69, 118
complete Enlightenment
20, 59, 96, 172
concentration 10, 58–9, 74,
110, 136
continuous 176
rudimentary 1
conditionality 126, 135,
286
cyclic 11
spiral 11
conditioned existence
108, 110
confidence 18–19, 34–5,
60, 73, 75, 161, 266, 271
Confucian teachers 242
consciousness 26, 33, 109,
117, 157, 159, 161–2,
203–4
contemplation 51, 207–8,
247
contradictions 7, 154, 196,
272
conventions 21–2
social 55
worldly 61
conversion ceremonies
233–5, 283
Conze, Edward 233
correspondence 236, 243,
254
cotton cloth 12, 171–2
craving 60, 66–7, 93, 109,
186, 223
crowds 63, 97, 108, 179,
235, 270, 283
cultures 23, 26, 76, 147,
150, 237, 252
cyclic conditionality 11

ḍākinīs 6, 73, 179–80
Dalai Lama 116, 186, 251, 256, 261, 267
Daochuo 225–6
Darjeeling 5, 68, 251, 258, 267
darkness 17–18, 115, 125, 129, 136, 146, 180, 187
Daśabhūmika Sūtra 160
death 55, 95–6, 98–9, 138, 176, 179–81, 240–1, 277
deer 4, 108
defilements 19, 104, 115, 177
delight 58, 73, 107–9, 119, 142–3, 251
delusion 26, 30–1, 33, 86, 93, 131–2, 221, 223
demon king 126–7
demons 49, 94, 112, 123, 125, 131
  local 178, 182
dependent origination 92, 154–5, 157, 161, 167, 185, 187
devas 61, 65, 103, 126, 128, 202
development 8, 34, 72, 153, 156, 162, 167, 175
devotion 34, 36, 63, 65, 82–3, 274, 280–1, 286
Dhamma, see Dharma
dhammachanda 32–3
dhammadhātu 94
Dhammadinnā 3, 11, 88, 108–12, 286
Dhammapada 30, 111
Dhardo Rimpoche 3, 6, 10, 228, 235, 249–55, 259, 261
Dharma 12–15, 39–42, 83–4, 99–101, 156–61, 174–5, 178–82, 270–5
  practice 78, 93, 229–30, 237
  teaching 11, 43, 69
  texts 12, 14, 41, 141–7, 214
  true 67–8
dharmacakra 69, 83
Dharmadhātu 84–6
Dharmākara 77–8, 222
dharmakāya 40, 71–2, 135, 242

Dharmapala 41, 273–8
dharmapālas 6, 201
dharmas, real 203–4
dhūtagunas 106
Dhyāna 197
Diamond Sūtra 191, 231
Dīgha-Nikāya 65, 123, 246
Dilgo family 264–5
Dilgo Khyentse Rimpoche 3, 10, 228, 235, 264–8
Dīpaṅkara 10, 14, 52–3, 62–5
disciples 89–93, 99–100, 105–6, 176–7, 192–4, 230, 253–5, 270
  chief 5, 11, 78, 90, 93, 178
discipline 62, 96, 171, 213, 216, 218, 250
disease 55, 253
disgust 57, 59, 106, 210
Dōgen 12, 206–7, 219–22
dogs 20, 242–3
dreams 1, 24, 30, 172, 176, 203, 209, 242
drought 178–9
dualism 38, 157
duality 121, 159, 161–2
  delusory 156
Dudjom Rimpoche 11, 137, 228, 235, 257, 261–4, 270
dzogchen 8, 242, 256–7, 262

education 105, 194, 198, 214, 218, 252, 278–9
ego 37, 39–40, 42–4, 223, 247
egocentricity 43, 45
ego-identity 31, 37–9, 43–5, 76, 271
egoism 221, 223, 247
elders 93, 167, 275
elephants 94, 96, 107, 119, 123, 131, 160, 162
elixir of life 124–5
emancipation 6, 211, 261
emotions 24–7, 36, 71, 81, 110, 114, 234
emperors 25, 83, 196, 198, 200, 205, 216, 218
empowerments 262, 267
  giving 265–6

emptiness 38, 52, 54, 73, 75, 80, 154, 157, 195
  ultimate 81, 154, 166
energy 49, 80, 122–3, 239, 245, 254, 276, 278
Enlightened mind 40–1, 81, 123, 142, 161, 176
Enlightenment, see also Introductory Note
  complete 20, 59, 96, 172
  experience 84, 114
  qualities of 19–20
  supreme 41, 64, 175, 212
enmity 97, 168
equality 75, 163, 280
ethics 34, 74, 110, 164, 166, 175, 276, 280
events, mental 157, 161
evils 58, 62, 74, 128–9, 137, 196
exile 225, 252, 261, 263–4
existence 154, 156–7, 161, 186–7, 203–4, 214, 216, 224
  conditioned 108, 110
  inherent 38, 75, 155–7, 271
  nature of 156, 177
experience 16, 19–20, 25–6, 43–5, 59–60, 145, 147, 156–7
  direct 40, 141
  spiritual 150, 275, 283
external objects 157, 203–4

faith 26, 34–6, 128, 131, 208, 210, 222–3, 226
  serene 68, 223–4
families 55–7, 59–60, 73, 80–1, 113, 240–3, 261, 263–4
  aristocratic/noble 81, 95, 175, 214, 262, 264
  Buddhist 33, 229, 274
family protectors 74, 76, 113–14, 119
fathers 54, 63, 98, 171, 175, 185, 265–6, 269
Faxiang School 162, 198, 204
fearlessness 70, 80, 112, 126, 130–1, 133, 269, 276

fictitious constructions 203–4

Field of Merit 6; *see also* Refuge Tree

five Buddha mandala 2, 41, 71–3

five Buddhas 14, 71, 73, 113, 136

five Jinas 12–13, 40, 49, 71–88, 135

flesh 57–8, 118, 158, 181, 230

flowers 40, 42, 66, 74, 76, 78, 126, 130
  lotus 1, 10, 78, 114, 130, 180
  wild 4

followers 57–8, 60, 62, 68–9, 95–7, 196–7, 212, 279–82

food 4, 31, 55, 74, 97, 99, 106, 244

forests 18, 78, 89, 96, 103, 106, 128, 131

foundation yogas 6–7, 9, 135, 261

freedom 45, 62, 143, 177, 257

friends 55–6, 59–60, 62, 64, 90–5, 229–30, 232, 236–8
  spiritual 100, 237

friendship 97, 254
  spiritual 90, 100, 230, 237

fruit 40, 66, 97, 101, 150, 160, 166, 202

Gaṇḍvyūha Sūtra 85

garlands 11, 85, 107, 122, 136, 273, 281

garuḍas 80

Gelu Rimpoche 241

Gelug monasteries 186, 250

Gelug School 12, 186

gem, wish-fulfilling 75–6, 125

generosity 74–5, 94, 164, 264, 266

geshe 251

gestalt 21–3

gestures 11, 13, 52, 70, 73–5, 77, 80, 84

teaching 12, 52, 70, 88, 170

gifts 75, 97, 168, 178, 200

girls 64, 105, 240, 267

goals 33, 107, 151, 177, 188

gods 13, 23–6, 65, 67, 74, 116–17, 122, 132
  jealous 82, 116

Going for Refuge 6–7, 15–16, 27, 29–36, 39–45, 229–30, 236–7, 285

gold 67, 78, 136, 143, 174, 183, 268
  pure 105

golden light 10, 75, 119, 124

golden vajra 11, 73, 123, 178

golden wheel 83–4

governments 55, 194, 248–9

Govinda, Lama 68, 233

grandeur 122, 142, 274

gratitude 1–2, 45, 78, 223, 286

Great Collection Sūtra 225

great compassion 41, 114, 127, 132, 158

great Refuge Tree, *see* Refuge Tree

green light 77, 81–2

Green Tārā 11, 80, 112, 131, 256, 258, 270

grief 172, 219, 234

Guhyasamāja Tantra 153

guidance 4, 37, 147, 234, 265, 267, 283
  Maitreya 67–8

gurus 173, 180–1, 183, 232, 237–8, 242, 270

Gyaltsap Rimpoche 265–6

hair 55, 57, 119, 124–5, 130, 136, 256, 263

Hakuin 12, 206–13

happiness 31, 60, 65, 68, 118, 120, 128, 173–4

Harsha 200

hate 82, 167

health 100, 221, 255, 267

Heart Sūtra 93, 116

heavens 59, 127, 159, 213

hells 76, 116–17, 125–9, 207, 211

hermitages 232, 242, 247–8, 257, 266

hermits 159, 163, 219, 229, 235, 238, 242–3, 257

hills 29, 108, 173, 232, 252

Himalayas 54, 63, 178, 184, 248, 262

Hīnayāna 7–9, 175, 200

Hindi 246, 252–3

hindrances 86, 123, 197

historical time 22, 41, 71–2

history 7, 23, 31, 41, 49–51, 149, 159, 194
  and myth 49–50

holy life 66–8, 97

holy woman 126–7

homeless life 67, 101

Hōnen Shōnin 222, 224–5

horses 75, 83, 179–80

household life 105, 195

householders 32, 60, 211

Hṛdaya Prajñāpāramitā Sūtra, see Heart Sūtra

Huiguo 215–16

Huineng 12, 190–4, 231

Huisi 195

hūṃ 13, 73, 116, 136–7

humour 62, 261, 270

ignorance 17, 57, 85, 110, 187, 197, 224, 226

images 21–2, 24–5, 36, 38, 40, 80, 85, 285–6
  mental 1, 3, 21
  visualized 15, 20

imagination 11, 17–27, 36, 38, 41, 59, 71–2, 155
  impoverished 25
  spiritual 26, 73

impermanence 31, 78, 85, 117, 172, 195

impressions 3, 38, 256, 265, 280–1

incense 1, 126, 215, 249–50

India 153–70, 174–5, 198, 246–9, 251–2, 255–8, 263–4, 282–3
  northern 60, 200, 245
  reviving Buddhism 273–4
  South 79, 153, 200, 232

Indian Buddhism 2, 12
  traditional 191

Indo-Tibet Buddhist
    Cultural Institute
    (ITBCI) 252–4
Indra 74, 124
inequality 278–80
infinite compassion 69, 118
infinite love 72, 114
influence, spiritual 34, 40,
    42, 44, 151, 229
inherent existence 38, 75,
    155–7, 271
initiations 5, 9, 11, 238–9,
    243, 260–1, 263–4,
    269–70
    Padmasambhava 11,
    260
    Tantric 9, 150, 255, 257
    Vajrayāna 175
inspiration 9, 12, 92, 149–
    50, 171, 175, 274, 283
instructions 16, 167, 220–
    1, 241–2, 262, 266–7
intellect 18, 25–6, 58, 71,
    86, 239
intelligence 82, 119, 127,
    197
intentions 15, 43, 58, 63,
    77, 108, 282
invitations, personal 99,
    141–2
ITBCI (Indo-Tibet
    Buddhist Cultural
    Institute) 252–4

Jagdish Kashyap 10, 228,
    230, 232, 244–9
Jambhala 76
Jamyang Khyentse
    Rimpoche 5, 11, 235,
    243, 260–1, 265–73, 286
Japan 2, 9, 12, 84, 114, 124,
    126–7, 207–28
Japanese Buddhism 196,
    213, 218
jealous gods 82, 116
Jinas, Five 12–13, 40, 49,
    71–88, 135
jñānasattva 20
Jōdo Shin School 222
Jōdo Shinshū 222, 225
Journey to Il Convento 24
joy 64, 66, 68, 173, 182,
    186, 218, 220

Jung, C.G. 24
jungles 84, 145, 232, 248,
    259

Kachu Rimpoche 5–6,
    10–11, 228, 235, 259–61
Kagyu School 172
Kagyupas 6, 12
Kālāmas of Kesaputta 144
Kalimpong 232, 238, 240,
    248, 251–5, 259, 261,
    263–4
kalpas 53, 128, 130
kalyāṇa 238
kāmachanda 32–3
Kaṇhāyans 124
Kapilavastu 54, 84, 98,
    101, 199
Kāraṇḍa-vyūha Sūtra 116
karma 82, 98, 117, 126–7,
    137–8, 172, 186–7
    bad 127, 171–2
Karmapa 184, 242–3
Kashyapji 23, 232–3, 244–8
Kāśyapa 104–8
Kauṇḍinya 60
khakkhara 125
kindness 23, 42, 44–5, 90
    loving 103, 167–8, 278
kingdoms 83, 157, 174,
    179–80, 267
kings 40, 54–6, 60, 62–3,
    103–4, 174, 178–83,
    199–200
    sage 146, 217
kingship 83–4
knowledge 17, 19, 22, 115,
    119, 142, 179–81, 187
    true 110
knowledge-body 20
kōans 207–8, 210
Kosala 56
Kōya, Mount 216, 218
Kṣitigarbha 11, 112, 114,
    125–9
Kūkai 12, 206, 213–18
Kyentse Rimpoche, see
    Jamyang Khyentse
    Rimpoche

labourers 183, 251–2
lamas 239, 251, 254, 259,
    261–2, 264–6, 268, 270

great 184, 250, 255, 267
    Nyingma 229, 255
Land of Bliss 78, 222
Larger Sukhāvatīvyūha
    Sūtra 77, 222
laymen 209, 225–6, 265
leaders 64, 68, 99, 234,
    280–1
legends 23, 59, 63, 113,
    116, 158–9, 163, 166
letters 66, 120, 136–7, 199,
    266
Lhasa 185, 250–1, 253, 257
Lhatsun Rimpoche 259
liberation 82, 86, 91, 97,
    110, 116, 118, 186
    path of/to 82, 91
life 31, 33–5, 53–6, 98–100,
    116, 176–8, 273–81,
    285–6
    holy 66–8, 97
    spiritual 32–4, 37, 39,
    42–3, 90, 93, 100, 236–7
light 14, 18, 29, 31, 49, 79,
    82–5, 136–7
    blue 73, 117, 123, 234
    golden 10, 75, 119, 124
    green 77, 81–2
    rainbow 82–3, 179
    red 79, 82, 117, 178
    white 14, 84–5, 136
lions 56, 83–4, 119, 131,
    179, 271
literal truth 23, 25
literalism 21, 23–5
livelihood, right 42, 44, 110
living beings 65, 67–8,
    81, 114, 117–18, 124,
    127–8, 130–1
London 230–1, 235, 278–9
Loter Wangpo 265
lotus 1, 10–12, 64, 67, 69,
    77, 118–20, 178
    blue 130, 132
    flowers 1, 10, 78, 114,
    130, 180
    thrones 12, 73, 75, 77,
    80, 83, 119, 123
Lotus family 77, 80
Lotus Sūtra 116, 124, 146,
    194–6
love 75, 77, 79, 82, 113,
    118, 276, 280

boundless 79–80
infinite 72, 114
mutual 62, 64
loving kindness 103,
167–8, 278
lust 109, 167, 177, 224
luxury 54–5

Madhyamaka tradition
12, 154, 156–7
Magadha 55, 65, 91, 95,
104, 248
Mahākāśyapa 11, 88, 104
Mahāprajāpatī 101
Mahāvairocana Sūtra 215
Mahāvihāra 165–7
Mahāyāna 7–8, 17, 144,
147, 156–7, 159–61,
163, 175
scriptures 93, 124, 135
sūtras 72, 120, 162, 200
Maitreya 10, 14, 52–3,
65–9, 81, 85–6, 158–60,
198–9
guidance 67–8
mandalas 2, 41, 72–3, 83,
85, 179–80, 216, 229–30
Mañjuśrī 11, 84, 112–13,
118–22, 142, 162
mantras 73, 75, 77, 116,
118, 120, 137–8, 242–3
Māra 58, 65, 74–5, 193
Marpa 172
marriage 54, 64, 179, 245
materialism 24–5
Maudgalyāyana 11, 90–8,
103, 142
meals 61, 91, 99–100, 106
medicine 102, 106, 159,
177, 226
meditation 89–90, 156–60,
172–3, 176, 216, 238–
40, 242–3, 276–8
deep 37, 62, 118, 154
mindfulness 159
practice 156, 167, 196,
220, 230, 259, 263
solitary 96, 104, 107
wrong 226
Megha 63–5
memories 3, 21, 38, 57,
119, 127, 266, 272

mendicant's staff 11, 112,
125
mental events 157, 161
mental images 1, 3, 21
mental processes 156, 161
mental states 110, 116,
159, 280
merit 6, 12, 14, 120, 126–7,
176, 181, 213
karmic 78
religious 202
Metteyya 65
Middle Way 153–4, 157
skilful 60
Milarepa 12, 49, 170–4,
273
mind 1–3, 18–19, 21–3,
55–8, 156–7, 176–8,
191–4, 280
clear 186
Enlightened 40–1, 81,
123, 142, 161, 176
unenlightened 53, 161
mindfulness 62, 86, 91,
104–5, 110
meditation 159
ministers 103, 179–80,
182–3
Mipham Rimpoche 264,
265
mirrors 75, 117, 146, 179,
191–2
Moggallāna 97
moisture 59, 146–7
monasteries 162–3, 165,
183–5, 191–2, 209–10,
216, 219–22, 259
Gelug 186, 250
Nyingma 265
royal 5, 259
Sakya 268
Zen 212
money 242, 254, 258, 260
monks 91, 100, 102–4,
142–3, 162, 191–2,
207–11, 276–7
Burmese 232
Chinese 200, 247
fellow 90, 99, 162, 195
Gelug 229
Trappist 247, 256
young 93, 219, 252
monotheism 25–6

moon-mat 123, 136
white 73, 83, 114, 119,
123, 130, 133
mothers 21, 90, 97–8, 102,
126–7, 131–3, 171–2,
240
mountains 96, 106–8, 128,
208, 214, 216–18, 257,
266
mudrā 74, 130, 216
Mūla-madhyamaka-kārikā
153–5
music 35, 74, 108, 117,
164, 237
mythic truth 23
myths 23–4, 49–51, 84,
113, 285
and history 49–50

Nāgārjuna 12, 23, 142,
152–6, 195, 242
nāgas 40, 154, 183
Nagpur 282–3
Nālandā 49–50, 162–3,
178, 199–201, 248–9
nature 71, 73–4, 141–2,
161, 204, 213, 220,
260–2
true 31, 135, 137, 224, 266
nectar 69, 117, 136–7
Nepal 120, 232, 255,
257–8, 263–4, 267
border 54, 171
nephews 17, 174, 269
nirvāṇa 67–8, 89, 93, 98,
110–11, 155–6, 187, 197
Noble Eightfold Path 35
non-Buddhists 218, 271
non-duality 121–2, 176,
219
non-existence 154, 157,
162, 187, 204
northern India 60, 200, 245
nuns 89, 102–3, 105, 108,
172
Nyingma
lamas 229, 255
monasteries 265
tradition 7, 12, 184, 257,
261, 263, 265, 267

oaths 171, 182–3, 254
objects 22, 32, 35, 38, 85–6,
161, 163, 203–4

objects (*cont.*)
external 157, 203–4
ocean 66–7, 124–5, 143, 224, 272
offerings 13, 74, 127, 130, 257, 260
old age 55, 272
open-mindedness 50
openness 77, 220, 262
ordination 4, 34, 160, 228, 232, 236, 270, 277
  Bodhisattva 235
  novice 232
  Tendai 225
  training process 9, 34
origination, dependent 92, 154–5, 157, 161, 167, 185, 187
other-power 37–40, 223–4

Padma 179–83
Padmasambhava 5–7, 9, 12, 49, 178–84, 257–8, 260–1, 267
  initiation 11, 260
pain 62, 125, 129
Pāli scriptures 17, 29, 123
parents 13, 105, 195, 207, 211, 241, 250, 252; *see also* fathers; mothers
passions 58, 67, 79, 154, 173
path of liberation 82, 91
patience 158, 161, 167
patriarchs 12, 162, 191–4, 209, 215
  Buddha 209, 211
  fifth 191–2
peace 15, 31, 100, 116, 118, 163, 277
Pema Ko 262
Penang 246–7
Perfect Vision 35
perfections 74, 115, 137, 164, 213, 220, 268
  Perfection of Wisdom 40, 112, 119–20, 154
  ten 118
personal invitations 99, 141–2
personality 14, 109
  origin of 109
phenomena 81, 86, 154–5, 187, 195, 203, 268, 271

philosophy 141, 180, 204, 231, 245, 251, 275
photographs 21–3
pictorial representations 22–3
pictures 16, 21–2, 274, 285
pilgrimages 27, 198, 232, 243, 251, 255, 270
pilgrims 12, 198, 200, 242
Piṅgiya 17–20
pity 115, 130, 212, 269
plants 40, 146–7
Platform Sūtra 191
pleasure 54, 56, 58, 66, 82, 111, 177, 215
poems 131, 209, 216
poetry 194, 214, 235, 271, 275; *see also* verses and *titles of individual works*
poisons 79, 81, 85, 124–5, 226
possessions 14, 39, 67, 94, 124–5, 171, 177, 197
posterity 100, 145, 193
poverty 127, 130, 171, 241, 279
power 18–19, 26, 54–5, 86, 123, 126, 195, 197
practice
  Bodhisattva 212, 224
  Dharma 78, 93, 229–30, 237
  meditation 156, 167, 196, 220, 230, 259, 263
  prostration 4–7, 15, 34, 36, 261
  spiritual 33, 43, 75, 149, 155, 226, 229, 237
  of spiritual friendship 230, 237
  visualization 3, 6, 20, 39
preceptors 168, 237, 276
precepts 179, 181, 184, 231, 233, 241, 245, 275–6
pretas 76–7, 116–17
pride 16–17, 75, 99, 131, 200, 208, 218
priests 201, 211, 221, 224, 226
princes 18, 54, 56, 65, 104, 114, 119, 130–1
privilege 66, 89, 99

progress, spiritual 26, 39, 41, 78, 129, 276
prostration 6, 13, 15–16
  practice 4–7, 15, 34, 36, 261
Protector of the Dharma 274, 276
protectors 72, 77, 84, 125, 127, 132, 163, 185
  family 74, 76, 113–14, 119
psyche 26, 58, 125
psychic powers 95, 98, 104
pupils 17, 40, 62, 103, 105, 174, 254
Pure Land Buddhism 12, 159, 162, 222, 224–5
pure lands 73–5, 77–8, 85, 132, 213, 222, 224
purification 135, 137, 166
purity 62, 66, 138, 185, 276–7
Puruṣapura 157, 160

qualities 19–21, 72, 74, 77, 79, 90–1, 146, 255
quarrels 102, 104, 115
queens 132–3, 182

radiance 14, 69, 258
rag robes 55, 84
Rāhu 125
Rahula Sankrityayan 246–7
rainbow light 82–3, 179
rainbows 77, 173, 232
Rājagṛha 90–1, 96, 104, 108
rationalism 25
Ratnasambhava 13, 70, 75–7
real Atman 203–4
real dharmas 203–4
reality 22, 24, 29–30, 39, 41, 55, 129, 204
  ultimate 22, 41, 185
realization of voidness 177, 187
Realm of the Imagination 23–4
rebirth 64, 66–7, 74, 78, 81, 126, 131, 138

red light 79, 82, 117, 178
Refuge Assembly 6, 9; *see
also* Refuge Tree
Refuge Tree 1–16, 21–3,
34–7, 40–2, 44, 49–51,
273–4, 285–6
refugees 252–3
Refuges 13–16, 34–6, 39,
44–5, 231, 233, 271,
275–6
Going for Refuge, *see*
Going for Refuge
Three 6, 15, 271
regents 174, 251, 257
reincarnation 250, 253,
255, 262
relative truth 155, 203
religious life 67, 219, 252
renunciation 105, 186–7,
243
reputation 57, 59, 93, 160,
175, 195, 245
great 200, 255, 257
responsibility 100, 129,
133, 236, 248, 252
Reting Rimpoche 257
retreats 34, 60, 98, 258,
263, 266–7, 269
reverence 13, 15, 132, 168,
202, 213
right hand 73, 75, 79, 85,
125, 136
right livelihood 42, 44,
110
Rimpoches, *see individual
names*
Rinzai Zen 12, 149, 207
rituals 113, 216, 246, 250,
253
rivers 40–2, 45, 53, 96,
128, 187
great 40, 42, 44–5, 78
robes 11–12, 89, 99, 102,
105–6, 125, 214, 246
rag 55, 84
white 83
yellow 10–11
rocks 53, 58, 94, 158,
217–18
rosaries 12, 16, 88, 112,
114, 131, 206
rūpakāya 71

Saddharma Puṇḍarīka 116
sādhana 119, 133, 137, 262
sage kings 146, 217
Sakya monasteries 268
Śākyamuni 41–2, 52–63,
65, 71–2, 77, 96–7, 123,
127
salvation 128, 193, 223
samādhi 96, 131, 160
Samaj 245–6
samayasattva 20
sambhogakāya 72, 83, 113
Saṃdhinirmocana Sūtra
156
saṃsāra 83, 129, 131,
176–7, 186–7
Samye Monastery 174,
182
sangha 11, 13–15, 29,
31, 61–2, 92–3, 95–6,
98–102
ārya 35, 40
Sangharakshita 5–7, 9–11,
228–40, 246–8, 252–61,
270, 273–5, 280–3
Sañjaya 91–2
Sankrityayan, Rahula
246–7
Sanskrit 26, 120, 131, 147,
175, 183, 200, 245–6
Śāntideva 12, 152, 162–5
Śāriputra 11, 66, 88, 90–7,
100, 103, 142
Sarnath 59, 232, 247
scheduled castes 278–9
scholars 12, 143, 153, 192,
198, 230, 239, 244
great 6, 175, 261, 264
scholasticism 153
schools 147, 150, 192–4,
203, 218–19, 252,
254–5, 275–6; *see also
individual schools*
scraps 89, 96, 106
sea 3, 79, 126–7, 224
security 39, 56, 285
self 5, 37–9, 42, 109, 159,
163, 221, 223
self-conceit 43, 45
self-contempt 43, 45
self-power 37–8, 174,
223–4

self-transcendence 39, 54,
113, 118, 285
sense-experiences 32
sentient beings 116, 131,
193, 203, 223, 241, 268,
285
serene faith 68, 223–4
setting sun 77, 79
shadows 102–3
Shenxiu 191–2
Shingon 12, 84, 124, 149,
213, 215–16, 218
Shinran 12, 206, 222–8
shrines 1–2, 29–30
Sichuan 198, 241
sickness 130, 177, 182
Siddhārtha 54–9, 74–5
Sikkim 5, 259, 267, 270,
272
silence 62, 106, 121, 197,
240
sins 194, 213, 226
skandhas 73, 82, 98, 109,
203
skill 90, 94, 166, 178, 269
slaves 123, 164, 171, 193
sleep 1, 93, 104, 106, 181,
244
*Smaller Sukhāvatī-vyūha
Sūtra* 77
snakes 12, 79, 122, 131,
152, 156
social status 39, 54–5, 95,
218
Sogyal Rimpoche 263, 270
solitary meditation 96,
104, 107
solitude 61, 172–3, 188,
219
songs 78, 96, 164, 170–3,
209
Sōtō Zen 12, 149, 207
sound 20–2, 74–5, 84, 86,
114, 137, 208, 244–5
South India 79, 153, 200,
232
sovereignty 74, 83–4
spiritual 133
space 10, 15, 40, 43, 53,
82–3, 85, 120
and time 10, 40, 43, 53,
71, 83, 135, 142

speech 2, 13, 15, 103,
    118–20, 130, 136, 176–7
spiral conditionality 11
spiral tendency 110, 286
spiritual experience 150,
    275, 283
spiritual friends 100, 237
spiritual friendship 90,
    100, 230, 237
spiritual influence 34, 40,
    42, 44, 151, 229
spiritual life 32–4, 37, 39,
    42–3, 90, 93, 100, 236–7
spiritual practice 33, 43,
    75, 149, 155, 226, 229,
    237
spiritual progress 26, 39,
    41, 78, 129, 276
spiritual sovereignty 133
spiritual teachers, see
    teachers
śraddhā 26–7, 35
Śrāvastī 95–7, 105, 199
Sri Lanka 165, 246–7,
    274–6, 278
staff, mendicant's 11, 112,
    125
states
    mental 110, 116, 159, 280
    supreme 82, 129
statues 1, 68, 105, 202, 252
status 37–8, 111, 195
    social 39, 54–5, 95, 218
stories 49–51, 106, 109,
    114, 117, 123, 130–1,
    285–6
stupas 63, 69, 104, 258,
    264, 267, 272
suchness 157, 159, 193,
    195, 212
Śuddhodana 54, 84, 98,
    101
Sudhana 85–6, 120
suffering world 16, 41–2,
    44, 69, 130
Sukhāvatī 78, 222
Sumedha 63
sun 56–7, 73, 84–5, 115,
    122, 132, 217, 258
    setting 77, 79
śūnyatā 38, 73, 157, 175
supernormal powers 63,
    93, 97

supreme Enlightenment
    41, 64, 175, 212
Śūraṅgama Sūtra 116
Sūtra of Huineng 191–2
Sūtra of Wei Lang 231
sūtras 72, 77–8, 126–7,
    154, 157, 159, 215, 231;
    see also individual titles
    Mahāyāna 72, 120, 162,
    200
Sutta-Nipāta 17
sweetness 17, 119
swords 11, 112, 117,
    119–21, 163
symbols 4, 6, 22, 24, 51,
    114, 117, 285–6
    empty 76

Taixu 241–2
Tantra 72, 124, 153, 163,
    175, 180, 185
Tantric colleges 251,
    253–4
Tantric initiation 9, 150,
    255, 257
Tantric practice 135, 171,
    175
Taoist teachers 241–2
Tārā 23, 113–14, 129–34,
    142, 174, 176
    Green 11, 80, 112, 131,
    256, 258, 270
    White 77
Tathāgata 40, 65, 84, 91–2,
    101, 103, 201–2, 224
tathatā 157, 159, 193, 195
teachers, see also individual
    names and Introductory
    Note
    Confucian 242
    of the Past 149–228
    of the Present 229–83
    Taoist 241–2
teaching seat 12, 163
temples 127, 209, 213–15,
    218, 255, 258, 263,
    276–7
Tendai School 194, 222
termas 184, 262
Tharpe Delam 5–7, 9, 11,
    261
Theragāthā 96, 101, 106–7

Theravāda 8, 12, 66, 149,
    165–6
thirst 32, 58, 117, 165, 212
thought 6–7, 21–2, 78–9,
    95–6, 157, 159–60, 213,
    267–8
Three Jewels 15, 27, 32–3,
    35, 38–40, 44, 126,
    235–6
Three Refuges 6, 15, 271
thrones 69, 79, 81, 254
Tiantai School 12, 149,
    194–6
Tibet 12, 116, 171–90,
    242–3, 252, 256–8, 262,
    264
    eastern 184, 257, 268
    western 171, 174
Tibetan Buddhism 5–6, 9,
    171, 184, 186, 251, 254,
    268–9
Tibetan monks 5, 249, 260
time and space 10, 40, 43,
    53, 71, 83, 135, 142
Tipiṭaka 166, 246
Tomo Geshe Rimpoche
    68, 252
tongue 158, 161, 178, 245
towns 63–4, 98, 131, 158,
    186
traditions 8–10, 33–4,
    143–4, 147, 149, 153–4,
    268, 271–2; see also
    individual traditions/
    schools
transcendental unity 9–10
transcendental wisdom
    12, 123, 128, 178
transformations 7, 15–16,
    20, 80, 127–8, 146
translations 26, 142, 147,
    198, 200, 212, 246–8,
    253–4
translators 147, 172, 198
Trappist monks 247, 256
Tree, see Refuge Tree
Tripiṭaka 141, 143, 147,
    160, 198, 240, 242, 248
triple world 132, 218
Triratna Buddhist
    Community 44, 122,
    236, 273–4

Triratna Buddhist Order
1–2, 4–5, 7, 9, 11,
49–50, 147, 149–50
Trisong Detsen, King 83,
178, 180–1, 183, 264
true nature 31, 135, 137,
224, 266
truth 26–7, 29–32, 83–5,
141, 144–6, 154–5, 197,
213
absolute 155–6
body of 71–2
final 41
literal 23, 25
mythic 23
relative 155, 203
ultimate 185, 214
Tsongkhapa 6, 12, 170,
184–90
Tusita Heaven 67, 158–9

Uḍḍiyāna 178–80, 260
ultimate emptiness 81,
154, 166
ultimate reality 22, 41, 185
ultimate Truth 185, 214
uncles 17, 171, 214, 219,
269
unenlightened minds 53,
161
unity, transcendental 9–10
unsatisfactoriness 30–1, 76
Urgyen 5, 178, 184, 260
Urgyen Sangharakshita,
see Sangharakshita

Vairocana 83–8, 119, 213
White 12, 70
Vaiśālī 101, 104, 199
Vajirapāṇi 123–4
vajra 12–13, 74, 112, 123–
4, 134, 136, 206
double 80–1
golden 11, 73, 123, 178
Vajra family 74, 123, 125
Vajrapāṇi 11, 74, 81, 112–
13, 122–5, 132, 270
Vajrasattva 13–14, 40, 74,
134–40, 242, 262
heart 136–7

nature 135, 138
Vajraśekhara Sūtra 215, 242
Vajrayāna 6–8, 20, 72–3,
215, 238
initiation 175
Vasubandhu 12, 142, 152,
156, 159–62, 198, 203
Vedas 17, 55, 90, 124,
245–6
verses 2, 13–15, 64, 96,
101, 111, 203, 211; see
also poetry and titles of
individual works
viharas 5, 235–6, 258–60,
276
villages 60, 90, 100, 116,
172, 247, 249, 258
Vimalakīrti 121, 240
Vimalakīrti Nirdeśa 121
Vinaya 89, 101, 143, 166,
175, 185
Visākha 108–11
visions 13, 24, 30, 35, 225,
230, 232, 242
deep 267
visualization 1–3, 6, 10,
14–15, 17–27, 38, 135,
137
practice 3, 6, 20, 39
Visuddhimagga 12, 152,
166
voices 17, 66–7, 115, 120,
126, 147, 213, 263
voidness 176–7, 187, 204,
240
realization of 177, 187
vows 73–4, 77–8, 117, 127,
129, 137, 271, 276–7
great 73, 77, 131, 222
Vulture's Peak 93, 96,
106, 199

wandering ascetics 55, 61,
89, 214, 231
water 40, 57, 59, 66, 79,
158, 163, 212
wealth 30–1, 54, 56, 59,
75–6, 95, 100
welfare 41, 60, 62, 81, 283
western Tibet 171, 174

wheel 30, 65, 83–4, 116,
121, 167, 197, 271
golden 83–4
white light 14, 84–5, 136
White Tārā 77
White Vairocana 12, 70
willed effort 39
wind 57, 78, 115, 145, 192,
199
winter 1, 3–4, 173, 214, 242
wisdom 18–19, 72, 74–5,
84–6, 112, 117–22,
166–7, 175–6
fourfold 213
perfect 30, 120
transcendental 12, 123,
128, 178
wish-fulfilling gem 75–6,
125
wives 55, 64, 105, 108–9,
111, 178–9, 261, 263–4
womb 180–1
women 13, 101, 111, 131,
226, 234, 236, 240
worldliness 176, 222
wrong meditation 226

Ximing Temple 215
Xuanzang 12, 49–50, 162,
190, 198–206

yidam 6, 161, 256
yoga 157, 172–3, 181
Yogācāra Buddhism 12,
38, 149, 156–7, 159,
198, 203
yogas, foundation 6–7, 9,
135, 261
Yogi Chen, see Chen, Yogi
youth 91, 198, 265

zazen 207, 212, 220–2
Zen 8, 106, 150, 159, 162,
191, 207–13, 221–2
masters 210, 219, 221
monasteries 212
Rinzai 12, 149, 207
Sōtō 12, 149, 207
zhiguan 196
Zhiyi 12, 190, 194–8

WINDHORSE PUBLICATIONS

Windhorse Publications is a Buddhist charitable company based in the United Kingdom. We place great emphasis on producing books of high quality that are accessible and relevant to those interested in Buddhism at whatever level. We are the main publisher of the works of Sangharakshita, the founder of the Triratna Buddhist Order and Community. Our books draw on the whole range of the Buddhist tradition, including translations of traditional texts, commentaries, books that make links with contemporary culture and ways of life, biographies of Buddhists, and works on meditation.

As a not-for-profit enterprise, we ensure that all surplus income is invested in new books and improved production methods, to better communicate Buddhism in the 21st century. We welcome donations to help us continue our work – to find out more, go to windhorsepublications.com.

The Windhorse is a mythical animal that flies over the earth carrying on its back three precious jewels, bringing these invaluable gifts to all humanity: the Buddha (the 'awakened one'), his teaching, and the community of all his followers.

Windhorse Publications	Consortium Book	Windhorse Books
38 Newmarket Road	Sales & Distribution	PO Box 574
Cambridge	210 American Drive	Newtown
CB5 8DT	Jackson TN 38301	NSW 2042
info@windhorsepublications.com	USA	Australia

THE TRIRATNA BUDDHIST COMMUNITY

Windhorse Publications is a part of the Triratna Buddhist Community, an international movement with centres in Europe, India, North and South America and Australasia. At these centres, members of the Triratna Buddhist Order offer classes in meditation and Buddhism. Activities of the Triratna Community also include retreat centres, residential spiritual communities, ethical Right Livelihood businesses, and the Karuna Trust, a United Kingdom fundraising charity that supports social welfare projects in the slums and villages of India.

Through these and other activities, Triratna is developing a unique approach to Buddhism, not simply as a philosophy and a set of techniques, but as a creatively directed way of life for all people living in the conditions of the modern world.

If you would like more information about Triratna please visit thebuddhistcentre.com or write to:

London Buddhist Centre	Aryaloka	Sydney Buddhist Centre
51 Roman Road	14 Heartwood Circle	24 Enmore Road
London E2 0HU	Newmarket	Sydney NSW 2042
United Kingdom	NH 03857 USA	Australia
contact@lbc.org.uk	info@aryaloka.org	info@sydneybuddhistcentre.org.au